"Philip Fradkin is much more than a first-rate journalist and writer. He is Trickster exposing the lies and assumptions of our culture with a fierce intellect, while at the same time creating a tenderness of heart toward all that is beautiful and just. His language is hard-edged, authentic, and clear."
TERRY TEMPEST WILLIAMS, author of *Refuge* and *Finding Beauty in a Broken World*

"Fradkin is an impassioned writer who knows his subject."
San Francisco Chronicle

"Fradkin experiences our worst public events as the very stuff of life. This lends his writing a stirring urgency."
Los Angeles Times Book Review

"With a reporter's eye for detail, Fradkin delivers in a most compelling fashion."
Sacramento Bee

Wallace Stegner and the American West

"A widely published author on wilderness and the West, the Pulitzer Prize-winning Fradkin was the first environmental reporter for the *Los Angeles Times*. Which is to say, he's thoroughly steeped in the very landscapes and conflicts with which Stegner spent his life grappling."
HAMPTON SIDES, author of *Blood and Thunder: An Epic of the American West*

"Fradkin's dynamic and probing portrait of Stegner brilliantly combines literary and environmental history, and provides a fresh and telling perspective on the rampant development of the arid West."
Booklist

A River No More

"*A River No More* makes a statement of the utmost importance and gravity."
WALLACE STEGNER, *The New Republic*

Everett Ruess

ALSO BY PHILIP L. FRADKIN

California, the Golden Coast (1974)
A River No More (1981)
Sagebrush Country (1989)
Fallout (1989)
Wanderings of an Environmental Journalist (1993)
The Seven States of California (1995)
Magnitude 8 (1998)
Wildest Alaska (2001)
Stagecoach (2002)
The Great Earthquake and Firestorms of 1906 (2005)
Wallace Stegner and the American West (2008)
The Left Coast (2011)

Everett Ruess

HIS SHORT LIFE, MYSTERIOUS DEATH,
AND ASTONISHING AFTERLIFE

Philip L. Fradkin

UNIVERSITY OF CALIFORNIA PRESS

BERKELEY   LOS ANGELES   LONDON

University of California Press, one of the most distinguished
university presses in the United States, enriches lives around
the world by advancing scholarship in the humanities, social
sciences, and natural sciences. Its activities are supported by
the UC Press Foundation and by philanthropic contributions
from individuals and institutions. For more information, visit
www.ucpress.edu.

University of California Press
Berkeley and Los Angeles, California

University of California Press, Ltd.
London, England

Library of Congress Cataloging-in-Publication Data

Fradkin, Philip L.
    Everett Ruess : his short life, mysterious death, and
astonishing afterlife / Philip L. Fradkin.
        p.   cm.
    Includes bibliographical references and index.
    ISBN 978-0-520-26542-4 (cloth : alk. paper)
    1. Ruess, Everett, b. 1914.   2. Poets, American—20th
century—Biography.   3. Explorers—Southwest, New—
Biography.   I. Title.
    PS3535.U26Z63   2011
    811'.52—dc22   2011011203
    [B]

Manufactured in the United States of America

20 19 18 17 16 15 14 13 12 11
10 9 8 7 6 5 4 3 2 1

In keeping with a commitment to support environmentally responsible and sustainable printing practices, UC
Press has printed this book on Rolland Enviro100, a 100%
post-consumer fiber paper that is FSC certified, deinked,
processed chlorine-free, and manufactured with renewable
biogas energy. It is acid-free and EcoLogo certified.

*For my parents,
and all parents
who have lost
a young son or daughter*

The publisher gratefully acknowledges the generous support of Marilyn Lee and Harvey Schneider as members of the Literati Circle of the University of California Press Foundation.

The publisher also gratefully acknowledges the generous support of the Humanities Endowment Fund of the University of California Press Foundation.

In the desert one comes in direct confrontation with the bones of existence, the bare incomprehensible absolute is-ness of being.

EDWARD ABBEY,
Confessions of a Barbarian

Nothing so augmented the interest in Ambrose Bierce as his disappearance. Obscurity is obscurity, but disappearance is fame.

CAREY MCWILLIAMS,
Ambrose Bierce: A Biography

*And they never found my body, boys
Or understood my mind.*

DAVE ALVIN,
the refrain from "Everett Ruess"

CONTENTS

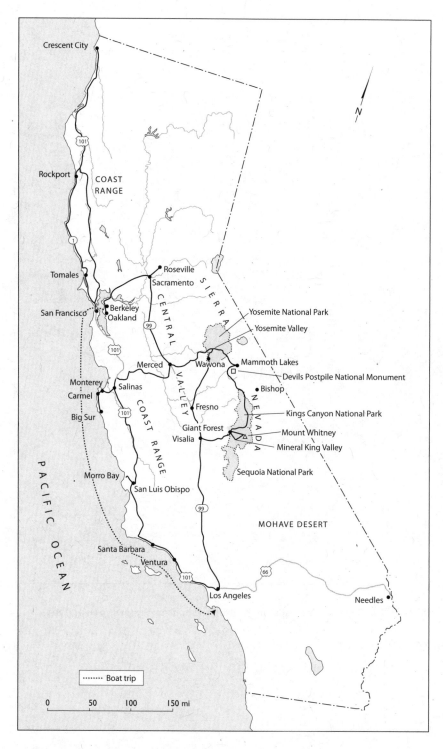

Map 1. Ruess's travels on roads and trails in California, 1930 and 1933.

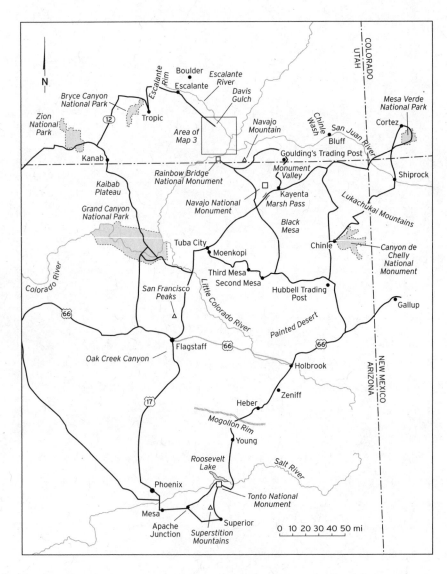

Map 2. Ruess's travels on roads and trails in the Southwest, 1931, 1932, and 1934.

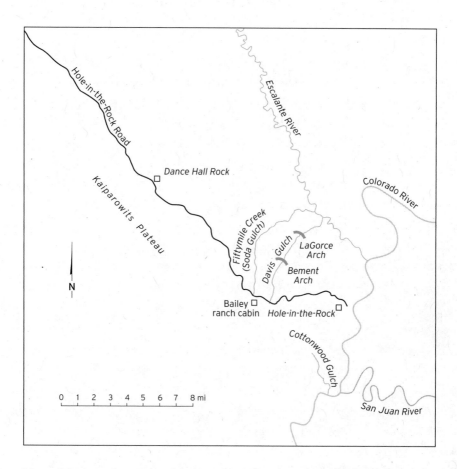

Map 3. The area where Ruess disappeared in November 1934 and where searches centered in 1935.

I

Davis Gulch

DARKNESS DESCENDED ON OUR SMALL GROUP about halfway across
the mesa that separated Davis Gulch from Fiftymile Creek. We had only
one headlamp. The last person in line played the light on the moving feet
in front of her. We stumbled on the uneven sand and rocks, but no one fell.
A rattlesnake warned us of his presence. We skittered sideways and shuffled
on until we found a rock warmed by the hot sun but losing its heat rapidly
in the early evening hours. We waited and contemplated spending the night
with little water, scraps of food, and only our T-shirts to keep us warm in the
Escalante Desert of southern Utah.

Our guide had become disoriented by the darkness. He took the headlamp
and went searching for the tracks we had laid down that morning coming
from camp. We saw his light shifting radically, then lost it. We sang songs like
"Show Us the Way to Go Home" and other campfire favorites. Inevitably, we
thought and talked about Everett Ruess.

It was in or near Davis Gulch that he had disappeared in late 1934. We had
seen his canyon haunts earlier that day and then gotten a late start back to
camp. We had made a mistake but were a group. He was alone and made a
mistake. What if he had been bitten by a snake, broken a crucial bone, fallen
off a cliff, or sunk into quicksand that buried him forever? Did he linger
long? We didn't know. We considered the loneliness of it all.

Our guide eventually found the route. We descended the steep sand and
rock slope and made it safely back to camp in time for a late dinner.

Davis Gulch is the black hole into which Everett Ruess vanished in November of 1934. The erratic crease in the wrinkled landscape is like many similar indentations in the desert Southwest across which Everett wandered. It differs from most, however, because of the fleeting presence of the desert pilgrim and the mystery of his disappearance. Emotionally moved by Everett's story, others have followed him into the canyon during the intervening years. Some left their marks, like Everett, in various forms.

The arid canyonlands of southern Utah, and Davis Gulch in particular, are a hard and unforgiving landscape redolent with ancient human presences. Nearly impenetrable, gigantic slickrock battlements encase green fringes of vegetation along intermittent water courses. The trail and now a rough road head south from Escalante, avoiding the slot canyon beginnings of the gulch. The dirt road ends at Hole-in-the-Rock and the Colorado River. These are the remote borderlands between Utah and Arizona.

The first time I visited Davis Gulch, the mouth of the canyon was submerged under the waters of Lake Powell. In a drought year the lower portion of the gulch was slowly emerging from under the massive weight of the reservoir, shaking itself free from a heavy coating of silt and just beginning to reveal its lost past. Our small party, arriving via a rickety pontoon craft, camped under a huge overhang of Navajo sandstone reached by climbing a sandy slope. The shrunken reservoir ended a few hundred feet to the west. Across the bent arm of the submerged canyon, from whose silty bottom dead cottonwood trees emerged like crooked lances, was LaGorce Arch. It was near the arch and farther up the canyon that Ruess had left two clues to his spectral presence. *NEMO,* a Latin word meaning "no one" or "no man," and *1934* were inscribed on the doorsill of an Anasazi ruin and a rock wall.[1]

A massive deluge of water descended from upstream on Lake Powell in 1983, and Glen Canyon Dam barely survived the onslaught. The rising water level of the lake inundated the floor of the overhang, Ruess's two inscriptions, and a panel of ancient Indian symbols listed on the National Register of Historic Places.* Since then the water level had dropped considerably, leav-

---

*When nominated for the national register in 1964, as Lake Powell was just beginning to fill, the Davis Gulch Pictograph Panel was judged to be safe unless the water level reached an elevation of 3,692 feet. The sixty-foot-long panel with thirty-five abstract designs was an outstanding example of rock art executed between 1050 and 1250 C.E. It was placed on the official register list in 1975, ostensibly to be

ing a strange tableau for us to view. A desert storm or storms had incised the silt slope, revealing a scene resembling installation art or a colorful kitchen midden arranged according to the age of various artifacts. Stacked from the bottom to the top were rusted tin cans; glass bottles of various ages, hues, and brands; and aluminum beer cans. I thought it possible that Everett had contributed to this layered collection of detritus.

At the back of the overhang the word *DUNN* was inscribed on the wall. It posed another mystery. William Dunn had been one of three men who left the first John Wesley Powell expedition down the Colorado River in 1869. The three men may have wandered separately or together. Three bodies that may have been theirs had been found but never identified. There was another, more likely, explanation for the inscription's meaning. Ray and Madeleine Dunn operated the Navajo Mountain Trading Post just across the Colorado River from Davis Gulch at the time of Everett's disappearance.

■

There is an overland approach to Davis Gulch that has a different set of reminders of past presences. I camped with two small groups at separate times on nearby Fiftymile Creek after that first visit to the mouth of the gulch. A short distance downstream on the north side of the canyon, locally known as Soda Gulch, was the following inscription: "E Rues *[sic]* Hunters, June 6, 1935. RS, HC, AT, HS, LCC." The hunters were from the Associated Civic Clubs of Southern Utah. Their initials were surrounded by ancient petroglyphs vaguely resembling antelope, bighorn sheep, circles, dots, and half-completed human figures pecked into the sandstone.

On other days I hiked across the mesa and descended the steep livestock trail hacked and blasted into the slickrock by local ranchers that was the only practical overland access to Davis Gulch. At the bottom of the steps was the large open space where Ruess's two burros were found in early 1935. Instead of the brush enclosure of that time there was now a broken wooden fence. Just downstream on the north wall was the overhang where some of Everett's belongings were found and the rock face where he had inscribed one of his enigmatic *Nemo*s. There were other incisions in the soft sandstone. They consisted of abstract designs, mazes, circles, slashes, and the

---

preserved. An overhang protected the panel from weathering but not the bathtub rings of Lake Powell that eventually covered it. The canyon is rife with such examples of disappearance.

signatures "J. E. Riding, 1923"; "Walter Allen, March 6, 1935" (Allen had been a member of two Ruess search parties); "Katie, 2002"; and those of more recent scribblers.

Other than these occasional human declarations, the canyon was a world unto itself. The sounds of trickling water, paired ravens, a canyon wren, and soft breezes passing through the grass, tamarisk, willow, and poplar trees came and went. The white-flowered Sacred Datura, more commonly known as jimson weed and used by Native Americans in rites of passage ceremonies, was in bloom. A marsh formed by the ponding of the stream by a beaver dam, gnawed tree trunks, and two beaver skeletons indicated the presence of those busy creatures. There were coyote and deer tracks in the softened soil. Six deer grazing on the opposite slope bounded away in gigantic leaps. The outside world was represented by the narrow panoply of passing clouds crossing the canyon's open maw. They carried messages from afar that could not be deciphered.

There must have been—and there still might be—wild turkeys in Davis Gulch. We found a seven-foot-high representation of such a bird outlined in faded red on the canyon wall. Flowing lines indicated feathers; there was an oval torso; and stick wings, legs, and splayed toes completed the pictograph. Near the giant bird was a four-foot-high male figure with a triangular torso and large feet, possibly encased in moccasins made from fibrous plants. A smaller, more rounded figure, with her hair arranged in buns on both sides of her head, completed what may have been a family portrait. Surrounding these more representational figures were arranged the usual painted, scratched, or deeply etched abstract designs.

Disappearance was a recurring theme in these arid lands. The Anasazi vanished from Davis Gulch around 1300 C.E. They left ruins, which Everett combed for artifacts. Across the stream were a well-preserved kiva and the remnants of storage structures under a massive overhang. The elliptical kiva had survived nearly intact for almost a thousand years. The three-layered flat roof of beams, thin sticks laid crossways, and an adobe roofing material partially covered the subterranean structure. It was nine feet in diameter and rose a little over five feet from the hard-packed dirt floor, in which a rectangular fire pit had been dug. Artifacts indicated a Kayenta, Arizona, cultural origin from the south side of the Colorado River.

Anthropologists had found seven corncobs with sticks stuck into them. I could see only one in the kiva. When I have encountered similar dried corncobs dating back a thousand years or so at other Anasazi sites in the Southwest, I have felt uncomfortably close to ancient peoples. I could almost see, feel, and taste what the teeth of the ancients had bitten into. It was a very intimate sensation.

Our last stop before retracing our steps was Bement Arch near the head of Davis Gulch. The arch was dramatically outlined against the blue sky with an expansive view from the shade of its graceful enclosure toward the head of the canyon. On one buttress was scratched *NEMO 34,* a crude imitation by a pretend Everett.

The depth of time and the variety of peoples who have passed through Davis Gulch are also represented by the impermanence of the names attached to the two arches. I have no idea what the Native Americans or early Mormon settlers called them, if anything. The locals called LaGorce Arch, in the lower canyon, Moqui Eye, Moqui Window, Roosevelt Memorial Natural Bridge, and, after Everett's disappearance, Nemo Arch. (*Moqui* referred to the Hopi and other early inhabitants of the region, such as the Fremont and Anasazi cultures.) What is now known as Bement Arch was called Davis Arch, Ruess Arch, and Nemo Arch.

Then the National Geographic Society took over the naming process, much to the consternation of the people who lived in the region. After a society expedition to Davis Gulch in 1954, the two arches were given new designations. Ruess Arch was named for Harlan W. Bement, the Utah state aeronautics director who had spotted it while flying low over the canyon. Bement brought the natural arches in the canyons of the Escalante River watershed to the attention of the society. The second arch was named after John Oliver La Gorce, one of the three original employees of the society and editor Gilbert H. Grosvenor's "man Friday," as he described himself.[2] Davis Gulch was named for Johnny Davis, who ran cattle in the canyon.

◼

The writer-teacher-conservationist Wallace Stegner led me to Everett Ruess, whose trail I followed until it ended in Davis Gulch. Both westerners were shaped by landscapes and transcended their respective eras in their own distinctive ways. I read Stegner's book *Mormon Country* in the late 1970s in preparation for writing a book about the Colorado River and the West. The Stegner book mentioned Ruess's brief life, its fleeting promise, and his mysterious disappearance. Thirty years later I wrote a biography of Wallace Stegner. I described a man who lived a long, full life. I now write about a youth who lived a short, fragile life.

I have had a personal investment in the books I have written, but none to a greater extent than this book. To varying degrees, we all searched for something during our early years. Like Everett, I was raised in the Unitarian Church, with its emphasis on independent thinking, had progressive parents who believed in letting children find their own way, traveled west when a teenager to work among strangers, and embarked alone on a quest, hitchhiking for six months through Europe. One major difference was that I returned with no written record of my journeys; Everett disappeared but left diaries, letters, and illustrations to document his wanderings.

This book is the story of all of us and our loneliness and confusion during the teenage years, only writ larger because Everett went to extremes. At that age our lives spread out like a topographical map before us, offering numerous diverging trails through the wilderness to choose from. How wonderful, how frightening, and how dangerous those years were. I hope readers, both young and old, can relate to Everett Ruess through either their own experiences or those of their children, a young relative, or a more distant youth. My parents and others experienced the wrenching grief following the loss of a child; that sadness and the process of healing are also part of this story. Everett's era forms the backdrop. His wanderings provide a snapshot of growing up nearly one hundred years ago on the East Coast and in the Middle West, the Depression years in California and the interior West, and the spaciousness of the national parks, monuments, and Indian lands in the Southwest.

In searching for a meaningful Everett Ruess, I sought the reality of who he was, or as close to that reality as I could get. I found the real Ruess to be far more interesting than the mythic one. I don't view him as a western Thoreau or a younger Muir, as some do.* Those two men described and thought about their respective regions. Everett described places beautifully. However, he thought primarily about himself, which is perfectly understandable given his age. I don't know in what manner he would have matured, but I do know he was exasperating at times. This quality alone made him more human and interesting, at least for me, than the patron saint of western wilderness, as he has been portrayed.

---

*Many have compared Everett to such luminaries, among them Stegner and the less known John P. O'Grady, a lecturer in English at the University of California, Davis. "Everett Ruess was a pilgrim to the wild, of the most extreme order—because he did not return," O'Grady wrote. John P. O'Grady, *Pilgrims to the Wild: Everett Ruess, Henry David Thoreau, John Muir, Clarence King, Mary Austin* (Salt Lake City: University of Utah Press, 1993), 19.

Everett was a hero, not because of what he accomplished, but because he persevered. His story dates back at least as far as Parsifal and the Arthurian legend of the innocent youth who embarks on a quest for the Holy Grail. It resembles the more contemporary tales of Huckleberry Finn, Holden Caulfield, and Christopher McCandless, who undertook odysseys of adolescence down the Mississippi River, on the streets of New York City, and into the wilds of Alaska, respectively.

Everett's unfiltered voice gives a tactile sense of who he was. Because he wrote so many words that form an autobiography within this biography, I have integrated his language into the text. I have differentiated his voice by the use of italics. The exact quotes of others are offset by the usual means: quotation marks for shorter phrases and indented paragraphs for longer passages. I make an occasional appearance in the narrative and notes to emphasize Ruess's relevance to the present and to other people. Given the facts that most readers don't read endnotes and that footnotes clutter pages and remind one of homework, I have sought a compromise. Notes that provide context or are particularly interesting are designated by an asterisk and placed at the bottom of the page. All other notes have been placed at the back of the book.

After I began working on this project, others supplied a surprising addendum. Everett's bones were supposedly discovered three-quarters of a century after he disappeared and one hundred miles from where he had last been seen. Misguided and sales-driven journalism, as practiced by a publication of the National Geographic Society, drove the bad science that resulted in two false DNA positives. The third test, by a more experienced laboratory, proved that the bones did not belong to Ruess and that science has its own types of fragility. Then the silence of the desert returned.

II

Wanderers

DISAPPEARANCES CREATE MYTHS, whose durability depends on the renown of the wanderers, the circumstances of their vanishing, and the fervor of their followers. Everett Ruess appears on almost every list of better-known individuals who have vanished:[1] writer Ambrose Bierce, Congressman Hale Boggs, hijacker D. B. Cooper, aviators Amelia Earhart and Antoine de Saint-Exupéry, explorer John Franklin, labor leader Jimmy Hoffa, mountaineer George Mallory, band leader Glenn Miller, outlaw Robert Leroy Parker (aka Butch Cassidy), anthropologist Michael Rockefeller, silk merchant Jim Thompson, and humanitarian Raoul Wallenberg.[*]

Around each of these men and this one woman a cottage industry of suppositions about their fate has developed, fed every now and then by some discovery or rumor. What these people have in common is that they pushed the envelope in some way, sought to go beyond known limits, became lost in attempts to find themselves, and were subsequently immortalized in myths.[†]

---

[*]In one of those odd coincidences, Everett's maternal grandparents lived next door to Ambrose Bierce's divorced wife and daughter in Los Angeles.

[†]On the need of creative people to become lost before they can find themselves, see Rebecca Solnit's excellent *A Field Guide to Getting Lost* (New York: Viking, 2005). She mentions Ruess, Earhart, Saint-Exupéry, and others. Of them she

Disappearance is "the place we go when we are ready, or forced, to throw down language and measurement," wrote an Alaskan author, whose state, like desert regions, has an unusually large percentage of the lost.[2] Alaska was where Christopher McCandless disappeared for four months and then was found dead in an abandoned bus just north of Denali National Park in 1992. The book *Into the Wild*, by Jon Krakauer, with eleven pages devoted to Ruess, and a film of the same name by Sean Penn elevated McCandless to the mythic status of a lost soul. McCandless and Ruess were wanderers who sought solitude in the wilderness under assumed names, Alexander Supertramp for McCandless and Evert Rulan for Ruess. That both were young added to the poignancy of their deaths, McCandless's from starvation and Ruess's from unknown causes since he simply vanished, adding mystery to loss.

Wandering is a form of separation from the tribe and parents and a rite of passage for youths, though perhaps not always in such extreme forms. In northern Europe there is the tradition of the Wanderjahr, the hiatus between the end of formal education and the start of a career. In Australia aborigine youths practice the walkabout. This is the time when the boy separates from his mother. "There is also a practical connection between initiation and wandering," wrote a Freudian psychologist. "Initiation begins with the separation of the boys from the mothers and ends with the readmittance of the boy, as a man, to the society of the mothers and other women. Between these two there is the transition period, the bush-wandering of the newly circumcised young man."[3] Ruess never emerged from this transition period.

There is a dark side to wandering. The symptoms are disorientation and suicidal tendencies. Ruess displayed these characteristics in his last years. A University of California anthropologist, who spoke the language of the Pit River Indians of northeast California, wrote:

> I want to speak of a certain curious phenomenon found among the Pit River Indians. The Indians refer to it in English as "wandering." They say of a certain man, "He is wandering," or "He has started to wander." It would seem that under certain conditions of mental stress an individual finds life in his accustomed surroundings impossible to bear. Such a man starts to wander. . . . People will probably say of such a man: "He has lost his shadow."[4]

---

writes: "They were all saddled with a desire to appear in the world and a desire to go as far as possible that was a will to disappear from it" (155).

Two fictional wanderers—Mark Twain's Huckleberry Finn and J. D. Salinger's Holden Caulfield—and McCandless and Ruess had the vast spaces of the American West in common. The West symbolized a place where they could find relief from their adolescent angsts. In the penultimate sentence of the Twain novel, Finn says he is going to leave the Midwest and "light out for the Territory" in order to escape being "sivilize[d]."[5] Caulfield, the New Yorker, ends up in a Los Angeles sanitarium after having fantasized about working on a Colorado ranch or hitchhiking west, "where it was very pretty and sunny and where nobody'd know me and I'd get a job."[6] For McCandless the desert West and then Alaska were empty spaces to escape to. Ruess repeatedly left Los Angeles in search of beauty in the mountains and deserts of the West. His most valuable legacy is alluded to in what Holden Caulfield's prep school teacher tells his former pupil:

> Many, many men have been just as troubled morally and spiritually as you are right now. Happily, some of them kept records of their troubles. You'll learn from them—if you want to. Just as someday, if you have something to offer, someone will learn something from you. It's a beautiful reciprocal arrangement. And it isn't education. It's history. It's poetry.[7]

III

The Legacy
1859–1913

VIEWED THROUGH THE EXTENSIVE DOCUMENTATION, there seems to be an inevitability about Everett's fate that extended back three-quarters of a century, to 1859. The Ruess family produced words and images in great quantities. There were letters, diaries, poems, essays, short stories, histories, miscellaneous fragments, book manuscripts, published books, bookmarks, note cards, block prints, watercolors, oil paintings, and photographs. Everett's family believed in the written word and were almost compulsive in their correspondence. They traded their journals back and forth, along with letters, to get a better idea of what each was thinking and doing. They were quite revealing and frank in some missives. At other times they described routine happenings, the stuff of life. The very private remained private.*

This belief in extensive record keeping started with Everett's maternal grandfather, William H. Knight, as did the family's on-again, off-again, and

---

*Not all the writings survive or survive as written. Stella Ruess, Everett's mother, burned her husband's journals after he died. She gave no reason. Michele Ruess, personal communication, April 8, 2009. Stella also edited Everett's letters and journal entries to make him appear to be the perfect son. Fortunately, the unedited versions still exist.

finally on-again presence in California. Beginning as a schoolteacher in his native state of New York, Will Knight emigrated to Michigan, where he worked in state government, and then joined a small wagon train at the age of twenty-four, arriving in San Francisco in August 1859. Finding California "a great country for change," the young man went to work for a bookseller.[1] The novelty of the climate, the nearby ocean, fresh fruits and vegetables, and the Unitarian church, where the renowned Thomas Starr King was soon to become the minister, enchanted him.

Knight published a combined business and education journal for H. H. Bancroft and Company in 1860. He worked for that mercantile and publishing firm for the next nineteen years, in charge of the publishing arm that churned out a series of histories and maps of the western states and territories. He credited himself with changing Lake Bigler, named for a California governor, to Lake Tahoe, a designation more closely matching its Native American name. But Knight's employment "ended bitterly" in 1879, he said, because he felt "unjustly treated" by Bancroft.[2]

The family moved to Cincinnati, Ohio, where Knight obtained a job purchasing manufacturing materials for a carriage firm owned by his brother-in-law. In 1868 he had married Ella Joanna Waters, with whom he would have seven children. Three of the four who survived to become adults were born in Cincinnati: Stella, his oldest daughter, married Christopher Ruess and became the mother of Everett; Emerson was a successful landscape architect in San Francisco; and Bertha married the actor Tyrone Power, who was known for his declamatory roles on stage and screen.* Alfred, born earlier in San Francisco, became the vice president of a large food company and his parents' principal financial support in their later years.

Knight was an active member of the Unitarian Church in Cincinnati and

---

*By naming his son Emerson, Knight honored his brother-in-law and employer, Lowe Emerson, and also Ralph Waldo Emerson.

Tyrone Power was the son of a famous Irish actor of the same name and the father, by a previous marriage, of the better known Hollywood actor also named Tyrone Power. He had little contact with his nephew Everett, as he and Bertha traveled constantly to fulfill his acting commitments. Moving from Shakespearean stage roles to the screen, he initially played leading men in silent movies and then switched to villains. His first talkie and last movie role was the villainous bull whacker Red Flack in *The Big Trail,* in which John Wayne had his first starring role. Power died of a heart attack in 1931.

the president of the church's literary society. As such, he arranged for speakers to visit, the first being Edward Everett Hale, an author ("The Man without a Country") and Unitarian clergyman. Besides church and literary matters, Knight vigorously pursued his interests in natural history and astronomy. He also wrote poetry, as did his oldest daughter.

The warmer climate of California beckoned after a dozen years in Ohio, and Knight moved his family to Los Angeles in 1891. He had little business sense and chose to rent and not participate in the real estate boom. When oil was discovered on the property, the family had to move. Bertha, who wrote her father's biography, said he was one of those men "of idealistic temperament who have not entrenched themselves in financial security."[3] It was a legacy he passed on to his daughter Stella, who handed it down to Everett.

Knight circulated on the fringes of the elite social, religious, cultural, and scientific circles of Los Angeles, attending countless club functions and recitals, organizing lectures, giving speeches, helping to found the Southern California Academy of Science and the local astronomical society, and serving as secretary to a business organization and to a philanthropist. He contributed articles to *Out West* magazine and the *Los Angeles Times,* traveling by train and buckboard and on foot at the age of eighty to report on the eruption of Mount Lassen. In 1925 Knight was struck by what he called "a machine," meaning an automobile, and died from the injuries.

A *Times* editorial praised his contributions to Los Angeles and called him "a victim of our modern speed craze."[4] His son-in-law Tyrone Power read Tennyson's "Crossing the Bar" at the memorial service, and a Unitarian minister was present when the family dropped Knight's ashes into the Pacific Ocean halfway to Catalina Island. The *Times* called this "a strange ceremony," but it was a practice the family adhered to through the years.[5] A plaque honoring William Knight was placed near a sundial memorializing his wife and a fountain of Spanish design erected by family members for the couple and one of their deceased sons in the patio of the First Unitarian Church in the 2900 block of West Eighth Street, Los Angeles. Stella wrote a poem honoring her father that ended: "Aspiring always high and higher," another goal she passed on to her son.[6]

■

The liberal Unitarian heritage with its emphasis on free thinking and veneration of culture, so influential in Everett's brief life, was a legacy derived from both sides of his family. The Ruesses came from the blue-collar end of the middle-class spectrum.* Everett's paternal great-grandfather was born in Ulm, Germany, and immigrated to the United States trailing a tradition of revolutionary activities and a love of books and beer. His son William married Katherine Keit of Fort Wayne, Indiana, in 1875. Everett's father, Christopher, one of three brothers, was born three years later on a farm near Sterling, Kansas. The farm was destroyed by a cyclone in his first year, and the family moved to the suburbs of Fort Wayne in 1879. "My people practiced of necessity simple, plain living and many homemade articles were used," Christopher wrote later in life. "Rigid economy and saving with endless self-help: Germanic thrift."[7] Christopher and his brothers walked three miles across fields to a one-room school that housed eight grades. The male teacher was frequently drunk, the walls were splattered with ink from inkwells flung by students, and the stove was riddled with bullet holes.

His parents sold the Fort Wayne home and, using the proceeds, traveled by train to Los Angeles, where illustrations of sun-blessed orange groves lured them and others in 1887. Southern California was in the midst of one of its periodic real estate booms, which was promoted by railroads, land speculators, and the Los Angeles Chamber of Commerce. "Never before," wrote the historian Carey McWilliams, had "individual boosters co-operated so successfully in promoting a region" with so few natural resources.[8] Midwesterners, such as the Knight and Ruess families, were particularly susceptible to such bait. The Ruess family bought their small piece of Arcadia (not the town, which actually exists in Los Angeles County, but the imagined rural paradise): a small house with a dog, chickens, cows, and pigeons in the Boyle Heights section of Los Angeles. Christopher's father worked for the railroad.

As in the Knight family, words and the Unitarian religion were important elements in the Ruess family. Christopher's eighth grade teacher, Anna C. Murphy, gave him a love of literature and poetry and the ability to memorize large blocks of text. She later married the poet Edwin Markham, who became a Ruess family friend. Another grade school teacher told him his first name meant "Christ-bearer."[9] The oratory of a Welsh preacher attracted the Ruess family to the "heretical" Unitarian Church, Christopher recalled, "so we all attended." Dinner guests at the Ruess home were somewhat eclectic:

---

*There are two ways to pronounce *Ruess,* a surname of Germanic origin. Family members rhyme it with either *goose* or *Lewis.* Kevin Ruess, personal communication, July 23, 2009.

a railroad man who read the philosopher Herbert Spencer and preached revolution, and a carpenter who was an atheist but later became a Christian Scientist. As a teenager, Christopher tended toward Christian socialism and religious skepticism.[10]

Young Ruess received high grades in his senior class at Los Angeles High School in 1897. One day Christopher earned twenty cents selling ads for the school newspaper and then "squandered" it (his word) on used copies of Ralph Waldo Emerson's first and second series of *Essays*. As corresponding secretary of the debating club, he came to the attention of the national secretary of the Lyceum League of America, a patriotic society and debating club. The national secretary "advised me to do the preposterous, to go to Harvard!" With the help of ten letters of recommendation (three of his high school teachers said he was the best pupil they ever taught) and a $250 prize, Ruess traveled east to Cambridge, where he took the entrance examination, finishing near the top of seven hundred incoming freshmen.[11]

Another student at Los Angeles High School was Stella Knight, whose grades were almost as high as Christopher's. She graduated one year after he did, in 1898. They began a correspondence in high school that continued through their engagement in 1902, when Christopher was still at Harvard. The couple came to know each other well enough through daily letters, Christopher said, that after their marriage in 1905 they "understood each other without discussion."[12]

Stella took a one-year course in art instruction after high school and then taught drawing in the Alhambra public schools. She also taught metalcraft in the Camp Fire Girls, an organization with which she maintained a long association. During this period she signed her letters "Starry" or "Star," *Stella* being Latin for "star." She outlined her creed in a letter to an uncle in 1900. It represents what was foremost in the mind of a young woman of a certain social class at that time and the ideals that were passed on to Everett.

> I consider these three things essential to the highest and happiest life; first, to be married to a fit help-mate, who can both help and inspire you and be helped and inspired by you, and to have a complete home and family life; second, to love and cherish the great books of the world, to live thus daily with the greatest and best of all ages, with the richest minds and fullest hearts of all times; third, to be busied, either primarily or secondarily, in some work for the sake of others than those of your own household, this work to be done, not at all for what it will bring to you but for what it will enable you to bring to others, to be done, in short, for the sake of the love you bear your fellows and the duty which you owe them; above all these

three, which I have mentioned in the order of magnitude and of probable and easiest attainment, is the fourth and greatest requisite to the highest and happiest life, which is this: to live and move and have your being consciously in the life of God, to act as knowing yourself a child of the great God of the Universe and to do all things as in His sight.

These ideals no one can ever perfectly attain; just on this account, life remains always more than worth the living. Given these four ideals as his own, no man will ever find life lacking in joy nor himself in faith, hope and love.[13]

———— ■ ————

Harvard University was in one of its expansion periods at the turn of the century. President Charles William Eliot was transforming a moribund institution into a modern research university that would serve as a model for the American educational establishment. His innovations reflected his Unitarian and Emersonian ideals of preparing young minds to think, make intelligent choices, and serve and lead. Spiritual goals should be grounded; specialized expertise should serve public purposes. Into this cauldron of knowledge, wealth, and privilege stepped the son of a painter of Pullman railroad cars from Los Angeles who later recognized that Eliot had gathered "the largest aggregation of truly great teachers ever together before or since."[14]

Christopher crammed four undergraduate years into three because he could not afford the extra year. There was no time for a social life. He graduated magna cum laude with a degree in philosophy but skipped graduation to work. Throughout his undergraduate career he could not decide whether he wanted to be a teacher, lawyer, minister, or social worker. He preferred the last occupation, but since there was no graduate school for such work, he chose to go to Harvard Divinity School. The divinity school was even more closely associated with the Unitarian Church than the university as a whole.

Unitarianism and the transcendentalists had an inordinate influence on the Ruesses. They named their eldest son Waldo after Ralph Waldo Emerson, and their youngest son bore the middle name of Edward Everett Hale, another prominent Unitarian. The couple's engagement motto was taken from Emerson's writings.[15]

The central tenets of the Unitarian Church in the first decades of the twentieth century placed an emphasis on the intellect and engagement with social issues.[16] The church was relatively small, urban, elite (meaning that a disproportionate share of its members were in *Who's Who in America*), centered on the East Coast, and appealing to educated, upper-middle-class worshipers. Facing a crisis of membership and identity in the mid-1930s, a Commission of Appraisal looked back at the church's history and stated in its report: "The most distinctive characteristics of the denomination[,] its emphasis upon intellectual qualities, its obvious natural ties with the more prosperous class in society, its cultural and educational advantages, its isolation from the main body of Christian churches," had resulted in a "self-satisfied body of church folk."[17]

The worship of beauty and the life of the spirit ranked higher than communion with the divine in the Unitarian value system. When transplanted westward to San Francisco and Los Angeles, the religion—or nonreligion, as some have called it—became even more unrestrained. The same assessment stated: "The outstanding difference is that western Unitarians somewhat less frequently affirm the traditional Christian and theistic values than eastern Unitarians do, while they more frequently affirm rationalistic and humanistic ones."[18] One of those humanistic values was the worship and pursuit of beauty, a legacy of the transcendentalists. There was beauty for Unitarians in their relationships with God, nature, and other humans that could be expressed in literature, music, and the visual arts. It was not just a simple beauty with tangible associations, but rather a sublime beauty—something far rarer, more fleeting, and potentially dangerous.

Beauty in the nineteenth century transcendentalist set of values was folded into the concept of the sublime in nature. "Vagueness, mistiness, and obscurity were favorable to the experience of the sublime," the Pulitzer Prize–winning historian Daniel Walker Howe wrote in a similar vein about the Unitarian experience. "There was just a touch of fear in the emotion, too; for whatever was sublime was powerful."[19] The art historian Reyner Banham transferred the concept of the dark side of sublimity to western deserts, of which he was a connoisseur, stating that "the awe, even terror" of such places was addictive. Deserts were "a sly and begrudging barrier, full of deceptions."[20]

Everett Ruess, who would set out on a quest for beauty in the desert, recognized the danger of the sublime in a piece of writing that lies buried in the archives at the University of Utah: *I think that beauty tends to become frightful as it becomes perfect, and that if we could see it comprehensively, the extreme of beauty is a desolating hideousness, and that the name of ultimate, absolute beauty is madness.* There is no clue to date this handwritten fragment, other than the fact that it mirrors the thinking of the last couple years of his life.

Before Christopher completed his studies at the divinity school, he had chosen his goals for the remainder of his life. He "scotched the snakes of love of either wealth or fame or promotion and substituted ideals of genuine quiet, inner-rewarding service." The realities of life that intruded in later years would bend but not break this commitment. Did Stella concur? She replied from Los Angeles, "I shall be happy to live with you even in a tent in the desert."[21]

Back on the West Coast, Ruess worked for a religious charity in San Francisco for a year before moving across the San Francisco Bay and becoming the minister of the Alameda Unitarian Church. Stella Knight and Christopher Ruess were married in Los Angeles on April 2, 1905. Ten days before the San Francisco earthquake on April 18, 1906, Ruess wrote a long, rambling letter to his father-in-law announcing that he was resigning his ministerial position because of long hours, poor pay, and the fact that he was preaching Christian socialism, not Christian religion, to an indifferent congregation. He didn't want to remain where he didn't belong.[22] The devastating earthquake and three days of firestorms presented him with the opportunity for a different type of service, and he went to work as the representative of the American Unitarian Association to the Red Cross. He and Stella lived in a tent and then a one-room apartment in San Francisco's Sunset District.

Christopher became chief probation officer for Alameda County in 1907, giving him a role in the liberal causes of preventing child abuse, creating a juvenile justice system, and gaining probation for criminals. He helped formulate the California juvenile court law of 1909, gave speeches about various aspects of probation work, and extolled the merits of the new juvenile court system in the *Pacific Unitarian* magazine. Ruess was part of the growing progressive movement in California and contributed articles to the *California Outlook,* a weekly publication that supported Governor Hiram Johnson. He also wrote poetry. One poem to his wife was sung to the tune of "Fair Harvard." Ten years after graduation, Ruess told his Harvard classmates that he had selected the Bay Area as the place to do his work because it was "the greatest sociological laboratory west of Chicago." His interests were people, reading, poetry, walking, and gardening. His religion, he said, was Unitarian with a dash of Quaker.[23]

During the years of Christopher's work in Alameda County, the couple had three children: a daughter, Christella ("star of Christ"), was born in 1908 but lived only six weeks; Waldo was born in 1909; and Everett was born on March 28, 1914.* In her annual anniversary note on April 2, 1914, Stella addressed her dead daughter, saying that she was missed but thanking her for sending them a substitute—a brother named Everett. "His name, Everett, will endow him with attributes of kindness and the helping hand for which Edward Everett Hale was noted, the beloved preacher whom Christopher knew in Boston." Five days after his birth, Stella noted that Everett was sleeping peacefully on the sun deck: "I call him Mr. Contentment, he is so satisfied with the world as he finds it."[24]

The yard of their postearthquake-constructed Oakland home was transformed from bare dirt into a romantic version of Valhalla. Happiness and beauty were the objectives. A memorial sundial for Christella was surrounded by daisies planted in honor of Stella's little sister Daisy, who also died at a young age. The branches of eucalyptus trees formed a honeysuckle-laced ramada under which the family and their friends dined on warm nights. Roses covered a Japanese-style arch, symbolic of leaving the mundane world behind on entering the lush garden. Red gravel pathways circled the garden. A grove of bamboo served as a backdrop and a screen.[25]

Stella drew up a mock will describing the family as she perceived it in Oakland:

To Sir Christopher the Strenuous—a portion of calmness and gentleness, and receptivity for music.
To Waldo the Serious—my Pollyanna disposition, and my fondness for walking.
To Everett the Flyaway—a strain of quietness.[26]

---

* Ninety-five years later Everett would be termed a "red diaper baby" in an article on the conservative *American Spectator* magazine website about the supposed discovery of his bones. Bill Croke, "Man-Child in the Promised Land," *American Spectator,* http://spectator.org/archives/2009/05/22/man-child-in-the-promised-land, May 22, 2009. This label designates the offspring of parents who were members of the Communist Party or sympathetic to its aims. There is no evidence that either of Everett's parents was that far left on the political spectrum. Rather, they were comfortably situated closer to the political center but just far enough left to make some people, like William Knight, squirm.

IV

_____

Growing Up
1914–1929

PERHAPS EVERETT WAS A WANDERER because his family wandered, moving eight times in the first fourteen years of his life.[1] None of the moves bothered the youngster; rather, he seems to have taken them as exciting adventures, with educational overtones supplied by his mother. Movement fit the character of the physically active, talkative child. His father displayed a certain restlessness too. After eight years of probation work, Christopher returned to the Unitarian fold in 1915 as the minister of a Fresno church in the San Joaquin Valley, a far different place than the Bay Area. The valley was steaming hot farmland in the summer and blanketed by cold, gray tule fog in the winter. The surrounding farm towns of Dinuba, Reedley, Hanford, and Clovis were also within his religious orbit.

By the age of two, Everett had shed his earlier placid nature. When the family went to the Kings River in the foothills of the Sierra Nevada to cool off one summer, he nearly drowned. So the youngster was tied to a rope while he flung rock after rock into the fast-flowing water. At home he had to be tied by one foot in his crib or on the porch to prevent him from wandering away. He had the choice whether Jupiter or Juno—the names his mother gave his feet—would be secured. Despite these precautions, one day Everett escaped and toddled across a bridge and railroad tracks. When a frantic Stella called the police, they told her he had been found by a family who were entertaining him with a wagon.

The family spent one year in the valley, and then moved to Los Angeles when Christopher resigned his ministerial position in September 1917, citing the need to support his parents.[2] To meet this obligation, he went to work as a salesman for Lewis E. Myers & Company, manufacturers of the Chautauqua Industrial Arts Desk. It was a product that Ruess could relate to, and he threw himself into the work with enthusiasm. "I was trying to turn the business into a social service," he said. "I was a promoter, a crusader, I had missionary zeal, I had fire and could mildly set others on fire."[3] He traveled extensively, sold desks, managed branch offices, ran sales conventions, wrote sales literature, and worked long hours.

The desk embodied the progressive educational philosophy of Everett's parents and John Dewey, who taught at the University of Chicago. Its concept was based on an antiauthoritarian approach to educating children. The wooden desk was portable and folded open and closed—not unlike a laptop computer—and had a steady surface on which to draw and cubbyholes where educational materials could be stored. The desk was designed to solve the restless "Boy Problem" in the home by keeping youngsters engaged.[4] Everett and his brother were given the children's model. "So the atmosphere of the home from the beginning," Stella said, "was one of child-interest and child-study and child experimenting."[5]

After an eleven-month stay in Los Angeles, the family moved across the continent to Brookline, near Boston, where the brothers' extracurricular education continued under Stella's supervision. They visited churches, Revolutionary War sites, and their father's Harvard professors and went Christmas caroling on Beacon Hill. Everett was in the second grade. "E was too talkative and was inattentive & slow with his rhythm work but he advanced from the bottom to the top group by the end of the year," his mother said.[6] Young Ruess took walks with a bird club; was photographed with the statue of his namesake, Edward Everett Hale, on Boston Common; and visited Hale's home in Roxbury.

When Christopher was transferred from the Boston to the New York office of the desk company, the family moved to the Bay Ridge section of Brooklyn in July 1920. There were more excursions and lessons: trips to Coney Island, the Statue of Liberty, the Bronx Zoo, the Metropolitan Museum of Art, sculptors' studios, art classes, and a woodmaking class in a Greenwich Village settlement house. On the couple's sixteenth wedding anniversary in 1921, the family took the subway to New York, the train to Newark, and the trolley to Montclair, New Jersey, where they ate a picnic lunch on the hillside. Their view of the skyscrapers of New York City over the fourteen miles of towns and swamplands reminded them of the view of San Francisco from across the bay. Christopher read Walt Whitman's poem "Song of the Open Road," and then the family continued their trolley ride, through Verona to West Caldwell.[7]

The Ruesses moved to Palisades Park, New Jersey, in May 1922, where they settled for a short time near the Hudson River. Young Everett led an active, outdoor life there. He had a Rolls Racer, a tricycle resembling an airplane with stubby wings and a tail, on which he sped around. He explored a nearby creek with a friend in the summer and went ice skating on a lake in the winter. Christopher, now sales manager for the eastern division of the desk company, commuted to his job in the Flatiron Building in New York City. Stella and Christopher had stationery printed with their names, a drawing of a sundial, and the words "Glorify the Hour." They called their home on Washington Place "Cherry Croft." Under Stella's tutelage Everett was exposed to a continuing range of cultural activities in the metropolitan area, including theater performances in the city—one being *The Wandering Jew* with uncle Tyrone Power in the cast.

By the age of eight Everett was a voracious reader, dispatching whole books in one day. He was also a constant sketcher. When a particular scene interested him, Stella said, "E whipped out his pocket notebook and made many sketches."[8] He drew and painted on his Chautauqua slate, an accessory for the desk. He took art classes at New York's Pratt Institute on Saturdays, sculpting wood with a coping saw and clay with his hands. Afterward mother and son ate soup and lemon pie at a corner store.

Everett and Stella took the train to Los Angeles to care for her ailing father in March 1923. The trip served as an introduction to the interior West and had a lasting impression on the nine-year-old. He would return in a few years with his burros to some of the places they had visited on this trip. One was the south rim of the Grand Canyon: *Saw the Grand Canyon of Colorado. When I first looked over I was scared, but the next time I could see better. There are red and grey stone turrets rising up. The canyon is a mile deep, and I couldn't even see the river. I looked at it through a spyglass in the lookout tower. Mother went down to the bottom on a horse.*[9] That night Everett said his evening prayer on the edge of the canyon, an experience "long to be cherished in his memory," said Stella.[10]

Mother and son were welcomed to California with a bouquet of golden poppies, the state flower. They arrived at the Knights' home in Los Angeles on April 6. The next day Everett was enrolled in Grant School—near the Fox Motion Picture Studios—one room of which was reserved for child actors.

Everett and his mother visited friends in the San Joaquin Valley and then proceeded north to Yosemite National Park, where they had the complete tourist experience, which Everett would duplicate on his first solo journey seven years later. A print of a stag with large horns being fed by a small boy appeared on the Ruess's Christmas card that year with the caption "Everett's happiest memory of Yosemite." Then it was on to the Bay Area and more friends and home to Palisades Park in September for the start of another school year, his last in New Jersey.

Valparaiso, Indiana, where the company Christopher worked for was head-quartered, was the family's home from 1924 to 1928. The small city lies forty-three miles to the southeast of Chicago on the Sauk Trail, which connected Rock Island, Indiana, to Detroit, Michigan, and was traversed by Native Americans, white explorers, and early settlers in their times. Named for a coastal Chilean city, Valparaiso became the county seat of Porter County in 1836. Kettle lakes, formed by the melting of large chunks of ice buried in glacial sediments, dotted the landscape. Creeks drained marshy ground. Both features were small boys' delights. Truck farms in the surrounding fields supplied fresh produce to Chicago and Everett with arrowheads. The Lutheran-dominated Valparaiso University, choosing to have no athletic teams or secret societies, furnished the area with an intellectual presence.

"All Boy" was the title Stella chose for her edited version of her son's "secret diary" for these years.[11] He certainly was an all-American boy. Everett was an avid Boy Scout and reader of the Boy Scouts of America magazine *Boys' Life*, whose mascot was Pedro the Mailburro. Pedro signed his letters to readers *UU*, which represented his hoofprints. Stella joined the local chapter of the Daughters of the American Revolution and enrolled Everett as a member of its related Children of the American Revolution. To be eligible for member-ship in either group, a child must be a lineal descendent of someone who served in the Continental Army or who materially aided the cause of free-dom during the Revolutionary War. A relative of Stella's collected taxes for George Washington's army and petitioned the General Assembly to set slaves free in Connecticut in 1777, thus allowing Everett's membership.[12]

Everett was raised mainly by his mother during the Valparaiso years. Waldo and Christopher were home only intermittently. Everett's brother worked summers on a Montana ranch and attended college; his father traveled exten-sively on business. What is striking is how happy and normal Everett was and how idyllic were his surroundings. His Norman Rockwell boyhood was a poignant reminder of what times were like in the Midwest during those long-ago years.

Against this backdrop, a typical year for Everett unfolded.[13] The year began with snow on New Year's Day and a cold spell during the first week of January. He went sledding, skiing, and ice skating. Everett chopped wood and then wrote doggerel verses about the cold weather and the need to constantly feed the furnace so it would coo like a baby. In school he got a 100 in spelling and an 80 in arithmetic. *After school I and Sheldon and Harold built a snow fort. Two boys, about fourteen years old each, started fighting us. Harold ran into the house. Then they chased us all over.*[14]

In February he wrote a story titled "My Visit to Niagara," having gotten the idea and the title from an 1835 essay by Nathaniel Hawthorne. Everett thought the falls in Yosemite National Park were the equal of Niagara Falls. He used the adjective *swell* to describe the Saturday trips with his mother to art classes at the Art Institute of Chicago. He began looking forward to those classes on Thursdays. *There were millions of things to look at in the Institute and it would have taken me months to see it all.*[15] Lunch at the Automat was a treat. Another constant was church on Sundays, where, in his opinion, the sermons varied widely in quality. Everett liked one sermon in particular. *He told how important it is to be outdoors and see the things of Nature to really know God.*[16]

Everett memorized the presidential oath of office before it was administered to Calvin Coolidge on March 4. He had a pillow fight with friends, and some of the pillows ripped open, spilling feathers across the room. With his close friend Harold Gast, Everett performed a play he had written, "A Tragedy of Two Kings." A stage hidden by a curtain and lit by six candles was constructed in the cellar of the Ruess home. The boys attracted an audience of four, charged admission, and grossed twenty-five cents. During a spell of warm March weather, Everett and a friend gathered wood, nailed it together, and launched a raft in Platt's Pond. It sank when they stood on it. His English teacher was surprised to learn that he had seen two Shakespeare plays in New York and that his uncle had played the leading role in one of them. *It is only six days before my birthday.* Finally, March 28 arrived on a Saturday, and Everett rose at 5 A.M. and caught the 6:40 A.M. train to Chicago. *I drew three pictures today.* His mother and father gave him art books. On another birthday he got a microscope through which he examined dirt, blood, tissue paper, cotton, leaves, moss, dust, and hair.

March of 1928 was quite different. Everett was exhausted, not his usual physical condition. He wrote his brother that the doctor thought he had pernicious anemia. Stella added in an accompanying note to Waldo: "Everett sounds downhearted, doesn't he? I think he will stay in bed all week, and then see about getting up."* Everett solicited recommendations for a contest advertised in that month's issue of *Boys' Life.* The prize was a free trip to Africa for two Boy Scouts.[17] Christopher put in a good word for his son, writing to the local Scout executive who needed to approve Everett's application: "Everett has been brought up not so much to take orders, as to think and decide for himself."[18] Unfortunately, Everett had to drop out of the contest because of an illness. Stella was vague on the specifics, but it may have been pernicious anemia again.

On the first Saturday in April, live rabbits served as models for the children's clay sculptures at the art institute. Everett made a rabbit and a baby squirrel. Then he went to the Field Museum and drew twelve pictures. The weather was unsettled that month. *There was a regular tornado today. It lightninged and thundered and rained and hailed.*[19] Everett got 100 in music. There were thirty-seven more school days before summer vacation began. Everett planted a garden, put sod around the house, swept the porch, and watered the lawn. He went to see the silent film *Janice Meredith,* about the Revolutionary War, in which his uncle played Charles Cornwallis, the British general.

In May he took his friend Harold to see *The Thief of Bagdad,* starring Douglas Fairbanks. *He was tickled pink and I knew he would be.* Everett dug a hole under the faucet in the yard, filled it with water, and then made a harbor for his toy boats in the shallow pool. Waldo was home. *At night Waldo and I had a water fight, threw golf balls and soapy water and sponges and cold water at each other. I was dead tired this morning.*[20] Everett and Harold went fishing and caught two turtles. They put them in Everett's shallow pool, but the turtles got *crawling fever.* Harold's turtle was named Prince Crawlaway I and Everett's Prince Crawlaway II. The turtles disappeared and were later replaced by Clark the box turtle and Snap the snapping turtle. Clark wandered away and Snap was butchered for his meat, which Everett sold for fifty cents.

---

*The letter is undated. Whether Everett actually had pernicious anemia is unknown. Following the doctor's diagnosis, there was to be a blood test. I could find no results of that test. Pernicious anemia is caused by a deficiency of vitamin B_{12}, either in the diet or because the body is unable to absorb it. Symptoms include fatigue. The treatment at the time was eating raw liver or drinking liver juice, both of which contain B_{12}.

When school finally ended, Everett took long bike rides into the country. *I rode on dirt roads, paved roads, brick roads and gravel roads (especially the former and the latter). I saw ponds and brooks and squirrels and cattle and the like. It was hard going.*[21] The family, minus Christopher, visited Marengo Cave in southern Indiana. With headlamps and a guide, they descended into the dark silence of the cave. When he returned home, Everett dug a cave with a pick and a shovel in the backyard. Three friends helped. *Tonight Father came home. He had been away since February.*

In the first five days of June, Everett read eleven books, including *The Adventures of Tom Sawyer* and some of L. Frank Baum's Oz books. He fixed a flat bicycle tire, helped his mother clean the house, and made firework sparklers with his chemistry set. He also rode his bicycle barefoot and with one hand. *I did it for about an hour. It's fun. Try it for yourself.* Everett and a friend went to the nearby creek with their toy boats. *There were natural harbors, natural straits, and many other things.*[22] They caught tadpoles and put them on the boats, which they then stoned. Everett began to keep a list of the birds he saw: blue jays, flickers, red-winged blackbirds, woodpeckers, sparrows. He drew them all.

On July 4, young Ruess went to camp, where he detonated his homemade and store-bought fireworks. Two exploded in his hands and two backfired, giving him burn blisters. Stella credited a Boy Scout nature teacher at Camp Bryan in Michigan with awakening her son to the wonders of nature at the age of twelve. "Of Mr. Bristol Everett might have said what John Burroughs said of Walt Whitman: 'He started me on an endless quest.'"[23] Everett rose to the rank of Star Scout, accumulating merit badges in signaling, art, swimming, cooking, map reading, nature study, bird study, star study, forestry, leather working, and safety—all skills he would use in future years.[24]

He worked on developing his Native American expertise at camp by using friction to start a fire and fashioning a tomahawk. At home he combed northwestern Indiana for Indian beads but gave up on the search when he was informed that what he thought were beads were actually fossil shells. He then hunted arrowheads with an even greater fervor. Everett also played with his homemade bow and arrows. *I never knew I was such a good shot. I punctured a paper box, knocked a ball out of a girl's hand, hit trees from a distance, and many other things.*[25]

He saw a number of movies in August and particularly liked *Code of the West*. His mother was delayed getting home. *In consequence, the beds are unmade, and all meals are very crude. The table is a mess. A mother is a pretty necessary person to have.*[26] Everett acquired a BB gun and shot at a cast-iron boot scraper in the shape of a cat, hornets, a board, a telephone pole, and other objects. Switching from shooting a gun to shooting photographs, he took his first photos of a rose, horses, and creekside scenery. Returning to the gun, he targeted butterflies, water skaters, and two lightbulbs, which he broke. He got his first photographic prints back. *I am to get nothing but Nature in my [photo] album. No people or buildings.*[27] There were other summertime diversions. With many lakes nearby, Everett became an excellent swimmer, at one time swimming one mile across a lake.

Everett had an extreme reaction to poison ivy in September and was sidelined for a few days.* Christopher wrote advice to him from all parts of the country, the following originating in Georgia: "Make up your mind to be among the winners whatever you do—but don't neglect the things you *like* to do, your art and Indians and other interests."[28] Two days after school began on September 8, Everett and a couple of friends engaged in a series of pranks. They honked the horns of unlocked cars, rang doorbells and ran, and rigged a water trap—a string attached to two cans that collapsed when tripped, wetting shoes and feet. Two men emerged from the library and sprang the trap. *They were good sports though and laughed.* Everett had a dog named Ginger, who went everywhere with him, including camp and school. *Today when I came home, Ginger was so happy to see me that he licked my face and then ran in big circles, as fast as he could, rushing by me like a whirlwind. Then he would lie down on his back at my feet, inviting me to pet him.*[29]

The family took a long drive out into the country in early October in their new Dodge. *The car has a thing you clean the window with when it's raining. All you have to do is turn a thing, and if the car is going it will go.*[30] Waldo left for Antioch College. *I am very sorry to have him go. We were getting along much better than in the old days when we threw things at each other.*[31] Everett got an excellent in spelling and passing grades in arithmetic and self-control. *One of my greatest faults is that I often leave disagreeable but necessary work to the last minute, especially school work.*[32] The weather was getting colder.

---

*This was not Everett's only such outbreak. His father had similar reactions to poison ivy and poison oak, both of which contain urushiol oil. Poison ivy grows plentifully in parts of the United States and southern Canada, while western poison oak is found in northern California and the Northwest. Everett's worst case occurred in Zion National Park, where a western variety of poison ivy grows. There is confusion between the species, so I have left the family's references to both plants intact. The oil and the symptoms are the same.

Wild geese passed over the house, heading south. *Tonight I dreamed I was back in California.*[33] He saved his money for a Scout axe and leather sheath, paying $1.85 for them. He then chopped branches, made stakes, and hammered them into the hard ground with the new axe. Halloween arrived, and he went out trick-or-treating with two friends. *We waxed windows and threw corn and rang doorbells. We got some taffy at Wise's and it sure was good. I cut my pumpkin today.*[34] He thought his mother made the best pumpkin pie.

There was time in November for a Saturday drive to the Indianapolis home and museum of James Whitcomb Riley, the Hoosier poet. Everett had his own museum in his crowded room. *I have an Indian basket and a totem pole and a string of beads in one corner of my museum. I also have a shell corner, a butterfly corner, a corner with minerals in it, a corner with nests in it, a corner with things from all over the world in it, and a corner with different kinds of elephants in it. There is an ivory elephant, a bone elephant, a bronze elephant, a clay elephant, and a china elephant. I have 170 kinds of butterflies, moths, and beetles and things from Japan, Jerusalem, France, Germany, Cuba, Mexico, Alaska, and Bermuda, as well as many different states.*[35] He also had an unspecified number of coins; between 2,200 and 4,000 stamps (65 from Greece alone), depending on what day they were counted; and 20 different types of arrowheads. The menu for Thanksgiving dinner was turkey, mashed potatoes, celery, Jell-O salad with pineapple, ice cream, and mince pie. Following dinner the family and three guests played a game. They were given cards with *Plymouth Rock* on them. Each letter in those two words served as the first letter in a new word they used to describe what they were thankful for.

It snowed on December 5, and Everett went sledding with three friends. He threw snowballs at milk bottles and knocked down three. An old lady with spectacles came out and scolded the boys. At the Myers company holiday party all the children received new adjustable Chautauqua table desks. There were prizes for drawing, and Everett won $15 for being the most improved artist. He got a shiny bugle from his parents and a set of drawing materials and a Scout knife from his brother for Christmas. Harold and his mother came over to the Ruess home for New Year's Eve. For noisemakers at midnight there were four alarm clocks and three large piles of tin cans. Everett wore his brother's cowboy hat, boots, and neckerchief. *Finally the whistle blew and I heaved all these piles of tin cans onto the floor, picked one up and hit it with a spoon, piled them all up and knocked them down again and when the Catholic Church bells started ringing like mad and the whole town was in chaos I received three telephone calls.*[36]

And then the Valparaiso years were over for Everett at the age of fourteen, just as he began emerging from his chrysalis stage. All the accounts, including his own, indicate that he was a cheerful, well-adjusted boy with an inquisitive nature. His love of art, fascination with Native American artifacts, and outdoor skills would blossom with time. He had friends and was a social animal. That would change.

The desk company went bankrupt on the eve of the Depression and wound up in the hands of receivers. Christopher was reduced to selling desks directly to customers. That was "quite an experience," he said.[37] The family headed to California in late July 1928 for another new life.

———■———

The nearly two-month trip in Dorinda Dodge, as the Ruess family had christened its new vehicle, was leisurely, educational, and inexpensive. Everett was designated the official trip photographer. He was also constantly on the lookout for arrowheads. The family stayed in tourist camps to save money. There were stops in St. Louis and Denver, Rocky Mountain and Yellowstone national parks, and Craters of the Moon National Monument in Idaho. The route south was via Portland, Mount Shasta, Mount Lassen, Lake Tahoe, and Yosemite National Park once again.

They settled, this time for good, in Los Angeles. Their home at 1332 N. Kingsley Drive in the Los Feliz district was christened Plumosa Palms, The House of Ruess. The rambling one-story, seven-room home was on a quiet street between the busy Santa Monica and Sunset boulevards. There were two palm trees in front and a green lawn, the best maintained in the neighborhood, Everett boasted. *You can always hear the ambulance sirens or an airplane buzzing here.* The dog barked at every passing emergency vehicle. Los Angeles was different.[38]

In September they were off again in the Dodge for a three-day familiarization tour of Christopher's new sales territory. The journey was a lesson in the diversity of landscapes and the fecundity of Southern California. They drove through the suburban and rural enclaves of Pasadena, Ontario, San Bernardino, and Redlands and out into the desert, where they camped the first night in Indio. Nearing the Salton Sea the next morning, Everett wrote in his journal: *I saw several road runners, desert birds, shaped like pheasants, and a gray color. As we approached the sea, a Great Blue Heron flew off and several sandpipers were in the water, which is extremely salty.* The road crossed the Laguna Mountains. *I counted six kinds of cactus.*[39] The border closed at 5:30 P.M., so the family waited in San Diego until the next morning to enter

Tijuana, Mexico, where Everett took note of the dog racing track, gambling casinos, and saloons. The brothers purchased stamps for their collections in the Tijuana post office.

Returning to Los Angeles along the coast, the family stopped at the seaside village of La Jolla, where Everett explored a sea cave and watched cormorants catch fish. As they drove north, the region's agricultural richness unfolded. They passed groves of dates, oranges, lemons, olives, walnuts, avocados, and mulberry trees, the last supplying food for the silkworms that supported the small local silk industry. Flames and a dense column of smoke from an oil well fire signaled the approach to the Los Angeles Basin.

Los Angeles was a city of near-instantaneous metamorphoses spread over vast distances in a reclaimed desert. From 28 square miles in 1850, it had grown to more than 410 square miles by 1928. There was a great spurt of growth in the 1920s, which consisted mainly of people of moderate means from the Midwest, like the Ruess family. The city, which was just beginning to cohere, was still an "enormous village" dominated by a suburban mentality and conservative and religious interests. As the short orientation trip had demonstrated, Los Angeles was trapped within a vise of landscapes. "Facing the ocean," wrote the social critic and historian Carey McWilliams, "Southern California is inclined to forget the desert, but the desert is always there, and it haunts the imagination of the region."[40]

In this land of physical and human instabilities—"a vast drama of maladjustments" due to "incessant migration," in McWilliams's words—Stella chose culture as the anchor for her family. Los Angeles was going through one of its periodic cultural renaissances in the 1920s. Out of the amalgam of places and people came "the amusingly confused culture of the region" and, given time, a more unfettered imagination.[41] Stella chose poetry and the visual arts as the two major flukes of the family's anchor. Dance (à la Isadora Duncan), prose (mainly journal writing), and gardening (landscape architecture) were more minor blades inserted into the holding ground.

Culture came in a number of forms. Poetry, McWilliams had noted, was proliferating: "There are more poets per square mile in Southern California than in any other section of the United States. They have poetry societies, poetry magazines, poetry breakfasts, and poetry weekends." The results were "pallid verses" that did not transcend "the period of awkward self-consciousness" of the new arrivals. Southern California, said its most astute observer, was not all "sunshine and poppies."[42] For admirers of prose, there were literary circles within literary circles, well-stocked bookstores, active book collectors, and specialized libraries. Art, as practiced and appreciated in Los Angeles, was democratic, because, as the historian Kevin Starr wrote: "Los Angeles itself represented a triumph of the commonplace."[43] Attention was focused outdoors for the entire year in this balmy region; thus sketches, etchings, and paintings of landscapes predominated. Printmaking became popular. The artists had the same problem as the poets, an inability to see beyond placid surfaces.

As the 1920s merged with the 1930s "a golden age of California as a regional American civilization" began to bloom in all the arts. The movement came to be known as Edendale, and artists working within various cultural organizations, rather than in lone garrets, sought their inner selves, essences, souls, and truths through self-expression. "Their community nourished them emotionally, sustained them economically, and provided a locus for their aesthetic debates." This predominantly middle-class society coexisted with the "unprecedented wretchedness" of Depression-era urban and rural poverty.[44] There were also intimations of an emerging culture more attuned to the diverse realities of the Southwest, which Everett might have become part of had he lived long enough.

Stella was at the center of this movement. She patterned herself after Isadora Duncan, another California native, and Ruth St. Denis, who had influenced Duncan. Both interpretive dancers gave women a sense of freedom from traditional restraints and permission to be themselves. Waldo noted on his mother's death: "She lived poetically, artistically, beautifully."[45] This also became Everett's goal.

His mother dedicated her life to beauty and was what was known in the newspapers of the time as a clubwoman, meaning she was active in organizations outside the home. In Stella's case these were the National League of American Pen Women, the Poetry and Music Club, the Ruskin Art Club, and the Camp Fire Girls. She danced in a performance with St. Denis, whose Denishawn School of Dancing and Related Arts in Los Angeles had such distinguished pupils as Martha Graham. Stella also studied dance under Michio Ito.

Stella was part of a dance extravaganza staged in the Rose Bowl on September 20, 1929. Nothing like it had been seen before in Southern California. Ito, a Japanese choreographer and dancer, brought his stylized movements to Pasadena to celebrate the installation of stadium lights at the Rose Bowl. He dealt in natural gestures, symbols, and metaphors, as did Duncan, who had influenced him. He dressed the two hundred women dancers in flowing white silk gowns with pastel velveteen bodices cinched tight at the waist, and they swirled before a 40-foot-high and 125-foot-long gold screen that served as a backdrop. Lights played on the screen as the dancers swayed to the music of Chopin, Tchaikovsky, Dvořák, and Grieg. The event also included a symphony orchestra, choruses, and five thousand spectators. A newspaper reporter said it resembled a scene from an ancient Greek tragedy. Everett described the performance: *Several male dancers with bare brown bodies moved in sticklike styles across the sward, faster and faster with whirling bodies, as the music rose and fell. All the time an orange light was on them, making their bodies gleam and turning the green of the grass to an ominous copper color. In the background was a huge screen, bronze colored from the lights that played upon it.*[46]

The sponsoring Tournament of Roses Association hoped to make the Pageant of Lights an annual event, but that was not to be. In a little more than a month the stock market plummeted, and the Depression put an end to such extravagant celebrations of minor accomplishments.

Everett concentrated on poetry, essays, and a play and created paintings, posters, and Christmas cards. The *Hollywood Citizen* newspaper published some of his written contributions; one of his poems appeared in the *American Indian* magazine, published in Tulsa, Oklahoma; and he won $25 in a poster contest sponsored by the Los Angeles Chamber of Commerce to promote trade. Ruess was a member of the high school literary society, named Tabard Folk.[47] A newspaper item noted that his poem "The Tropic Pool" had been voted the best of those by the society's members. In an essay for his English class he compared Los Angeles to Valparaiso, citing the bigness and wealth of the large city but also noting its lack of friendliness. Sounding a bit wistful, Everett compared himself to the frog who preferred a small puddle where he could make a large splash to a lake where his impact would be minimal.

Ruess pondered how he could make his splash. By August 1929 he had decided to become an artist. *The train of causes is endless.* Stella and California had played major roles in this decision. His mother's artistic sensibilities had greatly influenced him. She had introduced him to the splendid paintings in museums and to the libraries that contained countless volumes of illustrated books. He was taking classes at the Otis Art Institute.[48] In California, where his grandparents and parents had lived and met, there were the ocean, mountains, forests, and deserts to inspire him. *Here, surely, is the Artist's Paradise, and I intend to know it and enjoy it to the full.* He had no intention, however, of limiting himself just to California.[49]

For Everett, there was also a life besides culture. He counted twenty-five species of birds and animals in Los Angeles. He explored the caves and the bee colony near Bee Rock in nearby Griffith Park with two smaller boys. He tried to climb a hill with a friend. They lost their way and had to bushwhack through the prickly undergrowth, getting scratched and cut in the process and giving up before they reached the top. Outside Los Angeles the family encountered new sights. They spotted a coyote on a dry lake in the Mohave Desert. *The coyote was quite tired when we saw him, and we chased him until we got within five feet of him. He traveled at the speed of 30 miles an hour. He was a magnificent specimen with sleek gray fur and sinuous body. We didn't want to run him down, so he got off safely.*[50] The flat desert lakes, so alien to someone familiar with the kettle lakes of Indiana, fascinated Everett. The family could drive in all directions. A mirage split a passing train into two parts.

Everett briefly attended Los Angeles High School, where he took the poetry class taught by Snow Longley Housh. Stella said Mrs. Housh was one of the major influences on Everett. She was an "outstanding teacher of creative poetry" who, Stella believed, gave Everett the means to survive in the desert.* "During his wanderings it was often the chanting of poetry that lifted his spirit and gave him courage to go on," Stella said. It took more than chanting poetry, however, to stay alive in the desert.

The budding artist-poet transferred to Hollywood High School, a two-mile bike ride along busy Sunset Boulevard from his home. He would spend his two remaining school years there. Everett showed signs of restlessness and a romantic yearning for the road in an essay titled "Trails" for his English class. *Whenever I consider trails a strange deep longing to be rambling on a winding path fills me.*[51] Three-quarters of his short life was now behind him.

----

*Stella Ruess, draft of "Youth Is for Adventure" (partial photocopy), undated, xi. Housh, Stella's schoolgirl friend from Cincinnati, was an admired figure in the Los Angeles poetry movement and edited the *Anthology of Southern California Verse* in 1930, which included contributions by Hildegarde Flanner and the bookseller Jake Zeitlin. Three years after Ruess disappeared, Housh encouraged another student at Los Angeles High School to become a poet. Ray Bradbury did not think he was a very good poet, but Housh included his "Death's Voice" in the *1937 Anthology of Student Verse*. Bradbury, who had attended the same poetry class as Everett, dedicated one of his novels to Housh. Sam Weller, *The Bradbury Chronicles: The Life of Ray Bradbury* (New York: William Morrow, 2005), 82, 83.

V

On the Road

1930

TWO MYSTERIES ARE EMBEDDED IN THIS TALE, the more commonly mentioned one being what caused Ruess's disappearance in 1934. The other, which very few have noted, is why, at the age of sixteen and not yet having graduated from high school, Everett began wandering. And how did his parents feel about his leaving home? Because familial discussions about this, if there were any, took place at home, there are no letters covering Everett's specific reasons or any written reactions from his parents during the spring of 1930. There are also no surviving Ruess diaries for that year. What came before is all there is to consider. I have supplied the background: he was raised to be freethinking and venturesome. Everett chose to remain relatively close to home and visit familiar places the first summer. It was a period of trials and experiments that lead to longer forays into more distant and far stranger lands, presaging the road trips of youths in the 1960s and 1970s. His parents both encouraged him and worried about his well-being.

Lugging a heavy backpack over which was draped a bedroll, Everett Ruess began hitchhiking north from Los Angeles in late June. It took the cherub-faced teenager one long day and a lot of good luck to reach Morro Bay, a small vacation and fishing village on the central coast whose harbor entrance is dominated by a huge granitic cone named Morro Rock. He had no trouble getting rides. A sailor's wife, a salesman, a dishwasher, a druggist, and five others transported the youth northward through rolling hills and seaside vistas.

State Highway 101 bisected the farmlands of the San Fernando Valley and left the Los Angeles city limits behind among the orange and walnut groves of Calabasas. The road snaked through dry hills whose yellowed summertime grasses, transformed magically each year from rain-soaked iridescent green, were dotted by dark, umbrella-shaped oak trees that stood like chess pieces waiting to be moved.

It was hot and dusty, and horse-drawn wagons and old Ford trucks from nearby farm communities mixed with sleeker cars from the city. The northbound traffic had to squeeze between the brush-covered Santa Monica Mountains on the left and the rounder Simi and Las Posas Hills on the right. The road dropped down the Conejo Grade to the fertile delta of the Oxnard Plain, laced with beans, sugar beets, and orange and walnut trees. It bisected coastal Ventura, a small city of eleven thousand people, known for oil, lima beans, and poinsettias, and then was once again confined, this time more tightly, by the chaparral-covered hills of the San Miguelito Oil Field and the ocean, pacified here by the protective presence of the offshore Channel Islands. Everett chatted loquaciously with the various drivers and took careful note of what he saw.

Four lanes and ice plants characterized the roadway through the millionaire's enclave of Montecito, where people with such last names as DuPont, Pillsbury, and Stetson lived at the end of long, private roads. Beyond Santa Barbara the highway paralleled the Southern Pacific Railroad tracks along a coastal bluff backed by the Santa Ynez Mountains and with a view of the cobalt-blue waters of the Santa Barbara Channel on the other side. Coastal travelers comfortably ensconced in railroad club cars gazed down upon sandy beaches edged by palm trees.

The road turned rightward at a 90-degree angle and ascended Gaviota Pass, the coastal entrance to and exit from Southern California. The presence of oak trees on hillsides and sycamores along creek beds intensified, as did that of farmland on flatter ground. Miles of bean fields surrounded Santa Maria. Flat Pismo Beach was celebrated for its clamming.

Everett left the druggist in San Luis Obispo and hitched a ride to nearby Morro Bay. He found shelter behind a sand dune and lit a small fire. *I found that we had eliminated so many things that there wasn't much to eat.*[1] He slept without a tent and woke up soaked by the heavy ocean mist. The druggist knew where Everett was camped and sent an employee around in the morning to haul the sodden and hungry young man to San Luis Obispo, where he was fed. This was the first of many such kindnesses the youngster encountered on the road.

He left that morning for Carmel. The highway took a more inland and warmer route northward and passed through Atascadero, once envisioned as the site of a real estate scheme for the rich but consisting of chicken and turkey ranches in the 1930s. The landscape became drier, with a hint of desert. Everett entered the Salinas Valley, which John Steinbeck was just beginning to celebrate. The arrow-straight highway pierced flat land where cattle, lettuce, alfalfa, and flower seed farms predominated.

A man who gave Everett a ride mentioned the photographer Edward Weston and that he lived in Carmel-by-the-Sea. The Village, as it was called by locals, was nestled in pine trees and rose from a dazzling, white-sand beach. From the beginning it had been conceived of as a special place. The Carmel Development Company had sent out brochures shortly after the turn of the century addressed to "the School Teachers of California and other Brain workers at Indoor Employment." Professors, artists, poets, and writers were attracted to the Village.

By the time Everett arrived, there was constant warring between commercial and artistic interests, the latter being dominant in 1930. The city council gave first priority to the Village's residential character. Interest in the theaters and art galleries was rampant. The weekly newspaper decried "tincan tourists" who left litter on the beach and along the banks of the Carmel River. The small community was considering constructing a wall to keep out the growing number of visitors. A strict zoning ordinance was enforced. There were no streetlights, unsightly utilities, house numbers, or sidewalks in the residential area. A permit was needed to cut a tree, and only trees native to the region could be planted. Billboards and outdoor electric lights were banned. The aesthetics of the quaint European architectural styles favored in the business district clashed with the regional architecture of redwood-sheathed cottages in the residential areas.

Everett explored the beach, the river, the town, and the Catholic mission, founded by Father Junípero Serra. *When I got back in town I went to Edward Weston's studio and made friends with him. I saw a large number of his photographs. He is a very broad-minded man.*[2] Weston photographed vegetables and nudes, was separated but not divorced from his wife, and was living with his photographic assistant and young lover, Sonya Noskowiak. That was Weston's breakthrough year. His assistant brought him sensuous peppers to photograph, one print of which became the famous *30P, Pepper 30, 1930* image. Besides peppers he photographed Sonya nude, Point Lobos in muted light, tangled kelp on Carmel Beach, bananas, the poet Robinson Jeffers (he lived nearby), the Mexican painter José Clemente Orozco behind thick-lensed glasses, and the wealthy residents of the Hotel Del Monte in his studio. Weston detested his rich clients, calling them "unhealthy parasites," but they paid the bills. He also had his first New York show in 1930. Weston wrote in his journal that summer: "Sittings, sales, fresh contracts, future possibilities, everything points to success in more than one way. My stars must have changed!"[3]

Everett showed his work to Weston, who had strong opinions and was dismissive of mediocre art. The photographer said Everett was "a boy who has potentialities in painting and writing."[4] Poor Everett. He would be forever unaware of this praise, confined to Weston's journal and not published until 1966.

Everett was welcomed into the unconventional Weston family on June 30. *Mr. Weston invited me to supper, and I met his two sons, very nice boys. I slept in his garage, which is empty. This morning I swept it and cleaned it out.*[5] Neil and Cole Weston split their time between their father in Carmel and their mother in Glendale. Neil was Everett's age; Cole was a little younger. The brothers fought frequently. Everett went down to the Carmel River with Neil and Cole and met another boy named Sam, who had caught his limit of trout. Ruess cooked pancakes, trout, and bacon, and then the boys went swimming in the river. Neil and Sam told the editor of the children's section of *The Carmelite* newspaper about their good time on the river, and she wrote that the river was the place visiting children should go for warm-water swimming and fishing.

The next day Everett hiked to Point Lobos, which was then private property and is now a small gem in the state park system. *The surf booms and thunders and the waves seem to climb the cliffs. The whole thing is tremendous.*[6] The combination of bowed Monterey cypresses, pounding surf, and fissured rocks made a strong impression on Everett. *Point Lobos is really the one place I have seen which I prefer to all others.*[7] He returned to Point Lobos the next day, where he met his friend Harry Leon Wilson Jr., the son of a writer and the brother of Weston's next young mistress and future wife, Charis.[8] Harry, Charis, and Everett had attended Hollywood High School together.[9] The Wilsons had a home in Carmel Highlands, five miles south of Carmel. Both boys worked with watercolors. They hiked over the rocks to the tide pools, where they saw starfish and sea anemones. They listened to the barking of the sea lions and hurled stones at various objects. They sketched some more and then hitchhiked to Carmel. *That evening I had supper with the Westons and we sat around the fire while Mr. Weston read "Moby Dick" aloud. When Cole went asleep, we all went to bed.*[10]

Weston liked to get up early, sip coffee, and contemplate his work. He awoke on July 4 at 4:30 A.M. and described what he saw. "Well, what luck! Here comes Sonya at this ungodly hour—couldn't sleep with an ungodly cold—and Everett rushes from the garage with paper in his hand bound for the woods on a hurry call."[11] Ruess climbed a hill with Harry Wilson. They sketched and then playfully tumbled down the slope, sketched again atop a bluff, and then descended to the water's edge. Everett returned to the Weston residence. *At home, Mr. Weston showed me some pictures he had and we had some interesting discussions.*[12]

The next day Everett received a check from his father and a query from his mother about his health. Everett was plagued by a bad case of poison ivy. He visited the office of *The Carmelite,* whose editor was interested in his block prints. He would take three and pay $1.25 for each.[13] Everett came to a hasty conclusion. *There is money in Art if you know how to find it.**

Because of arriving guests, Everett had to move out of the Westons' garage. Neil, Cole, and Sam helped Everett put his camping gear in a small boat and shove and pull it up the river. Suddenly, the pack fell out and got wet, spoiling some of his watercolors. They reached a small tidal island, where Everett made his camp, and the other boys departed. Ruess bought fresh vegetables from a Japanese farmer, chopped some wood, and made his dinner over a fire. In the full moonlight, he could see the mission a few fields distant.

He hid his belongings in the brush during the day and returned at night. Cornflakes and condensed milk and fresh vegetables for dinner were Everett's basic diet, supplemented with peanut butter, four loaves of bread, and several cans of peas and corn. He made some money gardening and caddying at Pebble Beach. *There are some interesting fellows at the caddy yard. There are two one-armed men, an aviator, a mechanic, a fisherman, a boy from New York, a man from Hawaii and an assortment of boys, beggars, and street urchins.*[14] He returned to Point Lobos with Harry Wilson. The boys went swimming in

---

*Everett Ruess to Christopher Ruess, July 19, 1930. *The Carmelite*'s editor and publisher J. A. Coughlin was the first person to recognize the commercial value of Everett's poetry and art. *The Sky-Seekers,* a linoleum-cut print of dramatically upthrust mountains, dominated the front page of the weekly newspaper on July 11, as did an untitled print of waves crashing against rocks on July 31. A smaller print of New York skyscrapers accompanied a poem of Everett's titled "Ballad of the Lonely Skyscraper" on page nine of the August 7 issue, by which time he was in Yosemite National Park.

the ice-cold water, floating in and out of arched sea caves on the swells and avoiding the knifelike edges of the surrounding rocks. *We were almost numb when we got out.*[15] They made a fire and were warmed.

Everett set off to the south for Big Sur with his fifty-pound pack on July 21. He hitched a ride to the nearby Highlands Inn, then got a ride in a lumber truck. The dirt road, mostly one lane, rose high above the white fringe of booming surf. Precipitous cliffs 260 feet high towered above Bixby Creek, where convicts were widening the road and construction crews were beginning work on a gracefully designed bridge. *So I slid and slipped and tumbled down the mountain 'till I came to a valley at the bottom, through which a small stream meandered.* Everett ate his lunch perched above a sea cave and watched the sinuous movements of the kelp. *Below me were many brown seaweeds, waving their strands with every motion of the sea, and writhing like octopi.*[16]

Ruess was present on the eve of great changes on the Big Sur coast. The bridge was completed in 1932 and the work on Highway 1 shortly thereafter, thus ending the isolation of the dramatic coastline and making it accessible to tourists. The road had been first a path trod by Indians, then a horse and cattle trail, then a wagon road, and now it was about to become a highway for automobiles. The dirt road had followed every indentation of the coast; the new highway would impose its own course across headlands and over creeks.

There were practical camping lessons to learn in Big Sur. The boy burned his fingers and spilled his peas when he lifted a hot can from a campfire beside the river. He crawled into his blankets only to be told by the landowner that he was on private property. But the man said he could stay the night. In the morning Everett left his pack under an oak tree and hiked down a canyon to the ocean. Inner tubes from a wreck littered the beach. Sand blew onto his watercolor-in-progress, sticking to the wet paint and making an interesting effect but dulling the colors. The smell of a dead cow and the mock charges of a live one caught his attention. He climbed into the Santa Lucia Mountains, sketching oak and sycamore trees as he ascended. That night he camped in a small hollow on the inland side of the coast highway.

The youth returned to Carmel by noon of the third day. *Then I went to the Weston house, and Neil and Cole and I went down to the beach to meet Mr. Weston, who was photographing kelp. Then we continued up the coast. We stopped at a very rocky place and started to gather starfish. We finished up by having sixty starfish in one small pool. They were of all sizes, and colored red, brown, purple, blue, yellow, and vermillion.*[17]

Everett had begun altering his name, a quirk he would repeat the next year. *Evart* was "a cheap corruption of a good name," his father said in a stern letter, and *Evert* was "worse." But Christopher leavened the criticism with praise for his son's work that had been published in *The Carmelite*. Then followed some fatherly advice. Christopher attempted to steer his son toward a more conventional lifestyle. He should study forestry and marry "the right kind of a girl who also loved outdoor life." He could be an artist on the side. His experiences that summer, said the salesman who was job hunting, would teach him how to meet and please people, "which is the art of personal charm."[18]

During his last week in Carmel, Everett earned $14 doing odd jobs. He planned to not waste more time making money but rather devote all his time to traveling and painting. *I went to Point Lobos for the last time, and then said goodbye to the Westons.*[19] He slept on the beach the last night and was on the road for Yosemite National Park at 8:30 A.M. on Sunday, August 3.

———————— ■ ————————

It took Everett twenty-four hours to cross the rounded hills of the Coast Range, the hot, dusty San Joaquin Valley, and the gently inclined foothills of the Sierra Nevada. He began his cross-California odyssey by walking and then riding with a man who had hiked across the continent. Everett walked again for six miles, then got a series of rides. The drivers offered him advice on lives of crime or good works and discussed whether he should own an automobile or not—as if he had a choice. There was one flat tire, which he helped fix. He spent the night by a creek on the outskirts of Merced, the gateway to Yosemite and a farming center with a population of seven thousand. It was *the most miserable night of my life. At first it was so hot that my blankets were covered with sweat. But I had to swathe my face in a towel to keep out a few of the millions of mosquitoes. Burrs got stuck to my blankets. After a fitful night's sleep, I woke up in the hot sunshine, and found that thousands of ants were swarming through my pack.*[20]

More walking and riding in the valley heat followed. A disabled World War I veteran, who lived on a $20 a month pension, gave him a ride to the foothill community of Mariposa, where the shadows cast on the sidewalks by tin roofs offered little relief from the burning heat. Everett got a ride in a laundry truck to El Portal, near the entrance to the park. The driver had ridden freight trains all over the country. Entering Yosemite National Park for the third time in his life, Everett found a space on the bank of the Merced River in Camp Seven, laid out his bedroll, and ate supper. The ranger-led entertainment at the campfire circle that evening consisted of songs, harmonica selections, and a girl dancing to bagpipes. *I have never known such a deadly monotonous sound as the bagpipes. He wouldn't stop playing them, it* *seemed.** Everett had a difficult time locating his campsite in the dark that night. He had attended both a firefall and a bear show with his mother when he first visited Yosemite in 1923.

———————— ∎ ————————

Everett's wanderings would eventually take him to many of the national parks and monuments in the West. His observations would provide a portrait of those places of human refuge and natural repose in the early 1930s, as well as a snapshot of the people who occupied them. In an era when the number of visitors was the standard for gauging the success of policies and careers, the national parks were places of entertainment where everything from manufactured spectacles to untouched wilderness was provided for visitors.[21] "Before, during and after the Depression, plans everywhere were the same—to accommodate rather than limit the influx of new visitors," wrote an authority on park policies.[22] The can-do, paramilitary aspects of the National Park Service at the time of Everett's visits were evidenced by the superintendents of Yosemite and Sequoia national parks, both of whom were addressed as "Colonel" by their rangers and had military backgrounds.

Although the overall number of visitors dropped in Yosemite and most other parks because of the Depression, people tended to stay longer. The campgrounds were crowded with season-long campers, many of them families who made the park their temporary home. One month before Everett arrived, 9,585 people were camped in Yosemite Valley on July 3. The park superintendent noted in his annual report: "This prolonged and intensive use congested the campgrounds in the Valley to a point that fully justified the criticism received and imposed some critical administrative problems."[23] Crowding remains a problem at Yosemite.

Falling fire and hungry bears drew hordes of gawkers. The tradition of the

———————————

*Everett Ruess to his family, August 5, 1930. The campgrounds were numbered then and named in the 1970s. Individual campsites were not designated. Campground Seven was wiped out in the January 1997 floods and was not replaced. Yosemite was different in other ways when Everett visited. There were no recreational vehicles, such as crowd the campgrounds today. "In those days people in the campgrounds either slept in tents or out in the open." Fernando Peñalosa, *Yosemite in the 1930s: A Remembrance* (Rancho Palos Verdes, Calif.: Quaking Aspen Books, 2002), 46–47. And inspired by a popular radio amateur hour program, rangers sought musical talent among the campers.

firefall supposedly began with Indians sending smoke signals from Glacier Point, but that sounds like a contrived account to give it historical legitimacy. In the nineteenth century, commercial interests attempted to attract tourists by pushing burning coals, fireworks, dynamite, and oil-soaked gunny sacks from the heights, creating a chute of fire. When David Curry came to Yosemite at the turn of the century to establish a camp, he regularized the ceremony. The fire, consisting of pine bark, pine cones, and dead timber, was started at 7 P.M. and first served as a bonfire for guests at the Glacier Point Hotel. The fuel was reduced to walnut-size embers in two hours. Curry—and later a Yosemite Park and Curry Company employee—hailed Glacier Point at 9 P.M.: "Hellooo, Glacier Point!" Back came: "Hellooo, Camp Curry!" The lights were turned off in the camp, from where the command was then given: "Let the fire fall." The answer rebounded: "The fire falls." The fire tender used a long-handled hoe to push the embers over the edge of Glacier Point. The cascade of fire dropped 1,400 feet to a barren rock ledge, echoing in form, if not substance, the water that spilled from the many falls in the valley.[24]

The Park Service initially endorsed the spectacle. Its director, Horace M. Albright, called the firefall "one of Yosemite's most beautiful and interesting customs."[25] The custom ended in 1968 because as many as six thousand people caused hours-long traffic jams in the valley, and Park Service policies began placing greater emphasis on the natural aspects of the Sierra Nevada.[26]

There was a double feature on most nights. After the firefall, visitors hopped in their automobiles and drove from one end of the valley to a less populated spot on the south bank of the Merced River for the 9:30 P.M. bear show. Rangers directed parking, and spectators stood behind a barrier located a safe distance from the performers. The stage was darkened. The park naturalist gave a brief lecture. Then, to use Director Albright's words: "All is quiet and dark. Suddenly the lights are flashed on across the river, revealing the 'salad bowl' with anywhere from half a dozen to a score of bears growling and feeding as the bear man dumps numerous garbage cans of supper for them. A tree stump in the middle of the platform is painted with syrup each evening, and there is great rivalry among the bears to get at this. Bears are like little boys in one respect—they prefer dessert to entrees, any day."[27]

In August 1930, while Everett was in the park, there were thirty bear lectures attended by a total of 18,250 people. During that year's season, which ran from May 19 to the end of August, 68,230 spectators watched them, for an average of 637 people per evening. Besides providing entertainment, the purpose was to lure the bears away from the more populated sections of the park, a tactic that was only partially successful. Ten people were injured by bears in 1930, compared to eighty the previous year. Bears searching for food broke into the back porch icebox of the park naturalist and the kitchen of his assistant. The Park Service wanted to shut down the performances, but the newspapers took up the issue of "bear rights" to free food and forced the superintendent to reverse his stand.

———■———

Everett had his own problems with deer, bears, and crowds.* He bought some groceries, which he found expensive, and walked about the valley. *What a relief it is to be here at last! Although the falls are mostly dry, everything is cool and green. The deer are tame as dogs, almost. I shall have to be careful that the bears don't find my bacon.*[28] But Everett was careless with his food: a deer ate a loaf of his bread. The campground was crowded. People from Oklahoma who had been on the road since June were on one side of him, and two young men who worked for a Los Angeles insurance firm were on the other. With a ranger-led group, he climbed the steep Ledge Trail to Glacier Point and then proceeded to Sentinel Dome, which was topped by a much-photographed Jeffrey pine tree bent double by the wind. Then he descended to the valley and was off that same night to the bear show with the Oklahomans, whom he described as an overweight, jolly pair. Back at Campground Seven a bear was investigating his pack. *He knocked it off the camp table and was about to tear it apart, when another camper who was sleeping directly on the other side of the table, raised himself up and shouted. The bear nearly fell over backwards in his hurry to get away. The rangers are having a little trouble with some of the bears and their depredations. The bear trap they use is not large enough to hold some of the bigger fellows.*[29]

The teenager was curious and inexhaustible. There were people to meet and discoveries to be made. *I fell in with a large party of men and women going on a nine day hike. They were in the summer classes of geology, botany, and hiking.* He hiked to the Little Yosemite High Sierra Camp with the group, where he was diverted by a search for arrowheads.[30] Everett found three partial arrowheads but sought a perfect specimen. He dug for three hours, finding only broken artifacts.† *I ran at top speed all the way down to Vernal Falls, hurdling all the rocks and obstructions, and banking steeply on the*

———

*Current visitors to the park are given dire warnings about the predations of bears and are required to place their food in bear-proof metal food cabinets at campsites.
† What occurs here for the first time on federal lands, and will be repeated frequently by Everett, is a clear violation of the Antiquities Act of 1906, which sought

frequent hairpin turns.[31] He was interested in what he weighed after hiking sixteen miles that day; he registered 143 pounds on the scales at Camp Curry.

Ruess rested and swam in the river the next day. He had never felt healthier, he assured his parents. *As to being lonesome for a good bed, I sleep quite well on the ground here and don't mind it at all, as there are no burrs, mosquitoes, or ants. I could very happily keep up this life indefinitely if I had the money.*[32] After one week in Yosemite he felt like an old-timer because of the constant turnover of tourists. He had no desire to rush through the park, as others did. Money for oil paints and the approaching school year were his main concerns.

Embarking on the popular loop tour of the high country with his heavy pack, Everett headed to the Little Yosemite camp, where he resumed his search for arrowheads, this time finding two perfect specimens. He watched a bear and her two cubs eat scraps of food behind the tent camp. *For several days there have been magnificent cloud effects. Thunder rumbles and crashes, but it hasn't really rained.* He climbed Half Dome. *I passed a cowboy guide who was passing the time lassoing sagebrush.* The quiet of the backcountry gave him time to think. He came to a decision. *It seems that my ambitions are always to be allied with the A's—artist, author, archeologist.*[33]

He climbed higher, to Merced and Booth Lakes. *The aspen soon disappeared, and cedar and pine took their place. There were wildflowers all along the way. I passed several small lakes.*[34] He met people, some of whom he knew: his Hollywood High School chemistry teacher and a Hollywood neighbor of his grandmother. Strangers gave him fresh-caught trout to eat. There was much to occupy him on the trail. *When I halt for a rest, I watch an ant climbing out of a footprint, or I toss stones, trying to see how near I can get them to the edge of the path without making them fall off. As I hike, I count the burro's shoes which have been cast. Or, if it is a steep climb, I feel the sweat drip from my face and hair.* He remarked on the behavior of his fellow humans in the wilderness. *People are certainly less indifferent.*[35]

From Tuolumne Meadows he hiked to Glen Aulin and then Lake Tenaya, where *the granite boulders and slabs were polished like mirrors from the glacier.* He read *Messer Marco Polo*, a fictional account of the explorer's travels, beside the lake before climbing to 9,926-foot-high Clouds Rest, where he had a dramatic view of the Sierra crest. *On the smooth granite summit, I perched precariously and ate my lunch and surveyed the lowered skyline. Patches of snow*

---

to protect such artifacts by imposing fines and prison sentences on pothunters, if convicted.

were visible on some of the distant peaks. In back was Tenaya Lake, glistening turquoise in the sunlight.[36]

The youngster completed the loop by descending to the Little Yosemite camp. Everett had the typical capacity of a boy to worship natural beauty at one moment and destroy it the next. Ruess and two other boys climbed a cliff behind the camp. *The three of us then took a log and industriously pried away at a large boulder at the edge. It finally slid off, and with a great flurry of sparks from the friction, it crashed down. There was a short silence, and then it struck the ground far below, crashing through the brush and over some trees.*[37]

Yosemite Valley was anticlimactic. *I was returning from the mountains and the solitude to the valley, the noisy, uninitiated tourists, and eventually to the city and its sordid buildings and business places.* During his hike, he had grown tired of comments about what a heavy pack he was carrying. He weighed it at Camp Curry: forty-eight pounds, or one-third his body weight. *Evidently I am not as weak as I thought I was.*[38] He thought he might substitute a lighter sleeping bag for his blanket roll and purchase a burro for his next trip. Everett collected his mail, read Henry James's *The American* in the Yosemite branch of the Mariposa County Library, and had new heels put on his shoes, the previous ones having lasted two hundred miles. He attempted to cook rice pudding but failed. He succeeded in cooking the Native American dish of roasted grasshoppers, obtaining the recipe from one of the books he read.*

That season was rated very successful by the park superintendent. A gift from John D. Rockefeller Jr. and matching funds from Congress had enabled the Park Service to purchase private inholdings in the Crane Flat area; the naturalist-led auto caravans to points of interest had been very popular; and the construction of a new sewage treatment plant had been completed. There were a few problems, however. The campgrounds were crowded, dust on the roads in the valley obscured views, and there was little money for trail work. Furthermore, the John Muir Trail along the crest of the Sierra Nevada was experiencing increased usage. The superintendent spent a few days personally

---

*How Everett obtained the grasshoppers is not known. The Indians ate them roasted, ground into a paste, or raw. Grasshoppers were also dried in the sun and stored for the winter. Herbert Earl Wilson, *The Lore and the Lure of the Yosemite: The Indians, Their Customs, Legends and Beliefs, and the Story of Yosemite* (San Francisco: Sunset Press, 1923), 25.

assessing use of the trail as the guest of a party of prominent New Yorkers who were accompanied by 117 pack animals.[39]

———————————■———————————

The family's patterns for the next four years had been established. Stella focused her attention on their new residence. At last there was a place to call home and to make beautiful. The garden became "a little Shangri-La, a setting for good times and poetry." Stella published "Poems in Trees" and sent a copy of the booklet to the university librarian at Berkeley, reminding him that it was her father "who organized the first books in California at Bancroft's in San Francisco."[40] Stella's block prints accompanied her three- and five-line poems, which described such Southern California arboreal wonders as Joshua, palm, eucalyptus, oak, and olive trees. She dedicated the booklet to the Ruskin Art Club of Los Angeles, where she had heard a lecture on Japanese poetry.*

It was a transition period for Christopher. He had lost $18,000 in desk company stocks and bonds. He was despondent and briefly contemplated suicide, but he bounced back, albeit with less enthusiasm for his work.[41] At the age of fifty, Christopher returned to social work in 1930 as a deputy probation officer for the County of Los Angeles. He wrote a memo titled "Suggestions to Ameliorate Evil Effects of the Depression on the Morale of Children and Adults." One suggestion derived from his son's experiences on the road. Inexpensive trekking expeditions could introduce children to the wonders of California and the "rough life."[42] Christopher settled into the routine work of office supervision and adult field service. "I am happy in service," he said. "I am not killing myself. I try to do an artistic job."[43]

The other brother lacked direction. Waldo graduated from high school with poor grades, worked at various odd jobs, and left college in his sophomore year. "I did not have my mind on studying. The wanderlust was too strong within me."[44] He went to sea, where he ran a passenger elevator on and worked as a wiper in the engine room of a United States Line passenger ship on the New York–to–England run. After coming home he was an

————————

*Founded in 1888, the Ruskin Art Club was the first women's cultural organization in the city. A club history states that rather than holding tea parties, the members "applied themselves lovingly and earnestly to the study and democratic availability of art."

indifferent night school student at UCLA, worked one week in the movie industry, labored in a gold mine in the Sierra Nevada Mother Lode country, and then returned to Los Angeles, where he drove a cab to earn money to attend the Foreign Service school at Georgetown University. That attempt at a career failed because he spent too much time partying in Washington, D.C.

He returned home because of his family's financial needs. He wasn't much help, however. "At this point I probably made another bad move."[45] He went east again and sought a job in the shipping industry in New York, then sailed to Los Angeles as an ordinary seaman on a freighter. He drove a taxi again and then went to work in the publicity department of a film company, running a mimeograph machine for $20 a week. Being a capable typist, he worked for a time for a writer of Broadway musicals. He traveled to New York with a probation officer who was escorting three youths. He stopped briefly in Washington, where he unsuccessfully sought a patronage job in the federal bureaucracy, and then the much-traveled and restless Waldo returned to Los Angeles again, via Chicago and New Orleans.

Employed in menial jobs, then unemployed again, then briefly employed once more, Waldo had a résumé, in the form of a neatly typed, eight-page letter to a potential employer, of dizzying proportions and laced with constant regrets. He attended Hollywood Secretarial School for nine months, acquiring the stenographic skills he would use in subsequent jobs and in typing lengthy letters asking for information about his brother's disappearance. In June of 1933 he went to work as a stenographer for the Metropolitan Water District, which was then constructing the aqueduct that would bring water from the Colorado River through the desert to the Los Angeles Basin. Waldo worked in an engineering office near Indio, south of Palm Springs and far from the bright lights of the city.[46]

The remainder of 1930 was anticlimactic for Everett after he returned to Los Angeles. He focused on getting through his senior year at Hollywood High School. This was one of two periods when he wrote under academic constraints, producing what was basically homework at Hollywood High School in the fall of 1930 and UCLA in the fall of 1932. His prose writing was stiff and self-conscious. A labored sentence in a short essay titled "Desert" reveals his overwrought style: *Above me was the illimitable expanse of the metallic cobalt sky, shot through with bolts of pitiless, piercing sunlight.*[47] His prose flowed more freely, and at times eloquently, when he was on the road and writing letters to his family and friends. The letters were minimally self-edited. His poetry was frothy. Everett used images from his Carmel experience to describe his imagined future in the poem "My Life Shall Be a Little Curling Wave."

My Life shall be a little curling wave
Gaily racing forth from the great blue sea.
A moment it will sparkle in the sun;
Jeweled and scintillating it will flash,
Then with a little tinkling tune
It will shelter on the cool brown sand
And turn to bubbling, milk white foam.
So, broken, slowly it will retreat,
Leaving the beach a little smoother
For the other waves that come.

The 224 seniors in the 1931 winter graduating class at Hollywood High School received their diplomas in the school auditorium on January 22.[48]

VI

Lan Rameau

1931

EVERETT BEGAN A YEAR THAT WOULD SEE HIM suffer heat fatigue in the Arizona desert after camping with a classmate high on the wintry flanks of the mountains above Los Angeles on New Year's Day. *We were above the clouds and could see them blowing by below us. Soon they enveloped us, and when we stood in front of our fire, we could see our shadows high above on the clouds. Night set in. No stars were visible. It began to rain heavily, while further up, above us, it snowed. There was no sound but the swish of the fir trees and the ceaseless patter of the rain on my poncho.*[1]

The two friends camped beside a steep cliff. They could hear dislodged stones clatter downward until their sound ceased. They fed the fire more fuel. There was a loud hissing sound when the raindrops hit the hot logs. The clouds parted, and the sunlight touched them. There was snow above on ten-thousand-foot-high Mount Baldy. Cornel Lengel stayed in camp, and Everett climbed higher. He found a mining claim dated 1916 and saw six bighorn sheep, a rare sight then in the San Gabriel Mountains and rarer now. He rejoined his friend, who had discovered the skeleton of a deer that had fallen from a cliff.

Again, Everett climbed. *I pulled myself by roots and boulders until I was within ten feet of the top. For half an hour I tried to negotiate those ten feet. I could not go back. Above me the ground was nearly perpendicular, and the earth was soft and gravelly. I would get within a foot of the top and slide back, almost*

going over the edge. At length I made a final effort, and pulled myself to the top.[2]
Cornel took an easier route.

They read poetry night and day and kept a fire burning constantly on the mountain. On the morning of the fourth day they descended to Camp Baldy, where Cornel's father met them in his car.

Poetry became an issue between the two friends later that year. Cornel wrote to Everett, who had criticized his poem "The Quest," to explain that the purpose of the quest was "to find a beautiful death; to do this I strive to overcome material obstacles." Omnipotence "is accomplished through self-annihilation." But he shouldn't have to explain his poetry to Everett, should he?[3] Neither could know that this romantic, Byronic concept of death might apply to one of them.

Everett had already made his plans for 1931. He was going to Arizona, Utah, New Mexico, and southern Colorado, a goal that proved too ambitious for a single year given his preferred means of transportation. *I shall buy myself a little burro, change my name and call him Everett. Then I'll travel through the Navajo country, hunt for Indian relics in the cliff dwellings, and travel with my burro thru the Painted Desert, the Kaibab, etc. I won't ride him, but will have him carry my supplies.*[4]

———————— ■ ————————

Everett set off for the desert as the Depression was closing in on Los Angeles. Fellow wanderers were numerous, and jobs and money were scarce. Labor and racial violence, nativism and provincialism, and screwy politics and religions—all of which California excelled in—peaked in the Golden State during the 1930s. Strangers were not welcome. They were known as Okies, Arkies, and Texies for the states that they had fled. For a short time the Los Angeles police attempted to seal the state's borders to keep out the unemployed. Mexicans were deported en masse. A historian noted: "The Depression years had put a new slant on the westward movement to California, turning what was once the great desideratum to the great fear."* Unemployment in the city peaked in 1933 at nearly 30 percent.

In the 1920s migrants had come from the Midwest in Dodges and similar

————

*Leonard Leader, *Los Angeles and the Great Depression* (New York: Garland Publishing, 1991), 186, 194. In one of those wonderful ironies that abound in Los Angeles, as thousands of Mexican immigrants were being deported in 1931, the city celebrated its 150th anniversary with La Fiesta de Los Angeles, and City Hall

vehicles. In the 1930s they came from the south-central states in Model-Ts. Along the way they encountered a hostile, desiccated, hot land while crossing the deserts. The spare, rolling landscape was interspersed with small islands of gas stations, tourist courts, and cafés strung out along Route 66, mostly a dirt highway when Everett traveled it. Gas cost from 12.5¢ to 20¢ a gallon and a room from $1 to $2 a night. Camping by the roadside was free. Flossie Haggard recalled this scene on Route 66 between Oklahoma and California two years before her son, Merle, was born:

> We were out of water, and just when I thought we weren't going to make it, I saw this boy coming down the highway on a bicycle. He was going all the way from Kentucky to Fresno. He shared a quart of water with us and helped us fix the car. Everybody'd been treating us like trash, and I told this boy, "I'm glad to see there's still some decent folks left in this world."[5]

Route 66 was a lifeline. It spanned two-thirds of the nation, from Chicago to Santa Monica, and was the primary corridor for that decade's two stages of migration. The first fled generally depressed places, and the second, beginning with the dust storms of the mid-1930s, left ruination behind. Both migrations were good for businesses along the road. A highway historian wrote: "The untold lesson of Route 66 during the Dust Bowl migration was not that people helped or did not help the pilgrims, but rather that there were people at the roadside, plenty of them, where there was a living to be made."[6] Prefab diners resembling railroad cars and adobe and wood structures were hastily constructed to serve the traffic.

Before he left Los Angeles, Everett drew up a handwritten "Program of the 1931 Artists' and Adventurers' Expedition." The program was adorned with sketches of sitting, grazing, and packed burros. It included the following: *Official location notice (worn nightly): silver bell; Official persuader: Pointed stick, 28 in. long. (Never actually used. Employed only for ceremonial purposes.); Official yell: 3 Brays, prolonged, and a Snort of Derision; Territory to be covered in 1931: The Great American Southwest.*

---

operators answered the telephones with a cheery *"Buenos días."* It was the Spanish heritage, not the Mexican legacy, that was being commemorated.

Whoopee, Ki yi, yo ho,
Shake your feet, little burro;
The faster you travel,
The sooner you'll get there.
Whoopee, Ki yi, yo ho,
Shake your feet, little burro.

Then he was off on the first leg of his journey. It was only a couple of blocks north to Santa Monica Boulevard and Route 66, and then Everett headed east in a series of rides, passing through Pasadena and the postcard landscapes of the tile-roofed, citrus-pungent foothill communities at the base of the Sierra Madre Mountains. The road bisected San Bernardino, the home of the National Orange Show, where more than one million oranges, lemons, and grapefruits were sculpted into various structures and shapes once a year. As it ascended Cajon Pass, the twisting roadway gave a clear view of the abrupt change in landscape: fertile orchards and vineyards to the south and barren mountains and a desert to the north. The Mojave Desert was described in a contemporary guidebook as "a bleak plateau furrowed by scores of untillable valleys, shimmering in the fierce sunlight." The roadside sign for a tourist facility declared, "Water Free with Purchases Only." Drivers pushed on as quickly as possible to Needles and the comforting, green fringe of vegetation bordering the Colorado River, "a lazy-looking stream that periodically goes on a bridge-smashing rampage."[7]

It was winter, and Everett had avoided the intense three-season heat at this lowest and hottest point of his trip. From an elevation of five hundred feet at the river, Route 66 rose gradually in a series of steps through the mining and ranching communities of Oatman, Kingman, Seligman, and Williams to its apex at Flagstaff, where it descended on its eastward course across Arizona. For the remainder of the trip to Flagstaff, Everett was given a ride by two Long Beach toughs, who begged or siphoned gas when they needed it. Three times the gas tank went dry. After the last stall, Everett chose to walk the remaining eight miles to Flagstaff.

The city of nearly four thousand inhabitants was perched at the 6,900-foot level of a volcanic island with green pine forests and three snow-capped mountains in the midst of a desert sea. The 12,000-foot San Francisco Peaks furnished the town with water and the nearby Navajo and Hopi with a sacred landmark. Flagstaff was a railroad and ranching center and the home of Arizona State Teachers College and Lowell Observatory, where astronomers had discovered Pluto.[8] The railroad police rousted hoboes off freight trains and marched them to the city limits, where they hopped another freight slowed by a grade and continued on their way to California. The local schools were swollen with the children of "gas buggy" migrants who had paused in Flagstaff. The mines were closing, the lumber mill had cut back its hours of operation, there were fewer Atchison, Topeka & Santa Fe passenger trains, and the local bank was about to fail. Desperate times loomed in northern Arizona.

Everett slept on pine needles in the adjacent Coconino National Forest that night. His experiment of melting snow for drinking water failed—it didn't taste good. There were no burros for sale in Flagstaff, so Ruess hitched a ride in a snowstorm to Kayenta with a Navajo mail carrier. They stopped at trading posts on Highway 89 and along the unpaved Kayenta road into the heart of the Navajo reservation. Beyond Tuba City, Everett noted, the dirt road passed the location where *The Vanishing American* had been filmed. *All the mountains are pink and red. No trees but pinyons.*[9] The biweekly mail truck had no difficulties with Marsh Pass that day, but the drivers of passenger vehicles were advised to deflate their tires and carry water, food, a shovel, tire chains, a tire gauge, and a tire pump.

■

Thus began Everett Ruess's first prolonged stay in the desert. It would shape his adolescent mind and body to near-adulthood. Thirty-three years previously a forty-two-year-old university art professor from New Jersey, also accompanied by a dog, as Everett would be for part of his journey, rode into the California desert and ranged on horseback and his feet across the arid lands of the West for the next three years. John C. Van Dyke survived to write a classic book on the subject, *The Desert*. Perhaps Everett would have done the same had he lived longer, although his likely would have been an illustrated work. Their journeys had separate endings but similar goals. Van Dyke spent his long life seeking beauty, and the climax of that quest was his time in the desert. He wrote, "There is a war of elements and a struggle for existence going on here that for ferocity is unparalleled elsewhere in nature."*

---

*Van Dyke, *The Desert* (Salt Lake City: Gibbs M. Smith, 1987), 26. It was perhaps no accident that Reyner Banham and Van Dyke were both art historians and perceptive observers of western deserts. Van Dyke and Ruess have been compared elsewhere: "They reveal the physical necessity of personal adaptation to the desert

A map is also an excellent way to assess a region. The "Indian Country" map of the Automobile Club of Southern California is the best two-dimensional representation of Four Corners country, or what could also be called Everett Ruess country. It is one of the finest road maps available, and I have been using various editions of it for more than forty years. There were fewer mapped roads in 1931, and far fewer were paved. Kayenta and the wider Monument Valley region are near the center of that country, a subsection of the Colorado Plateau. If any place could be called a nexus for Everett's desert wanderings in 1931, 1932, and 1934, that region would be it.[10]

Kayenta is surrounded by both vivid and muted reminders of the past. The structural ruins and relics of the Anasazi culture, which date back to before the time of Christ, are this country's most visible claims to a deep past. They exude a sense of mystery because their inhabitants disappeared, like Everett. As one discoverer of the ruins observed, "To know that you are the first to set foot in homes that have been deserted for centuries is a strange feeling."[11] The Anasazi melted into nearby cultures with more assured sources of water when the deserts they inhabited became drier around 1300 C.E. Their cliff-side and canyon-floor ruins and corncobs and squash rinds and utensils and weapons and skeletons preserved by the dry climate give mute testimony of past lives. There are echoes of our eventual fates in these relics, and Everett was attuned to the whispers of the dead.

The great expeditions into the Southwest that benefited so many institutions' collections and launched careers and fame outside the region, yet deprived native inhabitants of their heritages in the places where they lived, were about to come to an end. They were, for the most part, romantic quests conducted by wealthy coastal men. There would be one more such expedition, and it was being planned as Everett descended Marsh Pass and accompanied the mailman into Kayenta, where John Wetherill had his trading post. At the time, Everett didn't know he would be a small part of that last expedition, or that the Tsegi, the branch of the Anasazi culture in Kayenta, was located just a few miles from Marsh Pass, but Wetherill would soon direct him there.

The desert could teach, and Everett would learn, as Wetherill had over a

---

for survival, and although they reveal influences from the Romantic movement, their romanticism is counterbalanced by the necessity of realistic pragmatism for survival in a harsh environment." Judy L. Perkins, "John Van Dyke and Everett Ruess: A Comparison with the Spirit of Place Tradition" (master's thesis, Colorado State University, 1988), 4.

lifetime. "The desert will take care of you. At first it's all big and beautiful, but you're afraid of it. Then you begin to see its dangers, and you hate it. Then you learn how to overcome its dangers. And the desert is home," Wetherill said.[12]

No white man knew the area better than Wetherill. He had penned a handwritten description of nearby Monument Valley on a sheet of paper titled "Notes on Navajo Proposed Park." The idea for a Rainbow Bridge–Monument Valley National Park, which would extend eastward as far as Canyon de Chelly and take in three thousand square miles of the Navajo Indian Reservation, was just beginning to emerge.[13] The description Wetherill offered was for bureaucratic purposes, as he worked part-time for the Park Service. It did not resemble the promotion-driven paeans later employed to attract filmmakers, who made Monument Valley the "canonical image" of the American desert, exploited and instantly recognizable on millions of movie, television, and computer screens.[14] Wetherill's report stated, "Monument Valley area lies partly in Arizona and partly in Utah. Consists of many detached mesas, buttes and slender, towering pinnacles that are the product of heavy erosion over a large area. These 'Monuments' have a weird and unreal appearance. Most of the formations are brilliant red in color. The area is arid and vegetation is of the desert type."[15]

When Everett arrived in Kayenta on February 12, the sixty-five-year-old guide and trader was recovering from the rigors of a three-week scouting trip in January for the proposed national park. He had set off on the Colorado River with two Californians in a steel boat propelled by an outboard motor through the icy water. This experimental vessel lasted one day, and the ice threatened the lighter wooden craft they had been towing and were now forced to use. The men were constantly in and out of the frigid water. They lost their food and had only tea and sugar for sustenance. They located a food cache at Rainbow Bridge, made it upriver as far as Hole-in-the-Rock, and then returned to Lees Ferry. Wetherill's stamina was diminished after that ordeal, but he had led an incredibly active life up to 1931.

It was Wetherill and his brothers who had launched the collecting craze at the end of the previous century. From a ranch in southwestern Colorado and then their separate homes and trading posts as they grew older, Wetherill and his four brothers discovered Anasazi ruins, ignited the search by others for antiquities, and excavated the sites themselves or guided expeditions to them. The Wetherills didn't exactly prosper, but they made a living from these activities that led to the passage of the Antiquities Act in 1906. The act gave the scientific and museum communities, which had their own set of monetary imperatives, the edge over such nonacademics as the Wetherill brothers. The Park Service history for Navajo National Monument, formed for the protection of three ruins in the Tsegi Canyon system, states: "The specter of Richard Wetherill haunted American archeology. As a result of his widespread digging and the cottage industry that developed around it, the scientific community pressed for legislation to protect American antiquities."[16] The pothunter provisions of the act were more honored in the breach because of the lack of effective enforcement.*

John Wetherill was the brother who discovered Rainbow Bridge and two of the three major ruins in Navajo National Monument, where he was the sole government employee for a quarter century. He guided such luminaries as Teddy Roosevelt and Zane Gray into the backcountry. John and his wife, Louisa—who spoke Navajo and made important contributions to the understanding of the Navajo culture—kept the comfortably appointed guest quarters at their Kayenta trading post open for travelers. The Navajo referred to him by the honorific *hosteen,* a mark of respect.

The early 1930s were difficult times for traders and Indians alike. The tourist business was nearly extinct, Indians purchased fewer goods from the traders, and the financial condition of the trading post was so diminished that the bond covering Wetherill's federal government license was revoked, and he had to seek another one. To supplement the $12 a year he was sometimes paid to be the custodian of Navajo National Monument, the sole annual appropriation for the government park, Wetherill took a job supervising a 35-man crew building trails in the monument. Despite hardships, like living in tents and eating only passable food, the crew was thankful for the work. Their former occupations covered a wide range: a National Forest supervisor, two Indian traders, businessmen, filling station owners, a newspaper editor, a cow camp cook, and two ranking railroad employees.

Wetherill faced a unique problem in implementing the Depression-era work programs, which included stabilizing the ruins. His team had to contend with a Navajo witch, an old man who visited the camp every day and whose goats

---

*Maurice Cope, who was the ranger in Bryce Canyon National Park when Ruess visited it in 1934, told the following story. An Indian found a ruin no white man had visited. Cope asked him how he knew that was so. "Houses not torn down, pottery bowls not carried away, everything still on ground in plain sight." Quoted in Eivind T. Scoyen and Frank J. Taylor, *The Rainbow Canyons* (Stanford, Calif.: Stanford University Press, 1931), 64.

grazed in the monument. The witch had extorted a large herd from fellow Navajo, whom he had threatened with his powers and who had given him their oldest goats to avoid his wrath. Wetherill wrote to the regional Park Service superintendent that his men had faced many problems before, but "we find ourselves having to add a new one—Witchcraft!"[17]

For the Navajo, the winter of 1932 was particularly severe. They lost many sheep and cattle and were in rags when they came to the trading post. Using his connections—considerable because of his influential guests, his congressional and Park Service connections, and Louisa's cultural reputation and contacts—Wetherill sought funds for the Indians, citing the fact that closing the tuberculosis sanitarium in Kayenta would be a hardship for the hundreds of Navajo housed there. Besides the sanitarium, Kayenta had a spring, a few scraggly trees, a Bureau of Indian Affairs school, the missionary's residence, a few scattered Navajo dwellings known as hogans, and two trading posts. Between Kayenta and Bluff, Utah, there were a series of wandering dirt tracks across Monument Valley and up over a pass and little else, except Goulding's trading post on the northern edge of the valley and the Oljato trading post a few miles to the west of it. When Everett was in Kayenta, he divided his time between the Wetherills' and Keith Warren's trading posts.

◾

Ruess rarely traveled with anyone, so he was emotionally dependent on correspondence with his family and friends. Everett was constantly writing letters, sending parcels, and receiving the same. On his arrival in Kayenta, he wrote to his brother that if his parents *want to send anything, they could send food*.[18] He immediately assumed the name Lan Rameau in his correspondence. It was difficult for him to take on a dual role, Lan wrote to his family and a friend, both of whom misspelled his new first name, the difference between an *L* and an *S* in Ruess's script being difficult to decipher. Everett was very touchy about the imagined slight. He asked them to respect his *Nomme de broushe*, even though it was not the perfect "cognomen" for an artist. He said he intended to keep it.* Ruess's mother was worried and wrote to the proprietor of the Warren Trading Post, who assured her that Everett was fine.[19]

---

*Lan Rameau to his family, March 1, 1931. A name change, as Christopher McCandless also illustrated, was one way to disappear yet maintain a corporeal presence. Everett may have seen his name change as a "rite of passage practiced in many cultures," or it might have been a sign of "an incipient psychosis." John P. O'Grady,

Ruess swapped a block print with Harry Nurnburger, a clerk at the Warren Trading Post, for a decorated black-and-white Anasazi bowl in his first few days in Kayenta. When Harry finished working, Lan spent time in his quarters, talking and showing him his art. It was cold outside. A watercolor painting had spots in the sky caused by water freezing as the paint was applied. Nurnburger purchased a watercolor and had it framed. Lan received a Navajo blanket in return for designing Harry's Christmas card.*

The youth's first impressions of the resident population were that the Navajo were poor and lived in filthy conditions, and that Wetherill was the best guide in the Southwest. *The traders around here deride the "Indian lovers" who drive thru in cars and write articles about their picturesqueness and their wrongs.* He didn't think the Indians were mistreated by the traders. *I have had a few disillusionments about Indians, here. For one thing the Navajo are scrupulously dishonest. When I leave my hogan for a while, I have to take all my possessions down to the store. I once left a few pots and pans behind. When I came back they were outside in the mud.*[20] Perhaps he was being given a subtle message that it was not his hogan. Altogether, however, the territory, if not the weather, was all Ruess had hoped for. *It has rained, snowed, hailed, or showered every night since I have been here. Now it is blowing an icy gale. Heavy, lead colored clouds are in the offing. On one side, the hills are still covered with snow.*[21]

He began preparations for more extensive wandering, buying a burro for $6, a Dutch oven for $2.50, a Navajo-woven cinch and rope for $2, a frying pan for 35¢, and a tarpaulin to keep him dry for $8. *Has my equipment proven inadequate? Ans.: "Yes."* Since no store-bought bread was available, he learned to bake squaw bread, corn bread, and biscuits in the Dutch oven. He had stocked up on flour, potatoes, onions, beans, rice, raisins, baking powder, syrup, Quaker Oats, lard, bacon, canned milk, chocolate, and other

---

Pilgrims to the Wild: Everett Ruess, Henry David Thoreau, John Muir, Clarence King, Mary Austin (Salt Lake City: University of Utah Press, 1993), 13, 14.
*Harry F. Nurnburger to Stella Ruess, January 4 [1936?]. Writing after Everett's disappearance, Nurnburger said he had known Ruess quite well at that time but didn't see much of him during subsequent trips. "I do not know anything about art, but I always felt that he would have gone far as a painter. For one so young his water colors showed great strength, and he caught the 'feel' of the desert, which few painters do."

items to satisfy his nonnative diet.* He bought gun oil for his shotgun, of unknown gauge. Lan also carried a Colt .25-caliber pistol buried deep within one of his packsacks.† The $25 he had unexpectedly won in a poster contest he had entered to please his high school art teacher would help cover the expenses. Cash on hand was $79 before expenses of $35.80, leaving $43.20 in his pocket.[22]

Lan's burro, the first of many, was a bit of a joke, he thought. He described the burro as being dressed formally in a black coat with a white nose and eyebrows and clipped ears. The animal was stubborn, as most burros can be—perhaps because of their sense of self-preservation—and elusive, even when hobbled and most especially when Everett went to retrieve him in the mornings. The burro frequently got loose. There were other problems. *The first time I put a real pack on him, he ambled along for a mile and then lay down in the center of the path, but I think he is over that habit.*[23]

A burro, also known as a donkey, can carry a heavy load for long distances and takes less care than a horse. They are also companionable creatures. But they have minds of their own. The saying went: "Any single-blanket, jackass prospector will tell you that for every week of prospecting with burros you spend two days hunting them."[24] Lan called his first burro Everett. It was one year older than him.

His worried family thought about visiting Everett in Dorinda, the family car. He dissuaded them, citing the poor roads. *It would sink in the sand, rattle to pieces on the rocks, get stuck in a river bottom, slide off a cliff, or run out of gas miles from a service station.*[25]

He much preferred a trail and a burro to an automobile but ran into prob-

---

*Everett's supposed Navajo diet—shown here to be a typical Anglo diet of the time—and its effect on his teeth would become an issue seventy-eight years later when it was thought his bones had been discovered.

†Everett is assumed to have been unarmed, but that was not the case from the beginning to the end of his travels in the Southwest, though it might just as well have been. He would trade his shotgun for a burro, and his pistol was not readily available in a quick-draw situation. *About the pistol, I haven't looked at it for a month or so, but presume it's as per usual except for more sand in the barrel. I keep it in a small waterproof case tied in an ore bag, which is under a flour sack in a pack sack all tied shut, with a tarp over all. I could say other things about the deadly weapon, but I am getting writer's cramp.* Evert Rulan to Billy [Bill Jacobs], May 23, 1931. He was at the Grand Canyon when he wrote his friend.

lems on his initial outing to the San Juan River. *After sunset I kept going, trying to reach an old Navajo hogan of which I knew. Finally I tied the burro to a tree and floundered around in the darkness and sandhills until I found the hogan. Then I couldn't find the burro. Then I couldn't find the hogan, after locating Everett. After two more searches for each, I made camp with the burro. A flying spark burnt a hole in my packsack. My knife got lost.*[26] Rameau was embarked on a steep learning curve.

By March 21 Lan was safely camped on the bank of the river, where he was learning how to cook, build roads and stone walls, chop wood, carry water, and wash dishes in a mining camp. In return he got his board. He went swimming in the river and didn't fall for the old prank of going on a hunt for nonexistent snipe that two of the workers tried to pull on him. John Wetherill, who was in the camp, drew him a map of the Anasazi ruins near Marsh Pass. There was no paying job available for him, so he departed.

When he was on the trail again, the pack shifted off the burro's back, twice. Crafty burros had a habit of inflating their bellies when being loaded and then deflating them on the trail. There were snow flurries. He cooked spotted dog (rice and raisins) for dinner. In the morning three Navajo on horses stopped by his fire and silently watched him pack. It must have been a strange sight for them and unnerving for Lan. He arrived at the Oljato Trading Post on March 28, his seventeenth birthday. His letters had been forwarded to Kayenta, but there was a single package waiting for him in Oljato. He devoured the food it contained for lunch.[27] Agathla Peak, also known as El Capitan, a nearly sheer 1,500-foot volcanic plug, served as a landmark for Lan, as it did for the Navajo, and guided him safely back to Kayenta.[28]

———————————————— ■ ————————————————

Lan was off soon with Wetherill's map in hand for the nearby Tsegi Canyon system and the ruins of Betatakin and Keet Seel.[29] Perhaps because he had tired of the echo effect of calling his donkey by his now nonexistent first name, Ruess christened his ancient burro Pegasus in ironic tribute to the winged horse of Greek mythology. *The red dirt road wound back & forth for long stretches, with hogan & cornfields on each side. Vultures circled overhead. The burro slowed. Once we almost kept up with a young Navvy on an old red horse, but he swung the quirt back & forth gracefully, & though I whacked Peg, he didn't spread his wings. Soon the Navajo disappeared over the hill. We got on the wrong side of a little gully that became a great wash, & had to circle all around. There were twisted junipers up the canyon. A herd of goats stopped us for a few minutes.*[30] They may very well have been the witch's goats.

Lan didn't have much to say about either ruin. He was alone except for three college boys who climbed down the trail from the rim to Betatakin, the more accessible of the three cliff dwellings in the monument. Navajo National Monument was—and is—remote, and the ruins require a substantial hike, greatly reducing the number of visitors. However, Lan did leave his words in the log at Keet Seel, and he would return in three years for a more extended stay. The log read:

1931

Lan Rameau   Hollywood, Cal.
Hiked from Betatakin & back, Friday
afternoon, April 10. Some cross country
race. Revisited on Apr. 12, and
investigated each room. It would have been
a magnificent privilege to have seen Keet Seel
in activity, some centuries ago, but I'm
glad I didn't live then.[31]

Five days later he was back in Kayenta telling his parents what he needed sent to him: two pairs of heavy shorts, three or four pairs of wool socks, a pocket comb, a pair of tennis shoes, peanut butter, raisins, more money, and a tin plate and fork. He said the Indians didn't use such utensils, and thus the trading posts didn't stock them. In return, he had sent home three packages. Among the items shipped were the Anasazi bowl, a more contemporary Indian bowl, a valuable mother-of-pearl ornament he had found in Keet Seel, numerous pottery shards, part of a human jawbone with its teeth intact, and dried corncobs he estimated to be more than 1,200 years old. Collecting these items was clearly a violation of the Antiquities Act, but there was no one in the monument to enforce it.

For his friend Bill Jacobs, Lan had some advice. He didn't like the fact that Jacobs was purposeless. *Man, climb out of yourself. Raise yourself to another level. There's no necessity for being commonplace. You can alter your circumstances if you want to badly enough. A person has no right to be dissatisfied if he makes no effort to change.* The son recognized that the sermon stemmed from his father's influence. *You know, heredity and environment are powerful things. My father was once a preacher.* As for himself, things couldn't be better. *These days away from the city have been the happiest of my life, I believe. It has all been a beautiful dream, sometimes tranquil, sometimes fantastic, and with enough pain and tragedy to make the delights possible by contrast. But the pain too has been unreal.*[32] There were other downsides. Art needed an audience or it perished, he missed having a real friend, and he would like to have a small dog for company.

In addition to his friend, he criticized Waldo for not living life to its fullest, as he was, and he deflected criticism from his brother for being a financial drain on his family during hard times. The items he had requested could not be purchased on the reservation, Lan explained, and they were necessities. *I have made many efforts to find jobs, but hard times are here as well as elsewhere.* The Indians were given preference for government jobs. He would never take a regular job. *I myself would sooner walk a whole day behind the burro than spend two hours on the street car.* He was determined to live the imagined life of the artist. *But each day spent in stupid labor I shall consider wasted.*[33]

Lan outlined his plans for the future to his brother. He would wander through the West for the next couple of years practicing his Art. Then he would return to the city—not necessarily Hollywood, though—and paint in watercolors and oils on larger canvases. *As to ways and means, that problem will be solved somehow.* A studio would be a necessity. *It is my intention to accomplish something very definite in Art.*[34] Exhibits and sales would naturally follow. Next on his agenda came foreign travel, not to Europe, which was too civilized, but perhaps to the South Seas. Ecuador, with its volcanoes and jungles, was a possibility—he had just read *Green Mansions,* a romantic tale of love set in the Ecuadorian jungle.

He may have imagined or foreseen his future and begun propelling himself toward it. *I must pack my short life full of interesting events and creative activity. Philosophy and aesthetic contemplation are not enough. I intend to do everything possible to broaden my experience and allow myself to reach the fullest development. Then, and before physical deterioration obtrudes, I shall go on some last wilderness trip, to a place I have known and loved. I shall not return.*[35]

There was more prosaic but nevertheless exciting news. *My family group has been enlarged to three.* Curly, a puppy, joined his road family. *He is a little roly poly puppy with fluffy white fur, and blue brown patches on his head and near his tail. His eyes are blue, and his nose is short. I found him last night, lost and squealing for help.*[36] There had been a struggle to possess Curly, who Lan believed was homeless. That may not have been the case. A young squaw walked off with the puppy. Everett gave chase and grabbed her by the two strands of beads around her neck. She didn't stop, and the necklaces broke. *Even then I had to manhandle her and pinch her fingers before she would let go of Curly.*[37]

Ruess changed his name again, this time to Evert Rulan, the last name a contraction of *Ruess* and *Lan*. *Those who knew me formerly thought my name was freakish and an affectation of Frenchiness. It is not easy to chose a name, but Evert Rulan can be spelled, pronounced, remembered, and is moderately distinctive.*[38] Evert, having received the items he had requested from his family and feeling he was now properly equipped, set off for Canyon de Chelly. He told his parents he had filled sixty pages of the diary they had sent him.*

It took four days to cover the eighty miles to Chinle. Curly, who tired easily, was perched atop the pack on the burro's back. The donkey was unpredictable. *One day I covered 25 miles, but in the afternoon, Pegasus folded his wings, and progress was very slow.* On the first day there were intermittent sprinkles, and Evert saw a double rainbow, surely a sign of good luck. *For three days['] duration there were magnificent cloud effects, with rain, lightning and rolling thunder.*[39] Then they arrived at the Navajo settlement that was the gateway to Canyon de Chelly, which had just become a national monument on April 1.

———————— ■ ————————

Evert's letter to his friend Bill Jacobs on May 10, describing the trip and what he saw on arriving at Chinle, raises the question of Ruess's possible homosexual tendencies. The letter was signed "Love and kisses, Desperately yours, Evert." There was a short P.S., rendered as *S.P.,* that contained a series of silly questions ending with "have you fallen in love." The question mark was inverted. The postscript was signed "your comrade."[40]

Humor, tinged with longing for acceptance, covered up the loneliness, raging hormones, and the crisis typical of a teenager who did not feel comfortable with his sexual identity. As with Ruess's literary and artistic talents, no one knows what the outcome would have been—whether in time he would have been at ease with women, other than as close friends, or in what direction his sexual orientation would have evolved. Because the question has been inadequately dealt with in previous published works and bears on his wanderings, it deserves to be addressed as fully as possible while Evert pauses at the entrance to Canyon de Chelly.

———————

*Evert Rulan to his parents, May 2, 1931. The 1931 journal has not survived. There is no mention of Everett writing a diary in 1930. The only surviving journals written in his teenage years cover portions of his travels in 1932 and 1933. Searches were undertaken for a 1934 diary on the basis of the two that survived and the family's tradition of keeping journals. It has not been found.

First, what was the context for the letters? During Everett's travels in 1931, he signed his letters to Jacobs, who gave them to Everett's parents after he disappeared, "Your comrade" to begin with. They escalated to "Your alter ego," "Cheerily," "Your comrade of ancient days," the above-mentioned "Love and kisses," "Your indescribable pal," "Yours," "Your own cronie," and ended the year with "Your comrade of olden times." In an August letter, Evert complained that he was always making overtures of friendship and Bill did not reciprocate the gestures. There was an unsuccessful attempt to travel together with a third friend the next year. Everett sent Bill a note addressed to "Dearest Billikin" and a letter that pleaded: "Give me some advice, tell me my faults, my virtues, if any, open up your heart, and write lengthily if you love me."[41]

For a time Ruess was closer to Jacobs than to anyone else, at least on paper. Something kept them emotionally apart. It is doubtful whether Everett could have been close to anyone, given his self-absorption. Ruess, a connoisseur of beauty, commented on the good looks of both males and females he met or observed in his travels. The women he was close to were older and safe. After he disappeared, his father wondered if he ever would have learned "to like" women.[42]

There were unspecified intimacies with boys. Everett gave his coat to a young cowboy to use as a pillow when this friend lay down beside him in a barn near Zeniff, Arizona. They were wrapped in saddle blankets. A Navajo boy wanted to sleep outside with Everett and crawled under the covers with him. It rained. They moved inside. *I had an ugly dream about him.* He wrote a trusted woman friend two years later: *I had a strange experience with a young fellow at an outpost, a boy I'd known before. It seems that only in moments of desperation is the soul most truly revealed.*[43]

Undated fragments of quotes in Everett's handwriting give an indication of the state of his mind and emotions. The first concerns women and is not readily identifiable. *It is particularly important that a man should know how to circumvent women, for this and the capture of food form the basis of masculine wisdom.* The second fragment expresses the love of a woman for a man. *Did I say I loved him before? Then it was only my body that wanted a slave. Now it is my heart that desires a master! Now I know love for the first time in my life!* This quote comes from act IV, scene 1, of Eugene O'Neill's *Lazarus Laughed,* a play first performed in Pasadena in 1928 that deals with the raising of Lazarus from the dead by Jesus.

The gay issue arose when Waldo Ruess asked the editor of *Everett Ruess: A Vagabond for Beauty* to eliminate the reference to "love and kisses." The book was published in 1983 with the phrase intact. This bothered Waldo.

He thought the ending "might give people the wrong idea." The editor left it in because of its humorous context. Waldo wanted the phrase deleted from subsequent editions.* It remained, along with W. L. Rusho's comment in the preface that Ruess "was a highly complex young man with multiple consuming motivations. . . . That he may have concealed part of his nature even to his close friends and relatives is a possibility subject only to educated guesses."[44]

The next writer to address the issue went no farther than posing questions, which was sufficient to put the idea in readers' minds. Mark Taylor asked if Everett had traveled alone in the desert in an attempt to understand his sexuality. Could it be that he had a secret life, a dual existence, a shadow side? The questions raised possibilities without providing answers or even basic information. Nonetheless, this allowed Rusho to declare that questions had been raised in his 1998 introduction to Ruess's journals, where he stated that nothing in the surviving diaries hinted at homosexuality—but this was sidestepping the letters. A third writer, Gary James Bergera, concluded that the "complex question" was difficult to answer.[45]

Only one person could reveal what "love and kisses" meant after Everett disappeared, and that was Bill Jacobs. Jacobs said he was unaware that he was a homosexual when he knew Everett. That knowledge came later. Times were different in the 1930s, and such feelings were not often discussed openly, even if they were recognized. The man who questioned Jacobs in the late 1980s and provided this clue was C. Larry Roberts, a coproducer along with Diane Orr of a documentary on Ruess. Roberts, who was gay, also thought that Ruess sought solitude because of his confused sexuality.[46]

———— ■ ————

When Evert arrived in Chinle, just west of Canyon de Chelly and its branch, Canyon del Muerto, he encountered difficulties. *The Indians are not very lovable here. This morning, when I looked for my burro, I found his bell and tie*

---

*Waldo Ruess to Diane Orr, July 23, 1984. Waldo was adamant on the issue of his brother's sexual orientation. A lover of many women who had repelled men's advances in Hollywood, Waldo wrote Orr: "Whenever R was at home we had beds in the same bedroom and often talked together before going to sleep. And I think I knew him pretty well. And I think my parents did too. He definitely was not a homo, or homo-inclined." Waldo told Orr that he talked about his many woman friends with his brother at night, but Everett never mentioned any girls to whom he was romantically attached. Diane Orr, personal communication, June 17, 2010.

rope had been stolen (from his neck). Peg had evidently been mistreated, as his legs were skinned.[47]

Unlike many canyons in the Southwest, Canyon de Chelly was broad and tillable and did not have a large volume of water rushing downward. Its mouth was level with the surrounding countryside, meaning it was easily accessible. For at least two thousand years the canyon had year-round inhabitants: first the Anasazi, then the Navajo. It was remote from denser population centers, breeding intransigence, the bane of any ruler. The Spanish sent a punitive expedition in 1805, and the Navajo hid in a recess that would come to be known as Massacre Cave. The commander of the expedition reported that he had killed ninety warriors and twenty-five women and children and had taken thirty-three prisoners, only three of whom were fighting men. A Navajo artist graphically portrayed the progression of Spanish soldiers on horseback in black paint at Standing Cow Ruin. "A fearful chasm" was the phrase applied to Canyon del Muerto by the Spanish, and "a cursed land" was the description of others.[48]

Next came the U.S. Army: an overwhelming force of five hundred led by Colonel Christopher (Kit) Carson in 1863 with orders to conduct a scorched-earth campaign to drive the Navajo from the canyon stronghold and onto a reservation three hundred miles distant. Carson, who was fearful of the canyon, directed his soldiers from above. Orchards were burned, livestock killed, and hogans destroyed. There was sporadic fighting; twenty-three Navajo were killed and thirty-four prisoners taken. Hunger and cold were the impetus for the eventual surrender of thousands and the infamous Long Walk to Bosque Redondo in New Mexico. That experiment in forced relocation proved a failure, so the Navajo, after pledging peace, returned a few years later to Canyon de Chelly and the surrounding lands. The roving Navajo were encouraged to become farmers and herders, considered stable and peaceful occupations. The federal government gave them ten thousand sheep as an inducement.

During the early years of the twentieth century archeologists discovered the Anasazi's former presence in the canyon system. The Smithsonian Institution, Harvard's Peabody Museum, the Brooklyn Museum, and Richard Wetherill took part in the excavations. Two mummies were discovered in what was subsequently named Mummy Cave, in a branch canyon appropriately called Canyon del Muerto. One of the mummies was richly dressed in rabbit furs and surrounded by goods designed to accompany him to the spirit world. A tower distinguished this ruin, the largest and best preserved in the canyon. The skeleton of an old man with long, streaked, gray hair knotted behind his head was found near Antelope House. Across from Antelope House was a cave where the remnants of a massacre had been gathered and dumped into a storage pit. A wooden arrow was lodged between the dried skin and weathered bones of an old woman. Big Cave yielded a pair of severed hands, a body with two healed broken legs, and abalone-shell bracelets wrapped around the severed legs of yet another individual. The remains of eighteen infants stuffed into a large basket were found in what had been a storage bin.

The Anasazi departed from this grim place around 1300, a baseline year in the Southwest. Certainly drought was a factor. Four hundred years later the Navajo arrived. The numbers of Navajo and their livestock increased greatly in the early twentieth century, until by the time Rulan arrived at the start of the Dust Bowl years the federal government was greatly concerned about severe overgrazing. Evert noticed the Indians' resilience on the eve of the livestock reduction program of the 1930s, another traumatic experience for the Navajo. But the Navajo were hardy, Rulan believed. *The Navajo Indian is accustomed to hardships that few white men can endure. I have seen him curl up in a single saddle blanket and sleep soundly on the hard ground while a miserably cold March rain poured down, and raw, gusty winds blew all night. In the morning, he will get up ready and fit for a hard day's work.*[49]

The Bureau of Indian Affairs and the Navajo Tribal Council devised the unique form of the national monument. The Navajo owned the land and the Park Service had jurisdiction over the ruins, which were eroding and being vandalized and needed to be protected. The 131-square-mile monument was created in early 1931. There was no on-site custodian until 1934, leaving Evert and others free to roam about with no restrictions.

The stock reduction program was a failure, greatly alienating the Navajo. A historian of the New Deal noted: "Continued stock reduction and administrative blundering, coupled with the absence of any firm Indian governmental structure, had contributed to a condition of persistent poverty, land abuse, intertribal conflict, and societal disintegration that made the administration of the Navajo one of the major failures of the New Deal."[50]

It was against this historical background that Evert spent portions of three years on the Navajo reservation and bemoaned the minor thefts and scars on Pegasus's legs in 1931. Rulan was able to protect *old and virtuous* Pegasus from the advances of *homosexual love,* he explained to his friend Jacobs.[51] A young, white Navajo donkey pursued ancient, black Pegasus. Evert first tried to deter him with stones. When that failed, he assembled his shotgun, loaded it with buckshot, and discharged a load into the ass's rear end. Another load of birdshot in the legs seemed to do the trick, and Evert continued on his way to the canyon.

Rulan spent most of the next twelve days in mid-May in Canyon del Muerto, where Pegasus got stuck in quicksand three times. He used a stout stick to urge the burro out of the encircling sand. It rained. Evert was cold at night, even though he was covered by a sleeping bag, two blankets, and a quilt and slept in his clothes. He was learning the Navajo language and had mastered twelve words. He sketched and painted. Most of his time was spent exploring ruins. *Many of the ruins are well nigh inaccessible. I made a foolhardy ascent to one safely situated dwelling. Part of the time I had to make my way along a horizontal cleft with half my body hanging out over the sheer precipice. But the tombs had already been rifled. One room, however, was rocked shut, & on opening it, I thot for a moment I saw a cliff dweller in his last resting place. But the blankets, tho mouldering with age, were factory made, & a Navajo baby was buried therein. Odd, because the Navajos are superstitious about the Moquis. However, in sifting dirt in a corner, I found a cliff dweller's necklace, a thousand or so yrs. old. About 250 beads, 8 bone pendants, 2 turquoise beads, and 2 pendants of green turquoise. In another isolated cliff dwelling I found a cliff dweller's baby board, 3 pcs.*[52] He mailed the necklace home.

Emerging from Canyon de Chelly, Evert found an unexpected surprise, a package from his parents containing food and money. *I'm sorry the financial situation is so pitiful at home,* he wrote his parents. His father would experience several cuts in pay while Everett was on the road and receiving a monthly stipend from his parents. To emphasize his thriftiness in the face of their sacrifices, he said his budget—lacking rent, utilities, and savings— was $20 a month, most of that being for food. He was heading the next day for the Hopi mesas and then the Grand Canyon, where his post should be directed. *Whatever my name, I have no difficulty in securing mail.*[53]

∎

Evert encountered the fierce summer heat of the desert for the first time and was poorly prepared for it. A 1930s guide describes the road he took (currently State Highway 264) and its scenery. The description, with minor alterations, could have applied to many southwestern roads Rulan traveled.

> Graded dirt or graveled roadbed throughout; impassable immediately following snowstorms in winter or heavy rains in summer; supplies, water, and gasoline available only at trading posts and limited accommodations at trading posts.

This road, entirely within the Navajo and Hopi Indian reservations, traverses land that still belongs to the Indians—where the only white people encountered are those who depend on him for their livelihood—traders, missionaries, and government employees. Consequently the landscape has been little changed by civilization, and an occasional hogan, sheep corral, or Hopi village on a rocky mesa are the only evidences of this area's long and continued inhabitation.[54]

From Chinle, the dirt road led south, then Evert turned west at Ganado. The road signs were confusing, he took the wrong turn, and he had to backtrack, losing two days in the process. He found water every day or two. The Hopi pueblo of Walpi was disappointing. *There is an element of incongruity in the juxtaposition of old stonework and fences made of bedsteads. All the squaws tried to sell me pottery.* He passed quickly through the other Hopi settlements. *The dust and heat are extreme.* He and Pegasus plodded on. A young couple gave him a gallon of water. At Blue Canyon he found a pool of cool, shaded water enclosed within high rock walls in which he and Curly bathed. He was amazed at how tiny a wet Curly was. Fantastically shaped hoodoos with red caps sat atop white sandstone pedestals. *The next day I saw a weird thing, the dance of the tumbleweeds. A small whirlwind picked them up and tossed them in a large circle. They would slowly float to earth and then bounce up again. Around and around they went in fantastic spirals.*[55]

He passed through Moenkopi, another Hopi village, and was approaching the Little Colorado River through a barren stretch of the desert imprinted with dinosaur tracks and little else. Two teens in a small Ford pickup stopped and offered to take Evert and his entourage to the ranch one of the boys owned on the southwest slopes of the San Francisco Peaks near Flagstaff. Rulan accepted the offer. That was the story he told Bill Jacobs and his parents.[56]

The following is the boys' version. Randolph "Pat" Jenks and his friend Tad Nichols were seniors at the Mesa Ranch School in Mesa, Arizona.[57] They were returning to the school's summer camp in the Flagstaff mountains from the Hopi villages and the Painted Desert on June 7. When they met Evert, "he was without a hat and sunburned almost dark brown. He looked sick and forlorn, so we stopped. This boy was on his last legs."[58] Rulan was dehydrated and on the verge of heat stroke. Nichols gave him water but had to slow down his intake. They decided to transport Evert, Curly, and Pegasus to Jenks's 160-acre ranch, which had been given to him along with the truck by his wealthy father. The family of three could recuperate in the cooler climate. Evert's equipment was lashed on top of the cab, and the three boys pushed the balky burro onto the small truck bed. *Pegasus stumbled and [illegible] from side to side, but maintained his equilibrium. We sailed gaily through the desert and forest, with the donkey's shadow beside. At dusk we reached their school, which has five teachers and five students.*[59] The next day they went to the ranch.

Known as the Veit Ranch after its initial 1892 homesteader and as the Deerwater Ranch to Jenks, it was Shangri-La to Evert. *The mountain slope is covered with aspens, and wild life is very abundant. One of the boys, Randolph Jenks, is interested in ornithology. He wants to buy my painting of a cliff dwelling if he can procure the money. There is always some catch, you know.*[60] Jenks brought Evert groceries. Rulan showed him his artwork. They talked. "He was easy to talk to," Jenks said. In addition to ornithology, they had other common interests. Pat thought Evert was a loner and a distinct individual. In appreciation for his kindnesses, Evert gave Jenks the block print titled *Battlements of the Colorado*, which hung on his living room wall seventy-nine years later.*

For eight days Evert sketched, painted, hiked in the mountains, felled aspen trees, and made fencing. Pegasus and Curly rested. Then they departed, heading north for the Grand Canyon through the mountains. The youth spent six days in a sheep camp doing chores and earning his board. Two sheepmen made a pack saddle for Evert from parts of three old saddles, and he repaired two old panniers, wooden pack containers also known as kyaks or kayak boxes.[61] He traded the shotgun for a new burro, sturdier and more handsome than Pegasus. *The superannuated Pegasus was left behind, free to kick his heels as he wished.*[62] The younger donkey, whom Evert would shortly name Pericles, or Perry for short, had unclipped ears, a rich brown coat, and a

---

*Interview with Randolph "Pat" Jenks on the eve of his 98th birthday, March 16, 2010. Jenks and Nichols went on to lead interesting lives. After graduating from Princeton University, Jenks was curator of ornithology at the Museum of Northern Arizona and a cattle rancher. He was kidnapped, ran away from his kidnappers, and served as a bodyguard for the son of one of President Roosevelt's cabinet members. He searched unsuccessfully for buried treasure in Mexico and Arizona. Nichols, who snapped a photo of Pegasus being loaded onto the truck, graduated from the University of Arizona and had a career as a photographer and filmmaker. His book *Glen Canyon: Images of a Lost World* was published in 2000. Unknown to most Flagstaff residents, the log cabin ranch house Everett stayed in was hauled down from the mountain and reassembled near the Frances Short Pond in that city, where it serves as the backdrop for wedding photographs. Remnants of the ranch and petroglyphs on nearby volcanic rocks can be seen at milepost 4.5 on the Snowbowl Road.

white nose.[63] It rained. Evert stopped at a logging camp and bought supplies, selling a print to a clerk for $5. He was left, after the purchases, with 4¢. Fortunately, more money was on the way. A print his mother had made from one of his paintings had sold for $25, of which he would soon receive $10.

He walked from the logging camp to Grand Canyon National Park, arriving on June 30. Dinner that night among the cedar and pine trees near the rim was rice pudding. *I can take care of myself rather well now.*[64]

————————— ■ —————————

Between July of 1931 and September of 1934, Everett would explore the Grand Canyon four times and pass from rim to rim on three of those occasions. His accounts were minimal, perhaps because there were relatively few ancient dwellings, the summer heat in the canyon was crippling, and the immensity of the place was staggering. The few words he devoted to the canyon fell short of matching the breadth of the space. But how could they have captured it? Many words have been tossed at the chasm. Many people have driven along its rim with only a cursory look before uttering some inanity. Then they turn away to deal with something more immediate, like purchasing a souvenir.[65]

In a time of great economic despair, Grand Canyon National Park was experiencing its greatest building boom. An administrative history of the park states: "Superintendent Tillotson characterized the year 1931 as the 'biggest building construction program in the history of the park,' alluding not only to concessionaire investments but also to the number of NPS [National Park Service] structures built or begun in that year."[66] The number of visitors dropped, however, but federal funds and workers, thankful for any job, increased greatly. Money was pumped into the park to build tourist facilities, roads, and trails.* On any given summer day three hundred to five hundred laborers fanned out from six military-style camps to work in the park.

While the national parks had previously catered to more affluent visitors, marketing efforts were now directed at the middle class. With the ownership of automobiles greatly increased and the democratizing effects of the gas buggies having their impact, the cost to enter Grand Canyon National

———————

*In 2010 when I toured the national parks that Everett had visited, stimulus funds, designed to offset the lack of employment due to the recession, were being used to repair roads in most of the parks. It struck me as interesting that such monies were designated mostly for vehicular purposes and not the more diverse projects that were undertaken in the parks during the depression of the 1930s.

Park was kept at $1 with no fee for camping. It cost $7 a night to stay at the fancy El Tovar Hotel, which included meals; for a housekeeping cottage at Bright Angel Lodge, the cost was $1.50.[67] Structures rose in the village on the south rim, Phantom Ranch on the Colorado River got a swimming pool, a cableway was constructed into the canyon, and at opposite ends of the rim drive a watchtower was constructed at Desert View and a stone grotto where tea was served was built at Hermit's Rest.

Jobs and funds to stanch the hemorrhaging of employment and the failure of banks in northern Arizona were part of the reason for these activities, but there were others too: the fear of social unrest expressed by Park Service director Albright in the park's administrative history. "Recognizing social unrest during this period of economic decline, he wrote that 'in a time of anxiety and restlessness [the parks] were immensely useful to large numbers of our people' and were 'a strong influence for stabilization and good citizenship.'"[68] Evert Rulan may have seemed like a good target for such an influence. It wasn't that he was a real threat to society; he just seemed beyond ordinary laws, as when the superintendent said he couldn't take Curly across the canyon to the north rim on Park Service trails. He would have to walk the long way around the canyon on roads. *We didn't fight about it,* wrote Evert from the north rim, *but I'm here and so is Curly.*[69]

Rulan left one vivid description of the canyon from his first visit. *For a week I was in the depths of the canyon. The heat was over 140 degrees at one time. I followed obscure trails and reveled in the rugged grandeur of the crags, and in the mad, plunging glory of the Colorado River. Then one sunset I threw the pack on the burro again and took the long, steep uptrail. I traveled for several hours by starlight. A warm wind rushed down the side canyon, singing in the pinyon. Above—the blue night sky, powdered with stars. Beside—the rocks, breathing back to the air their stored up heat of the day. Below—the black void. Ahead—the burro, cautiously picking his way over the barely discernible trail. Behind—a moving white blotch that was Curly.*[70] After facing this immense space, he expressed doubt for the first time after returning from the abyss. *I think I have lost something of my boundless self confidence. What I may have gained remains to be seen.*[71]

A few days later Evert descended the Hermit Trail on his way to the north rim. Pericles balked at crossing the suspension bridge over the Colorado River at Phantom Ranch. Rulan went swimming in the river and waited until evening, keeping in the shadow of the bridge to avoid the direct rays of the broiling sun. To shoo the burro across the bridge, he banged an old shovel on the planks. Ascending the Kaibab Trail toward the north rim, Evert slept one night behind Ribbon Falls, the cool mist affording him some comfort in the still, hot air of early August.

◼

It took Rulan nine days, with rest stops during the midday heat, to walk 130 miles through varied terrain from the north rim of the Grand Canyon to Zion National Park. He crossed the nine-thousand-foot-high Kaibab Plateau, a cool island of green amid a hot sea of dun-colored desert. The sixty-mile long north-south plateau was covered with aspen, spruce, fir, and ponderosa pine trees. He noticed two animal species, both significant, but he missed their importance. The white-tailed squirrel was the Kaibab squirrel, which lived in the ponderosa forest, ate its pine nuts, and was found nowhere else in the world. Evert also saw mule deer, the object of a misguided conservation effort.

President Theodore Roosevelt established a national game preserve on the plateau in 1906 to protect the deer. Seven years later he visited the Kaibab and advocated hunting mountain lions in the preserve as a means of further aiding the hoofed animals. A violent, seesaw, life-and-death struggle was taking place on the Kaibab. The deer were on one side and their predators— mountain lions, bobcats, wolves, and coyotes—on the other. Bounty hunters, game hunters, game wardens, and scientists were involved on different sides of the issue. Starvation and the use of guns and poison were the means toward an end that tipped back and forth: the predators were slaughtered, the deer multiplied, the vegetation was decimated, and then the deer herds collapsed. "One may see this in north Germany, in northern Pennsylvania, in the Kaibab, and in dozens of other less publicized regions," wrote the noted conservationist Aldo Leopold.[72] Popular accounts and textbooks about predator-prey relationships attracted national attention to the plateau that Evert crossed on back roads.

Through Fredonia, across the Arizona state line, and into Utah on the gently rising terrain that ran through poplar trees, Evert eventually arrived among the red rocks of Kanab. *Next I was out in the real desert once more, camping in a sandy hollow, with the crescent moon low in the sky.*[73] Evert had problems getting Perry through the mile-long Zion–Mount Carmel Tunnel, a cavelike tube carved in the Navajo sandstone leading into the park. It was dark and dense with the choking fumes and clanking sounds of 1930s autos and trucks.

They entered the park on August 17. Motorists stopped to take photographs of the cute threesome who seemed to have stepped out of the past. The weather was hot and dry, the temperatures in the low one hundreds having set records that summer. The leaves on the cottonwood and ash trees along the Virgin River bore October colors. The deer were descending from the high country on the east and west rims to seek water in the canyon.

Disaster struck. *I developed a severe case of poison ivy, which has been raging for six days and is not past the crisis yet. For two days I didn't know whether I was alive or dead—ate nothing, simply writhed & twisted in the intense heat & swarms of ants & flies. Finally I managed to pry my lips far enough apart to insert food. My eyes did not swell shut.*[74] When the letter with this account arrived in Los Angeles, his parents were alarmed.

To Bill Jacobs, who wanted to travel with him the next year, Evert wrote a long letter from Zion. His illness had not deterred him from the lone life. *My friends have been few because I'm a freakish person and few share my interests. My solitary tramps have been made alone because I couldn't find anyone congenial— you know it's better to go alone than with a person one wearies of soon.* Evert was looking forward to his hike to the west rim the next day because he could resume his solitary existence. He hoped the cool air would calm his fiery skin.[75]

On September 2, eleven days after the onslaught of Evert's poison ivy, Ranger Donal J. Jolley and a seasonal ranger were establishing caches of fire-fighting equipment on the rim when they came across the suffering boy, whom Jolley identified in his official report as "Mr. Everett Rulon, of Los Angeles, California, who was spending some time in Zion painting pictures." The park superintendent described what occurred next in his monthly report: "After his face had started to swell he had retreated to this location in order that people would not see humor in his predicament. He was taken to the hospital at St. George and given treatment for his poisoning." Since he had no money, the county paid the doctor and hospital bills.[76]

Jolley and his family cared for Curly while Evert was in St. George. That was a treat for Jolley's children, who normally weren't allowed pets in the national park. Perry was boarded in the Park Service barn. After Evert disappeared in 1934, the chief ranger said the youth was a loner who loved the desert and was capable of taking care of himself in the wilderness.*

---

*Jolley's son, also named Donal, recalled that after Everett disappeared he was frequently warned by his parents never to stray far from the family home because "a young man was lost out beyond Bryce [Canyon National Park] and had never been found." Donal Jolley, personal communication, May 27, 2010. His father worked at Zion from 1920 to 1943.

Rulan returned to Zion on September 8 after five days in St. George. The next day he wrote his family a short note. *There isn't much I feel like writing. The poison ivy is still raging.* No, he wouldn't send them his diary, although the sharing of these journals was a family custom. *It is too personal to be read by anyone but the author.* There was a postscript. *Infection is what has delayed recovery.*[77] A worried Stella contacted the park postmaster, who assured her Evert was fine. He had just cashed a Los Angeles money order for $5 that was dated September 1. Should he call for his mail again, the postmaster would tell him that his mother had made an inquiry.[78]

His parents tried to coax Evert home. He said he intended to wander at least another year, he would need a studio in the city and artists' materials that he couldn't afford, and the pamphlet for the junior college they sent had left him cold. *The place must be like a jail, with all the rules and regulations. What an anticlimax it would be after the free life.* Besides, he couldn't just dump Curly. (He would do exactly that the next year.) He was, however, reverting to his real name. *I tire of experimentation, entanglements, and after all there's not much in a name.*[79]

On the way back across the Kaibab Plateau, Everett captured the change of seasons with image-filled words. *Winter is close at hand; the maples are crimson, and flurries of yellow aspen leaves swirl about with each breeze. On many hillsides the yellow leaves have blackened, and the trees stand bare and silent. Soon the snows will be here, but I won't.* A full moon rolled through the clouds. *The lunatic quaver of a coyote—silence and sleep.*[80]

———————■———————

On October 1, dog, burro, and teenager dropped off the north rim and descended into the Grand Canyon once again. *On my way across the canyon I took the Tonto Trail. No one else has been over it this year. It was always a rough trail, and washouts and landslides made it doubly so. In one side canyon that cut deep into the plateau, I found the skeleton of a mountain sheep in the middle of the trail. One horn was broken, but I have the other and am sending it home. I traveled after dark that night. Time and again the burro went off the trail, twice at dangerous places. We traveled on the edge of a cliff. I could hardly see where to set my foot. Only a white spot on Perry was visible.*[81]

He saw electric lights ahead. Some Fred Harvey employees Ruess knew were reopening Hermit Camp for a crew from the Fox Film Corporation who were going to shoot canyon scenes for the Zane Gray picture *The Rainbow Trail,* starring George O'Brien. To get the equipment and supplies to the camp for the crew of fifty, the Hermit tramway had been reactivated after having been closed the previous year by the Park Service, which had taken over the camp from the concessionaire.

The history of the camp followed a shift in priorities and policies. The park concessionaire Fred Harvey had opened it in 1912. It was the first development in the canyon and had once been a popular destination for tourists on horses, mules, and foot. The eight-mile trail, which dropped 4,700 feet, had been constructed like a carefully crafted parkway, with cut sandstone walls, fitted sandstone surfaces on level portions, and a tread design or stairs on steep sections. There were comfortable rest stops along the way. The tramway transported fresh food and drinks to guests. The camp had deluxe tents—connected by a concrete walkway—with wooden floors, stoves, beds, and glass windows. There were hot showers and telephone service to the rim. A two-story structure served as kitchen, dining room, and common area. For sightseeing trips in the immediate vicinity, a Model T Ford had been shipped in pieces down the tramway and assembled at the camp. The company sensed that tourist priorities were shifting in 1930 and decided to concentrate its operations in other, more lucrative sections of the park. The Park Service was now in the process of reclaiming or eliminating private operations in the public parks in order to provide more natural experiences.[82]

Evert talked to the film's art director, who gave him some helpful advice. He headed up the Hermit Trail to the south rim, where there was mail to be read and answered.

The desert wanderer felt guilty about his brother being chained to work while he was free to roam. *You are right that in spite of our differences there is much that makes us near to each other. Whenever I think of you I feel glad that I have a brother like you.* He felt obliged to give Waldo a financial accounting for the past eight months to prove he was not a drain on the family and was doing all he could do to make money. He had spent $136, with more than one-third going toward equipment and the remainder for food. He could not sell his art, however. *The world does not want art—only the artists do.* To escape the wind, he had gone inside to continue writing the letter. The noise of a World Series game between the St. Louis Cardinals and the Philadelphia Athletics on the radio disturbed him. He moved to another room and continued writing. *Whatever I have suffered in the months past has been nothing compared with the beauty in which I have steeped my soul, so to speak. It has been a priceless experience, and I am glad that it is not over. What I would have missed if I had ended everything last summer.*[83]

He would have missed being a uniquely gifted teenager. Everett was becoming a fascinating mix of a willful child and an insightful adult in a young man's body. He got along better with children and thoughtful, mature adults than he did with his contemporaries. The callowness of his teenage years was tempered with knowledge and feelings many adults would never achieve in their lifetime. The problem was, you never knew which Everett you would get at a given moment. These are the bridge years for adolescents.

Pericles was abandoned. Curly, Everett, and his equipment were stranded at Grand Canyon until they could find a ride south. A couple from Lakeside, California, offered the boy and his dog a ride to Mesa. Everett looked around before leaving and summed up his feelings. *Nothing anywhere can rival the Grand Canyon. I must come here again some day. There are things I must paint again.*[84]

———————■———————

The husband, who was a class odist and poet at Harvard University, was impressed with Everett's talents and aspirations. They talked about poetry on the drive south, and Everett showed the couple his art portfolio, hoping for a sale. They gave him a spare Kodak Brownie camera and a leather vest and dropped him off at the house of a friend in Mesa.[85]

Everett was in need of a burro, or burros, for the next leg of his journey. He traveled to the copper-mining town of Superior, where there were numerous Mexicans who used burros to transport firewood. For the first time Everett had a choice of donkeys, but he didn't know how to bargain. Two burros cost more money than he possessed. Everett asked his mother for money. She asked him why he needed two burros. *Neither Pegasus nor Perry were good burros. They were too old, and suffered under their loads. I had to travel light and carry part of the pack myself.*[86] He said the advantage of two burros was that each could be loaded with one hundred pounds.

He bought two burros for $11.50, which included a pack saddle. He loaded them both. One donkey promptly fell down. He returned it for another that cost less. A bargain, he told his mother. One ass was brownish gray with a white nose; the other was black with a white nose and breast. He named them Cynthia and Percival, the latter an alternative spelling for *Parsifal.* Everett bought film and food and had his shoes repaired. He had 12¢ left. The only available work was harvesting cotton, and he didn't fancy picking one hundred pounds for a mere 60¢. He had skinned a Gila monster and was going to dry and stretch the skin before sending it home. Everett directed his mother to attach it with fine thread to a piece of felt. He departed with his two new burros for the Apache Trail and a new landscape.[87]

———————■———————

Ruess is most closely associated with southern Utah, where he disappeared. He spent far more time, however, on roads and trails in California and Arizona. He explored Anasazi and Navajo territory in the northern one-third of Arizona and made a quick dash into southwestern Colorado to look at the ruins of Mesa Verde. He also passed four months—two in late 1931 and two in late spring of 1932—in the Tonto Basin east of Phoenix, a remote region of the American West that was not served by a railroad. The basin was neither-nor: neither high plateau nor low desert. It has been described as the middle slice of three geographic divisions of the state. "Between the southern and northern plateau is a rough, broken country of brush, timber, flowing streams of permanent water, and intermediate heat and cold," states a publication of the Museum of Northern Arizona.[88]

The Hohokum, irrigators from the Valley of the Sun, had migrated to the basin around 800 C.E., bringing the art of moving water through canals, a technique the whites would emulate in the Phoenix metropolitan area. They merged with ancestral Puebloan groups to form a distinctive culture known as the Salado, whose members began constructing one- and two-story multiroom stone, stick, and mortar structures in shallow caves around 1250. The Salado were gone by 1400. Shortly thereafter the more mobile Tonto Apaches moved into the basin, waged their losing skirmishes with the whites, worked on the dam, and established a meager settlement on the shoreline near Roosevelt.[89]

Everett entered the basin on a dirt road named for the Apaches. The Apache Trail became a recognizable road in 1904. It began at Apache Junction, just east of Mesa, skirted the Superstition Mountains for nearly fifty miles, and terminated at what would become Roosevelt Dam when it was completed in 1911. The dam, built by Italian stonemasons, impounded the waters of the Salt River and Tonto Creek in Roosevelt Lake, named, like the dam, in honor of that booster of the West from New York. It was the highest dam of its type in the world at the time and the first major dam completed by the Bureau of Reclamation, another Rooseveltian creation. Twenty-three workers died while building the road and the dam. The reservoir and the dam enabled the Phoenix area to grow until it needed more water. The construction activity attracted workers, gawkers, and tourists, not only to the dam site and a nearby hotel but also to what became known as Tonto National Monument in 1907, also created by a stroke of Theodore Roosevelt's pen.

The ruins in the monument needed to be protected from vandals and explained to the curious. Neither purpose was well served, because the Forest Service had nominal control and sent only an occasional ranger to check the ruins. The Southern Pacific Railroad had practical control of the monument but did nothing about it until 1929, when it constructed a road, parking area, trail, and pit toilet and appointed an Apache caretaker. This man ran the eight miles from the lakeside Indian encampment to the monument and back again each day from 1929 to 1932. The road, trail, and parking lot were expanded in 1932, and a small caretaker's lodge was built. As part of the movement to reclaim the parks from private interests, the Park Service took over the monument in 1933. "There was nothing new in the Southern Pacific Railroad's promotion of a national monument and nothing new in its partnership with a federal agency to promote tourism," a history of the national monument stated. "To the contrary, the national railroads were partners in promoting the establishment of the national parks, the National Park System, and the National Park Service."[90] Meanwhile, Salado artifacts kept disappearing from Tonto National Monument.

The monument consisted of two hillside clusters of adobe ruins. The lower ruin, more accessible and more frequently visited than the upper ruin, was in a natural cave nearly fifty feet deep and forty feet high. There were sixteen ground-floor rooms and a second story. Most of the rooms had fire pits. Hundreds of remnants of corncobs, beans, squash, and cotton were scattered about. The skeletons of two children and one adult were buried there. Both ruins had been extensively vandalized by pothunters by the time Everett arrived.

Four years before Everett Ruess appeared on the scene, remote Roosevelt Lake was the scene of an international incident. With Premier Benito Mussolini's blessing, Commander Francesco de Pinedo of the Italian navy was on his second extensive flight in a seaplane when he landed at Roosevelt Lake on April 6, 1927, to refuel. The torpedo bomber, named the *Santa Maria* in honor of Columbus's flagship, was towed to the landing at Apache Lodge. The commander, nattily dressed in knickers, oversaw the fueling. Pinedo and his two crewmen dumped excess gasoline into the lake. They then retired with dignitaries and the local Italian community to the lodge for lunch. A cry went up: the wood-and-fabric airplane was on fire; the twin engines dropped into the depths of the lake. A youth had flipped a cigarette into the water, which had ignited the gasoline. Il Duce was convinced it was an act of sabotage. Pinedo, a World War I pilot and advocate of seaplanes, resumed his journey in a similar plane shipped by boat to New York City. He died in an airplane accident in 1933.

Roosevelt Lodge had been renamed Apache Lodge and dolled up with Indian artifacts by the Southern Pacific when it introduced tours from

Phoenix in canvas-topped motor coaches over the Apache Trail. The two-story lodge sat on a bluff called Hotel Point. A "first-class" radio and an "electronic orthophonic instrument" were available for dancing. For Arizona residents desiring a vacation by the water during hot summers, the advertised advantage was that a vacation could be spent less expensively by the lake than on the California coast. Tom Mix and a movie crew of fifty from Hollywood stayed at the lodge while filming *Tony Runs Wild*. Tony was Mix's tame horse, who played a wild stallion in the film.

Everett was not entering a wilderness by any stretch of the imagination, although by 1931 the region had been forsaken by serious prospectors, who could find no riches, and the reservoir had displaced its ranchers. Everett veered off the Apache Trail and plunged into the backcountry of the Superstition Mountains, the supposed location of the Lost Dutchman Mine, sought in vain by treasure hunters. *I killed a rattlesnake, and forced the burros to descend steep mountains against their better judgment.* With this mention of a slain rattlesnake, Everett began a litany of similar episodes. The urge to kill a venomous snake was not uncommon in the West in the pre-ecology era.*

The youth arrived penniless at Roosevelt Lake around the first of November. A bootlegger said he might be able to offer Everett a job guarding his still in the mountains. The proprietor of Apache Lodge said he might sell his paintings, if they were framed. Then Ruess had a bit of luck. He sold a print for $1, driftwood collected along the shoreline fetched a similar amount, and packing supplies for four hunters heading into the Four Peaks area for three days paid $5 a day plus food. *I want to survive this panic and yet have my time free for work and travel.*[91]

He camped at the monument, where he met the Apache caretaker, Ray Stevens, whom he characterized as *a generous, childish soul.* Winter arrived. It would be a devastating winter across the Southwest. *For days the sky wept.*

---

*Everett Ruess to Waldo Ruess, November 13, 1931. A current guidebook for hiking in the Superstition Mountains states: "Don't kill rattlesnakes; just learn to avoid them." Jack Carlson and Elizabeth Stewart, *Superstition Wilderness Trails East: Hikes, Horserides, and History* (Tempe, Ariz.: Clear Creek Publishing, 2010), 27. I was in the Superstition Mountains on horseback with a Forest Service ranger in the early 1970s. He was checking on the armed prospectors who were looking for the Lost Dutchman Mine and fighting one another in the meantime. We came across a rattler, and the ranger drew, fired several shots, and killed the snake. I don't think that would occur today.

Drizzles and drenching downpours were accompanied by lightning and rainbows.[92] November was the wettest month in recent years in this semidesert. Everett was miserable. *I am all alone in a tent with my feet frozen.*[93] He wanted to see his friends and family, frequent city libraries, and transform his sketches into oil paintings. *It rained last night. I have been in several snowstorms.*[94]

The weather cleared. He walked the six miles to the dam, where he sketched, and then stopped at the post office on his return to the monument. Would Bill Jacobs, his father, or his brother come and pick him up? No, none were available. He was angry. He was not coming home, a petulant Everett told his mother in early December. *I'd never have thought of coming home if you hadn't spoken of it two or three times.*[95] Nevertheless, Everett and Curly hitchhiked home in late December.

His anger didn't last long. He gave Jacobs one of Percival's burro shoes for Christmas with an accompanying note.

From my desert nightingale to you
Comes this well worn burro shoe

It protected his feet while he slid down rocky slopes of wild cactus covered hills; it caked with snow as he climbed down mountain trails between white mantled pines; it scraped waterworn boulders as he gingerly felt his way through muddy mountain torrents. Following its imprint in the red soil I tracked him many weary miles till at last old longears stood before me, discovered; sometimes in nimble haste I dodged it. I heard it clatter over concrete bridges and crunch the pebbles in a river bed. Heedless of Percival's protest, a whiskered Mexican threw him down and nailed it to his hoof. An Apache jerked it off.

So look well at this shoe, from me to you & hang it high on the wall. Its days of use are over, but now it is something of which to dream and sigh.[96]

VII

The Misfit

1932

EVERETT, WITH HIS SIDEKICK CURLY, was home barely two months, time enough to experience the Tenth Olympic Games madness that consumed promotional-minded Los Angeles. Stella Ruess contributed to the hoopla, producing a booklet of prints and short verses titled *Los Angeles in Block Print*. She wrote in the foreword: "This little book is intended to give you, whether resident or visitor, a new appreciation of the charm of our City of the Angels, and a desire to seek out the unfamiliar spots. On such journeys you will find new beauty." The cover depicted crowds entering the main gate of the new Los Angeles Coliseum. One of the twenty-six prints showed a city park scene with the accompanying verse: "In sweet communion / Dwell the Palm and Brother Pine / In fog or sunshine."[1] Everett departed for Arizona long before the games began in early August.

For a short time while hitchhiking east on Route 66 in March, Everett was accompanied by another youth with similar interests and a similar style of travel. Alfred L. Law, a college student, left Ruess in Needles and made his way eastward; Everett headed in a more southerly direction, toward Phoenix. Law's boots were stolen while he slept on the ground outside Flagstaff, and he was stuck for three days without any food or a ride between Albuquerque and Santa Fe. He hopped a freight train that took him to Las Vegas, New Mexico, where he wired his aunt for money. Passenger trains and buses eventually delivered him to his home in Staten Island, New York.

Law couldn't find work, so he wrote short stories and poems. He admired Everett's poetry and sent him a poem that began: "Life is a sane insanity / A rational irrationality / A splendidly logical illogicality."[2]

Everett also had difficulties finding rides. He was forced to pay a man $5 to drive him from Phoenix to Roosevelt on the Apache Trail. The driver dented the fender of his car while avoiding an oncoming vehicle on the narrow, twisting road. A sunburned Ruess arrived in Roosevelt on March 22 to find that his friend Clark Tyler, who had preceded him, had made a favorable impression on the locals. Bill Jacobs would be joining them soon.

The burros were not available. Percival had been stolen and Cynthia was pregnant. Clark and Everett spun their wheels, waiting to acquire horses. *We have traveled in all four directions from Roosevelt.*[3] Everett had $4, and Clark was broke. Money was first on the wish list Everett sent to his parents, followed by such books as *The Magic Mountain* by Thomas Mann, *The Brothers Karamazov* by Fyodor Dostoyevsky, *The Satyricon* by Petronius, *The Life of Gargantua and Pantagruel* by Rabelais, *Candide* by Voltaire, *Mrs. Dalloway* by Virginia Woolf, and *Nana* by Émile Zola. He found a $12 money order and most of the books he had requested waiting for him on his return from an eight-day trip into the wilderness with Clark. Their food supply had dwindled to beans and flour. *As for myself, I am willing to walk if I have a pack animal to bear the burdens, but Clark feels that he cannot enjoy himself at all if he must walk.*[4]

To Bill Jacobs, who was still in Los Angeles in early April, Everett sent a rattle from a rattlesnake he had killed and a request to send a backpack and waterproof material to cover his sleeping bag. From a perch midway up the cut-stone facade of Roosevelt Dam, he wrote an ode to the spring winds in the desert, which he sent his parents. *Wild winds are shrieking in the wires, twirling in the dust heaps, and swishing the bushes. Clouds are scudding by, and the water from the power house is roaring out like a maelstrom whipping itself to froth before it flows to Apache Lake. The turbines are humming. Now the gale grows fiercer. The lake above is flecked with white caps and the willow trees bend low.* In addition to Dostoevsky, Ruess had been reading the Russian writers Maxim Gorky and Anton Chekhov. He had finished most of the books his parents had sent him by April 20 and requested two novels by John Dos Passos, *Fortitude* by Hugh Walpole, and *The Anthology of Modern Poetry.*[5]

Everett found a foster family and an island of culture abutting the fluctuating shoreline of Roosevelt Lake. Ben and Eleanor ("Billie") Reynolds had been married on top of the dam in 1922. Ben was a hydrographer at the dam. They had two young sons, a love of books and poetry, a basement museum, a radio on which Sunday classical music concerts could be heard, extra rooms for travelers, and delicious home-cooked food. Their house had a clear view of the dam, which the employees of the Salt River Project living on Government Hill were charged with operating and maintaining. The Reynoldses were gracious practitioners in hard times of the western custom in remote areas of feeding and lodging strangers, such as Everett.

From their first meeting, when Everett knocked on the door of the Reynoldses' two-story home to borrow some magazines, the family, and particularly Billie Reynolds, treasured his company. That night Everett stayed for dinner; one of their special dishes, clam chowder, was served. Mrs. Reynolds, like Everett, felt she was a misfit in her surroundings. She read, composed verses, and enjoyed classical music and art, but none of her neighbors had similar interests. She was lonesome, so when Everett "treated me to the tho'ts he'd expressed in verse," she felt she had found a kindred soul. "Somehow Everett was such a little boy to me and yet I always enjoyed talking with him as I have appreciated conversations with men my own age or older."[6]

Everett did not return to his camp four miles distant at the cliff dwellings until late at night after enjoying the Reynoldses' hospitality. The attractions were numerous. *They had a nice house. Mrs. Reynolds was an excellent cook, there were good books to read, and a radio over which I heard several concerts. The people were really intelligent.*[7] At the end of the year Everett wrote to the Reynoldses. *Of all the families I met, there was none I liked better than yours, and none where I felt more at home. I will always remember your hospitality to me. It was deep rooted and sincere, I know, and it meant very much to me.** Ruess had the habit of overstaying his visits with strangers he met on the road. He was sometimes viewed as a moocher and given a hint or openly asked to leave. Clearly, that was not the case with the Reynoldses.

Bill Jacobs arrived in late April or early May. On Friday, May 13, the three friends had a bitter argument. The disagreement, on the surface, was over money, but the real cause was that Everett was essentially a loner who had become entangled in a web of human relationships and could not find a graceful way to extract himself. Ruess was also having some personal ups

---

*Everett Ruess to Billie and Ben Reynolds, undated but most probably December 1932. Everett could be considerate. For the remaining two Christmases of his life, he sent the family a greeting. Billie had two of his block prints framed. Her sons used his discarded pup tent to play camp and circus.

and downs. He was feeling very unsettled. *I have gone through several stages these last few months.*[8]

Everett made up his mind to leave. *I shall be traveling alone again, and it seems the best way. Clark is unwilling to travel unless he can ride, and maybe he will travel with Bill. We might meet later in the year.* His friends were staying with a man named Wilson. On the morning of May 13, Everett traded an ungovernable Apache pony he had bought for $10 for Pacer, a pack horse owned by the Reynoldses. Taking his camera and canteen and mounting Pacer bareback, he rode to Wilson's place. There was an argument. He left. *I shook the dust of the place off my feet.*[9] He asked Bill later that summer to tell Clark he was *genuinely sorry that he wasn't equal to continuing with me,* but "the past is a bucket of ashes."[10]

■

Everett, Pacer, and Curly, the last with a rawhide strap attached to his collar, forded the thigh-deep Salt River and began their journey northward through the Tonto Basin on a dirt road that also served as a cattle trail. The road eventually climbed the Mogollon Rim and crossed the desert to the railroad and Highway 66 at Holbrook.[11] The ten days it took to reach Young, a remote settlement in the basin's Pleasant Valley, were among the most difficult in Everett's years of wandering. It was hot, his shoulders ached, and he had a racking cough and a minor dose of poison ivy. An old couple at a farmhouse would only give him water, not food. But as he gained altitude, junipers replaced saguaro cacti, and he found a place to camp.[12]

In the cool morning Everett ate rice cakes and read Walt Whitman's poetry. He inspected an abandoned asbestos mine and read old magazines in the shacks. That night after hobbling Pacer, he was reading *The Magic Mountain* and was halfway through eating his biscuits and gravy when he remembered to check on the horse. Pacer had gotten loose. He eluded Everett in the dark. Both horse and rider were drenched in sweat by the time they reunited.

Ruess returned to the campsite to find that Curly had eaten the rest of his dinner. He exploded with rage and severely beat the dog. When he woke in the morning, Curly was gone—forever, as it turned out. Everett called and called and thought he heard barking in the distance, but he didn't search very far, thinking the dog might follow. He didn't. By this time neither dog nor master was enamored of the other. *I wish he was shot. He kills chickens and steals food. I can't afford to feed him. Curly might drown in the river, but it's unlikely.*[13] There were limits. *A good dog is a fine companion, but Curly had disappointed me.*[14]

Everett regretted listening to Bill and Clark's advice to switch from burros to horses. He now knew that horses cost more to shoe and feed and couldn't carry as much as burros. He killed a rattlesnake and, having lost his pocket knife, used his fingernails to cut off the rattle. Ruess searched for cliff dwellings, and when he found them in Pueblo Canyon was disappointed that they were not more picturesque. He killed a scorpion he found in one of his packs. *Gnats and mosquitoes. Alone again. The crazy man is in solitude again. . . . The full moon, round and yellow, in the chalky blue sky over distant mesas. No Curly to pet.* He finished *The Brothers Karamazov* and gave it a mixed review. *It fell flat toward the end, and I didn't like Dostoyevsky's chatty way of speaking, but it was a real book.*

All was peaceful for a change. Pacer's bell tinkled as he grazed, a coyote howled, and the bars of a symphony echoed in Everett's head. *I often wish people meant something to one another, and one could find people to one's taste.*[15]

Leading Pacer, Everett walked into Young on May 23. There was $15 waiting for him at the post office and the immediate possibility of trading Pacer for two scrawny burros that had been used for plowing. He named them Peggy and Wendy. Everett did odd jobs, was paid with food, and fiddled with his equipment for three days in Pleasant Valley, whose history had been very unpleasant.

The Pleasant Valley War in the late nineteenth century resulted in approximately twenty deaths and the almost complete extinction of two large families, making it one of the deadliest family feuds in American history. The conflict involved cattle versus sheep, grazing and water rights, vigilantes, hired killers like the notorious Tom Horn, masked men, lynchings, confrontations, and cowardly ambushes. Only two members of the families survived the decade of bloody conflict. Zane Gray, who had a hunting lodge nearby, wrote about the war in *To the Last Man,* which was adapted as a movie starring Shirley Temple and Randolph Scott.

Everett was unmindful of this mournful history and began the 1,500-foot ascent from the basin to the Mogollon Rim with his burdened donkeys. They passed two flocks of sheep and camped where there was little grass. Dinner was squaw bread, peanut butter, beef jerky, and parched corn. *It was rather good.*[16]

■

Back on the Colorado Plateau, Everett was surrounded by an entirely different landscape. The familiar high desert was more to his liking. *The country changed completely in half a mile or so. There was plenty of good grass, and* the glittering green of the aspens showed against the gloomy green of the pines. Finding water was a problem, though, as was reading the Thomas Mann novel. *It is very depressing, about a young German who visits his cousin at a tuberculosis sanitarium in the Alps, and finds that he too has the disease.*[17] The gusting spring winds lowered his spirits further.

Every journey has its low point, and this moment was one of the deepest for Everett. *I wish I had a companion, some one who was interested in me. I would like to be influenced, taken in hand by some one, but I don't think there is anyone in the world who knows enough to be able to advise me. I can't find my ideal anywhere. So I am rather afraid of myself.*[18] He admired the affection the burros displayed when they stroked each other's necks with their noses. He gave them some bread and scratched and petted them.

They plodded on through Heber, a small town near the rim. The mail carrier stopped and gave Everett some water. The burros behaved strangely and seemed ill. In poor shape to begin with, they were tottering under their heavy loads. Everett would discover soon that Peggy was pregnant. The journey seemed over. *Felt that the trip was foredoomed to failure, that I'd be overcome with melancholy if I visited the places I've seen before. Afraid to go home because that would be an admission of failure & I'd be ashamed to face Bill and Clark.* Everett felt isolated from humanity, a position he had placed himself in. *I felt distinctly different from other people; already I've drifted too far away from other people. I want to be different anyhow, I can't help being different, but I get no joy from it, and all the common joys are forbidden me.*[19]

Supper was macaroni with cheese and eggs. Everett fed each burro an ear of corn. He didn't read that night, but rather gazed into the fire.

A short distance up the dirt highway from Heber to Holbrook was Claude Despain's ranch, on the west side of the road.[20] Everett was welcome to have meals without working, sleep in an adobe outbuilding, and play with the four children. *The food was rather good. Besides biscuits and beans (Mexican strawberries) there was rice pudding, pickles, honey, ham, milk, and corn.*[21] During the days he worked on repairing his kyaks, read newspapers, and talked with Grandma Despain about her early life on the Navajo reservation. In the evenings at the Despain Ranch there was guitar playing and singing, and Everett showed his photographs.

Three days at the ranch, and then Everett was on the road again, headed north toward Holbrook. He didn't get far. Zeniff was a relatively short walk. He was struck by the strange women's names in the Mormon community, like Zelma and Rilla. It rained. He stopped at the last ranch house, but the woman couldn't put him up without the consent of her husband, who was off somewhere. The sky cleared, and Everett filled his canteens with muddy water from the last cistern in the settlement. He camped, ate, petted his exhausted burros, and read more of *The Magic Mountain*. The fire blazed, and he felt almost content. *I am in the desert that I know—red sand, cedars, great spaces, distant mesas, and behind, the blue of the Mogollon.*[22]

He had walked half a mile on the morning of June 4 when a rancher stopped his car to talk with him. Tom Reed had heard of Everett's journey at a ranch in Pleasant Valley. He offered him a place to stay and rest for a few days, or as long as he liked. It was an offer Everett couldn't refuse, and he would remain in Zeniff and Reed's outlying ranch for the next twenty days. (Besides the town lot, Reed owned the Rocking Chair Ranch, halfway between Zeniff and Snowflake, and property in Pleasant Valley.)

Zeniff, now a ghost town, was a Mormon cooperative venture gone dry, another western failure due to the lack of water.[23] It was settled around 1910 by families who had been living farther north along the Little Colorado River. The water for the dry farms was hauled from a well three miles distant and stored in cisterns. An imagined aerial drawing of the settlement in 1922 showed a log-cabin schoolhouse and ten dwellings, of either adobe or logs, with Tom Reed's residence the farthest north on the road. More families arrived at the end of the 1920s, and the well began to go dry. Cattle being trailed north to Holbrook stopped for water in Zeniff. The cooperative charged a toll of 25¢ per head, a lucrative business as long as there was water. Herds from the Tonto Basin sometimes numbered two thousand. Cattle, sheep, horses, cowboys, and chuck wagons converged on the fenced pasture in the fall months. Campfires blazed at night. In 1933, one year after Everett's visit, there was a water shortage, and the post office where he had received his mail closed. By the end of the decade most of the families had departed, leaving their adobe structures to melt back into the earth. The Despain family wound up owning most of the land.

Everett briefly became part of the cowboy culture of Zeniff. *I have been riding for the last two weeks. I have a saddle and an old white gift horse that used to be a good cowhorse. I was thrown once by a big black when I was driving the burros in to water. I stayed with him for several jumps, but finally I sailed out of the stirrups and came down on my nose. I caught him and mounted again.* He suffered a cut lip. Everett did odd jobs for Reed and looked for a horse or two to purchase. He roped four calves and helped dehorn and castrate them. *We saved the marbles and had them for breakfast.*[24] At the age of eighteen he was now shaving and sported a mustache. He also smoked cigarettes.

He asked his parents to send him a copy of Homer's *Odyssey*.[25] Stella wrote that Mrs. Jacobs had driven to Roosevelt and brought Bill back to Los Angeles. Clark would return later on his own. *I haven't met anyone to talk to since Bill and Clark. Yesterday I wrote them a good long letter, with my irrepressible superiority showing through. Clark says I antagonize everyone and whoever learns to know me finally becomes disgusted. There may be some truth in that. I don't try to please people I don't respect.*[26]

From his bed, Everett looked up at a ceiling papered with yellowing newspapers. It wasn't the same as lying in his sleeping bag and gazing up at the trees and sky. He concluded that physical labor wouldn't cure him of his unnamed troubles but would only exacerbate them. *I will be glad when I am alone again. It is too much work for me to get along with other people.*[27]

Everett's favorite breakfast, hotcakes, was served for his departure meal on June 24. Being among the cowboys had converted him from burros—he left both of his behind—to horses once again, specifically an old white cowhorse that cost nothing, which he unimaginatively named Whitie, and a tough old bay that cost $6 and was named Bay. *I have been striving vainly to acquire a sense of balance, but I still flop in the saddle when the horse trots.*[28] Tom Reed gave him a saddle and directed him to the Cosby family in Holbrook, with whom he stayed for three days.

It was the weekend of the big rodeo. Everett cashed a $10 money order from his parents and purchased a black, narrow-brimmed Stetson hat for $9. It became his trademark headgear and was immortalized in Dorothea Lange's portraits of him. He also bought a gray shirt and a black silk neckerchief. He was now properly attired for the Saturday parade. *The streets were thronged with cowboys wearing gaudy shirts. Navajos came by in wagon loads. The whole town was like a bunch of manikins, showing off.*[29] The colorful display disguised harsh economic realities in Holbrook. Delinquent taxes had doubled, the town's principal business of shipping cattle and wool had dropped precipitously, and the president of the Arizona Industrial Congress had just told the Holbrook Rotary Club about the economic perils facing the entire state.

The attempt by Ruess's evangelically oriented host to convert him on Sunday failed. *I told him I didn't believe in Hell, that I had some faith in evolution.*[30] The pastor of the church Ruess attended warned the congregation about the dangers of Christian Scientists, Universalists, and Unitarians. Everett did not say a word.

With Ruess astride Bay and leading Whitie, the trio departed Holbrook on a Monday morning and headed north toward the Hubbell Trading Post at Ganado. For the next week Ruess traveled through the Navajo reservation, seeing no whites and dealing exclusively with Indians. It was his most sustained immersion in the Navajo culture.

He passed through badlands both external and internal. *There were no trees—no escape from the blistering heat.* He made a poor drawing. *My eyes are wretched. They have been paining me severely.* Everett crawled under a bush to escape the sun and read about a snowstorm in the Alps in *The Magic Mountain.* It rained one day, and that night was bitterly cold. *The beauty of the wet desert was overpowering. I was not happy for there was no one with whom I could share it, but I thot, how much better than to be in a school room with rain on the windows, or at home in my dreary bedroom. My tragedy is that I don't fit in with any class of people.** He spent the night with an Indian in a stone house. *There are many stone houses here and no white people.* Dinner was mutton, cornmeal bread, and coffee. He slept on goatskins. The next day he continued up Pueblo Colorado Wash.[31]

In return for their letting his horses graze in a hay field, Everett helped two Navajo scythe the tall grass. He killed another rattlesnake, his seventh that year. More mutton was served that night, and he was taught the Navajo phrases for *tired, I want to eat, Where is water?,* and other necessities. Indians gathered to witness the lesson. He carefully wrote the phonetic equivalents of the Navajo words and phrases in his journal. He worked the next day, and that night shared more mutton with four Navajo and again slept on goatskins. The following day he learned he had been fooled: the Navajo words and phrases he had been taught did not match their English equivalents. More mutton was served that night. *The men persisted in talking Navajo in my presence.*[32]

The fact that Everett couldn't understand them, that his ability to speak or understand the language was almost nonexistent at this time, casts doubt on whether he could speak it with any degree of fluency two years later, as his parents believed he could at the time of his disappearance. Everett was alone most of the time. His spare time on the road was devoted to reading books in

---

*Everett Ruess to his family, July 9, 1932. The corresponding diary entry did not include the ungracious phrase *or at home in my dreary bedroom.* He had little regard for his parents' feelings and needs at times, which is not unusual behavior for an adolescent.

English. He remained in California for all of 1933 and portions of other years. A few months before he disappeared, he wrote his parents that language was a barrier with the Navajo.[33] But two official reports written after his disappearance, based on information furnished by his parents, referred to his being fluent in the Navajo language.* That belief fed the unfounded rumors that he was living with the Navajo on their reservation.

At the Hubbell Trading Post the longtime employee Friday Kinlicheenie offered Everett a place to stay and food in return for helping him hoe the corn.[34] In addition to overseeing the post's agricultural operations, Kinlicheenie delivered the mail and herded sheep to the railroad at Holbrook. He could remember when the corn and alfalfa fields were dense stands of junipers. Then they were cleared, and water was diverted to the fields to make the crops grow.

John Lorenzo Hubbell had died in 1930. He was responsible, through buying from the Navajo and marketing to the whites, for the transformation of Navajo blankets into more profitable rugs. Hubbell was also part of the movement to allow Hispanics to vote, but he wanted to deny that right to Native Americans. Should they be given the vote, policies to the traders' advantage might change. "Something was wrong when traders like Hubbell were able to benefit from the use of Indian reservation land without paying the tribe anything for that use," wrote his biographer.[35] Hubbell's son, Lorenzo, was struggling with this legacy in the summer of 1932, when the Republican presidential incumbent, Herbert Hoover, was facing the Democratic challenger, Franklin D. Roosevelt. The Arizona attorney general had ruled that Native Americans could not vote in the November election. Lorenzo told the

---

*The language is immensely difficult for an English speaker to learn. My guess is that his parents assumed, or wanted to believe, that Everett spoke fluent Navajo, and relayed that information to the authorities after his disappearance. The supposition fit the romantic concept they had of their son's wanderings and helped them believe he was still alive and living with the Indians. In the daily police bulletin, Los Angeles Police Department, September 4, 1935, "Walks long strides like Indian; speaks the Navajo Indian language" followed a more mundane description. The only official report of his disappearance, made by Chief Ranger Donal J. Jolley of Zion National Park, stated that Everett "speaks the Navajo language well." But Jolley hadn't had any contact with Ruess since 1931, when Everett spoke no Navajo, according to his letters. Jolley, "Report on Search for Everett Ruess Who Is Supposedly Lost near the Colorado River," Enclosure 619 330, Department of the Interior, April 24, 1935.

newly elected Republican national committeeman from Arizona that nearly 100 percent of the Indians eligible to vote in his district were Republicans and asked what he should do.*

· Everett thought Kinlicheenie's daughter, Alice, was the most beautiful Navajo woman he had encountered. Alice was married to Sam Johnson, who took Ruess to their home seven miles distant in the settlement of Cornfield to help him hoe a cornfield and cut hay. Johnson didn't speak English, but the couple's home was adorned with white men's furnishings. *I have been observing more and more fully that the Navajo owes almost everything he has to the white man. His food is mutton, bread, and coffee. All these were brought by the white man. His clothes are borrowed. All he has left is his language, ceremonies, and a few customs. In spite of all the things he did not have before, he seems a pitiful creature to me. Yet he is always ready to laugh and sing.*[36]

The work was exhausting. For lunch they ate mutton, which Everett by this time had learned to swallow without chewing. Still, he ate only half as fast as the Indians. The Navajo diet did not appeal to him.[37] They talked about him in Navajo; he talked about them in French. Ruess hoed corn and cut hay in the afternoon. He slept with a Navajo boy that night. The next morning he quit work early because he was weak and tired. Fatigue and burning eyes were becoming more constant complaints. He ate mutton for lunch and read. *A Navvy came in, shook hands with me. Then he stood over me, pawing over my diary. Like the other Navvys who kept trying on my hat, I think less and less of these people.*[38] At the time Everett was reading a volume of collected letters from such classical composers as Mendelssohn, Liszt, and Wagner.

Two days later Everett left Ganado, and he reached the familiar village of Chinle on July 11. He rode directly to the stone house of Cordelia and Dick Dunaway, not knowing the welcome he would receive because of a troublesome encounter with Cordelia in 1931. *Mrs. Dunaway had had nerves last year and a few things I did set them on edge.* He had promised Dick a painting for Christmas but had only sent a card. As it happened, he was delighted by the reception of his unannounced visit. Cordelia, a former teacher in the Chinle Indian boarding and public schools, was working on a Navajo primer. Her husband repaired Navajo windmills for the Indian Service. Louisa Wetherill and Frances Gillmor

---

*Lorenzo Hubbell to Frank H. Hitchcock, June 14, 1932. Reminiscent of its recent passage of immigration laws aimed at Latinos, Arizona officially disenfranchised Native Americans from voting until 1948, and then it instituted certain barriers, such as literacy tests.

dropped by for a supper of rabbit meat. Everett was pleased that Louisa remembered him, and he recognized Frances as the author of the novel *Windsinger*.[39] After the meal, the two women departed for the Ganado trading post, where they continued their search for a Navajo without an accent who could be cast in the movie *Laughing Boy*, based on Oliver La Farge's novel of the same name.

Dick came home, and Mrs. Garcia, who operated the Garcia Trading Post across the street, joined Everett and Cordelia. *We had a good discussion about the Indians, banks, etc.*[40] After the others went to bed, Cordelia talked with Ruess about her divorce and remarriage, her daughter, and crowded California versus the isolation of the Navajo reservation. Everett tended to his horses in the morning, read, and talked with Cordelia about the beauty of the surrounding landscape. As with others, he had formed a bond with this safe, older woman.

Letters from home were waiting for him at the post office. Christopher was proud of his son. He wrote, "I told some people the other day that in the hard times you were the true philosopher, to go off into the wilderness, close to God and heaven, and to drink in beauty and feed on hardship, and live like Thoreau on next to nothing."[41] He enclosed collections of the fifty best English and American poems, a volume of poetry by Walt Whitman, three plays by Shakespeare, plays by Henrik Ibsen and George Bernard Shaw, essays by Thoreau and Emerson, a collection of short stories by Tolstoy, and "two quizzical works," *Rip Van Winkle* and *Through the Looking Glass*. Everett was undergoing a wandering version of home schooling.

Ruess also received a letter from his brother, to whom he wrote a five-page reply that took in a broad range of subjects. He gave Waldo permission to read parts of the reply to their parents.[42] *I have not met any intelligent girls out here. Before I left Hollywood I met a very interesting Polish girl, but it might have been better if I hadn't.* He had a hunger for music but didn't like listening to classical music in Hollywood with people who owned fine victrolas and were *offensively queer.* He switched subjects. *The country is fiercely, overpoweringly beautiful.* His lows were *fearfully low,* but they didn't last long. *A few glorious moments make me forget them completely.* He signed the letter and then added a thought that echoed his escalating refrain. *I've been thinking more and more that I shall always be a lone wanderer of the wilderness. God, how the trail lures me. You can't comprehend its resistless fascination for me. After all, the lone trail is the best. I hope I'll be able to buy good horses and a better saddle. I'll never stop wandering. And when the time comes to die, I'll find the wildest, loneliest, most desolate spot there is.*[43]

———— ■ ————

The happy, normal Everett of just a few years ago was no more. Now eighteen, he had reached the average age of onset of manic depression, currently known as bipolar disorder. His mood swings were probably symptoms of bipolar II disorder, less severe than bipolar I. These alternating cycles of profound despair and transcendent states increased in frequency and intensity over the next two years. Since much less was known about the illness in the 1930s, Everett was never examined for the disorder, and as his life ended abruptly in 1934, there can be no certainty about whether he was in the early stages of the illness or what the progression would have been had he lived longer.*

_____

*The present Ruess family, consisting of two nieces and two nephews of Everett's, disagreed with my interpretation that Everett had symptoms of bipolar disorder and withdrew their cooperation from this book when they learned of it. My evaluation was based on Everett's surviving written record, the relevant literature, and the input of qualified mental health professionals. To make such a diagnosis, the National Institute of Mental Health recommends that a doctor examine, interview, have lab tests performed, and conduct mental health and complete diagnostic evaluations of the subject. These are obviously not possible now, and Ruess didn't undergo them during his lifetime.

Comparing the evidence in Everett's letters and journal entries to the symptoms described by the nonprofit Depression and Bipolar Support Alliance, the National Institute of Mental Health, and the American Psychiatric Association (meaning the profession's bible, the _Diagnostic and Statistical Manual of Mental Disorders,_ fourth ed., text rev., 2000), I concluded that in 1932 Ruess displayed symptoms of the milder version of bipolar disorder and two years later was verging on the more aggressive form. I have come to similar conclusions about medical and scientific matters in which I had no expertise, such as the health effects of nuclear fallout and seismic events, in other books (and DNA in this book) after extensive research and consultation of experts. When I was seeking a publisher for this book in 2003, I wrote to Kay Redfield Jamison, a professor of psychiatry and the recognized national authority on bipolar disorders, and asked if she would be interested in collaborating on a book. I sent her the lengthy book proposal and other materials. She commented on the "fascinating proposal" and said she was overcommitted but added that she would comment on the book when it was published. I took this assent as collaboration of my layperson's evaluation of the state of Everett's mental health. Jamison, personal communication, August 26, 2003. I also consulted a family therapist and a psychiatrist who have treated bipolar youths. Both concurred with my opinion.

I hope mental health professionals will take an interest in Everett's case because,

Certain guesses based on medical literature and Ruess's letters and journals can be made, however. Other than Everett's mood swings, his heightened periods of euphoria and creativity were one indication of the presence of bipolar disorder. The flip side was the down times, of which he complained. And therein lay the danger. There was a 30 to 60 percent "completed" suicide rate for people diagnosed with having the illness before an effective treatment had been found.[44] A larger number attempted it, and an even larger number seriously considered it. Bipolar emotions also have powerful effects on human relationships, irritability and withdrawal into solitude being two symptoms. Teenagers were—and are—the most susceptible to all aspects of the illness.

The ancient Greeks identified mania and depression (what they called *melancholia*) but didn't link them. They attributed these mood swings to excesses of yellow and black bile, respectively. In medieval times the causes were thought to be witchcraft and demonic possession. In the mid-nineteenth century and the age of reason, a link between the two polar opposites on the emotional spectrum was first proposed, and at the end of the century a German psychiatrist defined the disorder as "a single morbid process" in a classic textbook on the subject.[45] But there was no effective treatment for the next seventy years, primarily due to the disarray of German psychiatry because of two world wars. Also, the influence of psychoanalysis prevailed in this country, and the "talking cure" was a useless method to treat the illness. It was not until the 1970s that the first helpful drug, lithium, became available.

Up to that time the more extreme cases of manic depression were confined to private homes or private sanitariums if their families could afford this, or public insane asylums if they couldn't. In such institutions, treatments were nonexistent, ineffective, or ruinous. Had Everett lived and this evaluation proved correct, the chances are that the milder form of the illness would

---

rather than them having to elicit a history from a patient, he is volunteering a description in his own words as the symptoms occur and without any knowledge of the affliction from which he is suffering. In this manner a contribution could be made to understanding and treating this disorder that cripples so many teenagers, including Jamison when she was young. Jamison experienced her first attack of manic depression at the same age as Everett and also attended UCLA, where, like Ruess, she received poor grades. She wrote about her attempted suicide in *An Unquiet Mind* (New York: Alfred A. Knopf, 1995). Lithium saved her.

have become more severe, perhaps evolving into an extreme psychosis. Kay Redfield Jamison, an authority on the subject who suffers from bipolar disorder herself, described the illness:

> Manic-depression distorts moods and thoughts, incites dreadful behaviors, destroys the basis of rational thought, and too often erodes the desire and will to live. It is an illness that is biological in its origins, yet one that feels psychological in the experience of it; an illness that is unique in conferring advantage and pleasure, yet one that brings in its wake almost unendurable suffering and, not infrequently, suicide.[46]

Pleasure is experienced as exuberance, high spirits, elation, euphoria, grandiosity, racing thoughts, flowing words and images, lack of inhibitions, and reckless behavior. "As the combination of euphoric mood and mental quickness develops," a colleague of Jamison's wrote, "the manic individual begins to feel tremendously self-confident, even fearless."[47] Using biographies, Jamison documented the heightened creativity in their manic phases of Lord Byron, Alfred Tennyson, Herman Melville, William and Henry James, Samuel Taylor Coleridge, Vincent van Gogh, Ernest Hemingway, Virginia Woolf, Anne Sexton, and others. The seesaw effect, however, could lead to a "strikingly" high rate of suicides during depressed periods. "That such a final, tragic, and awful thing as suicide can exist in the midst of remarkable beauty," Jamison wrote, "is one of the vastly contradictory and paradoxical aspects of life and art."[48]

Depression is characterized by pervasive gloom, sadness, a sense of loss, regret, hopelessness, guilt, shame, feelings of inadequacy, worthlessness, and incompetence, the dimming of bright and beautiful things, slower thinking, indecision, and fatigue. The writer William Styron could "feel the horror, like some poisonous fog bank, roll in upon my mind, forcing me to bed."[49] An early professional observer noted: "Many patients constantly play with thoughts of suicide and are always prepared on the first occasion to throw away their life."[50] One of his patients attempted suicide five times between the ages of ten and twenty-four. Given the drugs now available to treat bipolar disorder, the number of contemplated and completed suicides has been greatly reduced—if the sufferer seeks treatment in time.[51]

———————————■———————————

After two days with the Dunaways, Ruess departed on his second visit to Canyon de Chelly and its offshoot, Canyon del Muerto. *We made slow progress but I was drinking in the glory of the cleanly chiseled canyon walls.*[52] These were the same monumental walls immortalized by the photographer Edward Curtis in his signature photo of the Navajo horsemen crossing the sandy entrance to the canyon. Everett camped in a grove of cottonwoods where he had stopped with Pegasus and Curly the previous year and explored a nearby ruin. A Navajo dug in the sand and found some water for him.

The next day Everett continued up the main canyon, passing White House Ruin again and the places where his burro had gotten mired in the quicksand. He found a deserted hogan, cooked rice cakes, and read. The next afternoon, during a hard rain, Ruess made a dangerous ascent toward three small ruins in a side canyon. A sheer cliff deterred him, and he found a more accessible ruin where there were artifacts. The corn he ate for dinner and breakfast made him ill. Everett read all the letters he had received and burned some.

Time passed in this seemingly timeless place as Everett explored, ate, and read. Styron's fog settled over him. *I felt futile. It seems after all that a solitary life is not good. I wish I could experience a great love. I find that I cannot consider working on in art. To be a great artist one must work incessantly, and I have not the vitality. . . . More and more I feel that I don't belong in the world. I am losing contact with life.* More rain, more reading, more rice. And then the skies cleared. He chanted aloud the poetry he read by flashlight at night. *Somehow this raised my spirits greatly. . . . It was good to see the stars again.*[53]

The two horses and Everett made their way back down the canyon. *We had gone only a few turns when my eyes pained me intensely and I could hardly see.* He felt dizzy and swayed drunkenly in the saddle. By the time he reached the junction with Canyon del Muerto, Everett had recovered. It was the second time in twenty days he had experienced pain in his eyes. This attack was more severe. Lunch was *naneskadi*, Indian fry bread, with mutton tallow. It sickened him. Dinner was ground wheat mush he had acquired nearly two months ago and more mutton. Breakfast the next morning was more mush and mutton.[54]

They traveled up Canyon del Muerto past familiar places. *I lifted up my voice in triumphant rejoicing, making the canyon echo with my song.* A Navajo advised him to climb out of the canyon because there was quicksand ahead. He sought to purchase saddle blankets from the Navajo he passed but disliked their crude designs. He bartered unsuccessfully with an Indian named Old Yellow Mustache and then drank tea with him and ate some of his tortillas.

He felt ill. Mummy Cave did not interest him this time. In fact, he was losing interest in a lot of things. It was another low period. *Lunch and long thoughts. I think I have seen too much and known too much—so much that it has put me in a dream from which I cannot waken and be like other people. I love beauty but have no longer the desire to re-create it. Ambition is distasteful to me. . . . Everybody disapproved of my going off by myself. Actually, I am nearly satisfied with solitude, but I refuse to give up the independence I am used to. Physically I feel weak. I would not be surprised to hear that pernicious anemia had hit again. A slight bruise has taken three weeks to heal. My injured toe will pain me for weeks to come. Diet more trouble.*[55]

The horses' unremarkable names had displeased him for some time, so that night Whitie, referred to as Whity in recent journal entries, became Nuflo, whose name derived from that of a cantankerous old man in *Green Mansions,* a novel Everett had read three times. Sweet-tempered, gentle Bay was transformed into Jonathan, a short-lived appellation.

Off they went the morning of July 22 up Twin Trail, one of the few paths leading out of the canyon. The narrowness of the trail forced Everett to lead Nuflo and urge Jonathan ahead of them. Jonathan fell, or sat down of his own accord; Everett wasn't sure. The horse had been acting strangely for days. Ruess thwacked him with a stick, but the horse didn't budge. He unpacked Jonathan and transferred the load to Nuflo. While Everett was pulling off the horse's pack saddle, Jonathan slid off the edge of the trail, fell, turned over three times, and got shakily to his feet. The trio retreated to their previous campsite.

Jonathan walked in circles, staggered sideways, and fell into a clump of cactus. *He got groggily to his feet, tottered again and collapsed. Then I prepared myself for the worst and began looking at my map to see how near a railroad was. In a little while, I looked at Jonathan again, and he was dead—eyes glassy green, teeth showing, flies in his mouth. So for me, Canyon del Muerto is indeed the canyon of death—the end of the trail for gentle old Jonathan.*[56]

Everett hid the saddle in the same ruin where he had left the baby board the previous year. He didn't think he would return for either object. The discarded name *Evert Rulan,* which he had inscribed on the board fourteen months ago, was now obscured. He also left his old saddle blankets, worn by five of his beasts of burden. The ghosts of the cliff dwellers would watch over these discarded objects, he thought.[57]

Jonathan was left unburied. Everett thought the Navajo would help themselves to the four horseshoes. He vowed to take better care of his one remaining horse. Now on foot, he led Nuflo much as he had guided his lone burro. *In two days I reached the Lukachukai Mountains, but how I suffered on the way! Something seems to have gone wrong with my legs. They don't give me good service anymore.* He camped by a lake for two days, resting and reading two Shakespeare comedies. He saw a brown bear. *There were aspen glades and dark quiet lakes surrounded by pines and firs.*[58] Landscape can heal. *I still think at times that the future may hold happiness.*[59]

Descending the east side of the mountains, Everett used the 1,700-foot-tall eroded volcanic plug of Shiprock as a navigational aid, heading northeast toward the town of the same name in New Mexico. His legs were even weaker than before. His clothes were in shreds. His equipment was almost nonfunctional. He wanted to go home. Everett sat in a deserted hogan and smoked half a dozen cigarettes, blowing smoke rings upward toward the fungus-covered rafters. He would not quit, he decided, since the alternative of an ordinary life was too distasteful.

On July 28 the weary pair entered Shiprock, and Everett went immediately to the post office. There was one letter waiting for him. His mother cited the advantages of a life at home and asked if he was smoking too much. No, he answered, just enough to give him a sense of peace around a campfire at night. He had read all the books his father had sent and was returning them. Could she mail him something by William Blake and Charles Baudelaire? *As we left the town behind, my spirits soared again and I sang and sang.*[60] He was on his way to Mesa Verde.

At the Mancos Creek Trading Post in southwestern Colorado, shaded by cottonwood and elm trees beside the running water, Everett asked the way to the national park. He was given vague directions for the trail ascending Mancos River Canyon by a Ute Indian. Everett and Nuflo made their way up a narrow defile. Nuflo slipped. *He clawed the ledge frantically, then fell down into the current of the muddy Mancos. It was deep near the bank and he floundered about and wet his pack.*[61] The horse floated downriver. Everett jumped into the current and pulled him ashore. Everything was wet. While Nuflo grazed unconcernedly, Everett inspected the damage. It was a complete disaster. It should have defeated him, but it didn't.

Instead of heading back to nearby Highway 666, where he could have gotten a ride in the direction of home, a bedraggled Ruess soldiered on. He walked back to the trading post and bought a few necessities, such as cigarettes, candy, and a comb. *Though I had not let it show, I really felt overwhelmed by what happened.*[62]

In the morning he cleaned and oiled his pistol and set his clothing, bedding, food, and equipment out to dry in the sunlight. Then he set out again. The trail up the canyon was like a phantom presence: it was there, then not there, and then there again. He stopped to rest in the shade of two trees. A brief additional inspection revealed that his camera and flashlight, not to mention almost everything that was mechanical or perishable, were ruined. *Yesterday I was laughing at myself for feeling so crushed by the wetting, but it was not the last laugh. My photos are all stuck together, the matches are all wet, the soap is soggy, the baking powder is muddy—so on down the list.*

Again the trail vanished. Everett camped beside a small water source. Now that he was off the Navajo reservation and on Southern Ute lands, his diet had changed, and he felt better. He ate fried sweet potatoes with bacon and onions. *Smoked, peered into the fire, stargazed.* He was in no hurry to reach Mesa Verde. *It will mark the termination of my wanderings—my independence.* He feared he would be restricted to guided tours of the ruins. Still, Everett was excited. *In the evening I watched the fire with beating heart.*[63]

His spirits improved with altitude. He reached the mesa via a sunlit side canyon. *Once on the mesa we rolled along thru the pinyon juniper forest, I singing and whistling gaily.* He found the campground, hobbled Nuflo, and at park headquarters inquired for mail. There was none. He picked up a park pamphlet with information about guided tours. The group visited Spruce Tree House, Balcony House, and Cliff Palace. *Some of the tourists were rather stupid—physically feeble & the party seemed too large, but I enjoyed myself very much.*[64] Everett noticed that he talked a lot on the tour.

Mesa Verde National Park is on a tableland, 2,000 abrupt feet above the high desert. Its highest point is at 8,600 feet. The Anasazi had progressed from outdoor shelters to living quarters under overhangs that protected them from the elements and provided defensive positions. The problem was that in the 1930s the ruins were crumbling under the twin onslaughts of weather and the feet of thousands of tourists, some of whom inscribed their names and addresses on the walls, making it easier for them to be arrested and prosecuted. The Park Service put out a call, in the form of a press release, for "a clear, transparent, waterproof solution that when sprayed on prehistoric masonry will preserve it from weathering without obscuring it from view."[65] Needless to say, no such miracle preservative existed.

Like the smaller Tonto National Monument, Mesa Verde was off the main railroad and highway routes, and the road to the top was along the knife edge of a ridge. Never a wildly popular destination, it saw a drop in visitor numbers from 17,000 in 1928 to 10,000 in 1932. Salaries and maintenance budgets were cut by 10 percent the year Everett arrived. But for Ruess, Mesa Verde was the mother lode of the Native American experience he had been avidly seeking since his boyhood years in Indiana, and he spent most of August immersed in it.

The national park was an outdoor museum. The extent of its holdings was unknown even to its curators, the National Park Service. No survey of unexcavated sites had been made. Preserved in caves and mounds were at least ten centuries of Native American history in the Southwest. The Park Service now counts more than four thousand known archeological sites, including six hundred ruins, in Mesa Verde.

Since the accidental discovery of the Cliff Palace ruins in December 1888 by the Wetherills, who were grazing cattle on the mesa, the uses of and policies governing the cliff dwellings and surrounding lands have shifted through the years. Generally, the phases reflect national concerns, and therein lies a history lesson depicted in broad strokes. Southwestern Colorado was Indian country before becoming cattle country in the second half of the nineteenth century. There were no laws governing Native American artifacts. They were extracted for private pleasure, private profit, professional recognition, and public display, the last usually at the Smithsonian Institution in Washington, D.C. The establishment of park boundaries ignored the impoverished Southern Ute tribe, which objected to the original designation and subsequent infringements upon its lands. "The Utes responded that they had preserved the sites simply by leaving them alone, but their concerns were overridden by [Department of the] Interior officials and other national park proponents," wrote a Park Service historian.[66]

The year Everett visited Mesa Verde was a transition period for the park. The superintendent for the prior ten years, who was credited with achieving unprecedented development, had left, and the new superintendent, who would deal with the early years of the Depression, was in place. There was a new hospital, named after the prior superintendent's wife, with separate wards for white females, white males, and the sixty Indians employed by the park—the last ward presumably for both male and female patients. The campground had been expanded, and there were a new mess hall, bunkhouse, and club for rangers, all of which Everett used. The plans for a new hotel, in the Fred Harvey style, were being held up until the water supply was assured. Meanwhile, new ruins, artifacts, and skeletons were being discovered.

Civilian Conservation Corps (CCC) workers numbering more than two hundred would soon move into the park and lodge in a military-style camp. These workers, mostly from the surrounding region, would make some discoveries and supply much of the labor needed to upgrade the park. Everett would make his small contribution, being partly responsible for the naming of one ruin.

National park regulations that herded tourists into groups were not about to inhibit the teenager, who had twice smuggled a small dog across the Grand Canyon. First, however, he had to settle into his new surroundings. He asked his parents for a few dollars, some writing and drawing paper, pens and ink, and another diary, since he had filled the existing one. He was not in a hurry to return to Los Angeles, he told his parents, because he wanted to see more of the West. *You have no idea how flabby and pale the city is, compared with the reality, the meaningful beauty of the wilderness.*[67]

He had found some likable young men among the seasonal rangers, most of whom were college students. When it rained, he stayed in their quarters and ate meals in their mess hall that cost 37¢ and were very good. Everett made friends with one ranger, Fritz Loeffler, and they discussed music. "I discovered Everett had a very deep love for music," Loeffler said. Ruess showed the ranger his artwork. "I befriended Everett because I recognized in him a very brilliant mind but felt that he was lonely and needed companionship." He advised Everett not to isolate himself from people and to enroll at UCLA. "There was nothing unusual in our rather casual and short acquaintance," Loeffler wrote to Stella after Everett's disappearance.[68]

Then Everett was off on a trip within the national park for ten days, spending part of the time with a ranger. They explored Wetherill Mesa and in one of the ruins captured a buzzard. Everett held it by its wings, and his friend took a photo. The small ruin subsequently became known as Buzzard House.

Everett suffered from a bad case of poison ivy, did some sketching, fondled a skull, and pocketed pieces of pottery. He was back on a diet of rice cakes and spotted dog. While in Ute Canyon, Everett witnessed a flash flood for the first time. *I heard a rumbling and roaring, and ran to the edge of the stream bed. Below was the dry canyon floor, above was a foaming, boiling, brown torrent, rolling sticks and trash ahead of it, coming down like lava from a volcano. Soon it pushed past, and for several hours there was a torrent. By morning the stream was dry again.*[69]

On his return, he and the Park Service wrangler removed Nuflo's horseshoes and turned him loose with the other horses. *He is too old—his teeth are worn down so that he can hardly eat. His back was getting sore.*[70]

Everett was juggling future possibilities. He had been thinking about Loeffler's advice. *I don't feel in the mood for a big change now, but it is bound to come, I guess.* Los Angeles and more formal education were possibilities. There were problems with going home, however, like the lack of money and friends. He was estranged from Bill, Clark, and Cornel. *That leaves me completely friendless, and it is hard to start from the bottom again.* He wasn't really sure he wanted to be an artist. Writing about his adventures was another possibility. He was sure he wanted no part of a career that involved any kind of routine. There was one man he admired and who served as an exemplar of what he wanted to achieve. *I can't say I've ever met anyone whom I could really envy unless it was Edward Weston.* His unsettled emotional state echoed these uncertainties. *I've been having plenty of contrast, misery that heightened the ecstasies that would follow. For the moment, I am feeling blithe.*[71]

Having to carrying his own pack did not deter Everett from continuing his explorations of the park. He embarked on a four-day hike to Wild Horse Mesa, where his ascents to inaccessible cliff dwellings were breathtaking. *There was one small dwelling which could only be reached by a ledge, from six inches to a foot and a half wide. Below was a sheer drop of fifty feet or so. I had little trouble entering it, being right handed, but when it came to returning, matters were more complicated. I could not get by the narrow part with my back to the cliff, and if I faced the cliff, I had to go backwards and could not see where to set my feet. After three false starts, I finally reached level sandstone, by crawling on my knees.*[72]

In a ruin near Horse Springs, reachable only by climbing up a nearly vertical crevice and hanging by his hands at times, he found a bone awl. At the 8,300-foot level of a mesa, there was an incredible view. *The sun was just setting behind a smoky cloud, casting a lurid glow over the olive drab terrain. Small lakes and canals gleamed up at the cloudless sky overhead. The lights of Cortez flickered in the distance. Soon a cold wind sprang up, blowing a veil of fleecy clouds across the stars.*[73]

There were other lone outings across mesas, canyons, streams, and ridges. It was a wet summer, so there was plenty of water. From the heights, he looked down on towers, squat remains of dwellings, and other evidence of an ancient culture that presaged the coming of more recent Native Americans and then the whites, all of them seeking a way to survive in an environment that would not tolerate large numbers.

He returned to the adobe ranger quarters. After a shower and another good meal in their mess hall, he went looking for a California-bound tourist. His ranger friends thought he had little chance of catching a ride with the amount of luggage he had, which included the two wooden kyaks. But he found a willing tourist at the guided tours meeting point and got a ride to Gallup, where he mailed a postcard to his father stating that he was becoming interested in a college education.[74] He then persuaded this driver to take him to the Grand Canyon. *I always enjoy the Grand Canyon, and I couldn't resist going down again, so I swung my pack over my shoulder and went down into the depths of the glowing furnace. I killed a Grand Canyon rattler, and camped in a wonderful little side canyon with a stream. I went along the Tonto Trail and down to the writhing Colorado, and then did some tall hiking, climbing out between mid-afternoon and dusk.*[75]

A World War I veteran asked Everett to guide him down into the canyon so he could join some friends who were prospecting. When they returned to the rim, the prospectors gave Everett a ride to Kingman, where he shipped home his boxes and stuck out his thumb once again. He was stranded in Needles and wired home for help. The wire was never received. Eventually he got a ride all the way to Los Angeles, where he arrived in the fog. Home for one week, he was then off again to get one last hit of the desert, this time Red Rock Canyon on the edge of the Mojave. Home again, he enrolled for two semesters at UCLA, taking geology, philosophy, English history, English, gym, and military drill, also known as Reserve Officer Training Corps and seemingly antithetical to everything Everett represented.

In the city he sought reminders of the rural West. In return for mowing the lawn of the California Riding Academy in Griffith Park, Everett was given a frisky horse to ride. *A grand wind was sweeping down from the west, and it was good to be on a horse again.*[76] He chose trails up and down the steepest hillsides. As for more intellectual pursuits, he listened to classical records on expensive victrolas with his Hollywood friends and read *Saint Joan* by George Bernard Shaw and "The Waste Land" by T. S. Eliot.

During Christmas vacation, Everett hitchhiked to Carmel. He looked up Weston, but the photographer was busy filling Christmas orders and had no time for him. Everett had his own holiday business to attend to. He sold five Christmas cards decorated with his drawing of a sea horse for a total of 90¢. He revisited Point Lobos with his mother's married friend Grace Meinen. He seemed to form the closest attachments with safe older women: Billie Reynolds, Cordelia Dunaway, Grace Meinen, Doris Gray, Dorothea Lange, and Frances Schermerhorn. He would spend time with Gray in Visalia and with Lange and Schermerhorn in the San Francisco Bay Area.

Grace and Everett hitchhiked from Carmel to Point Lobos, something Grace hadn't done before and found exciting. They slid down a grassy slope toward the edge of a cliff, and then Everett pulled her back up by the arm. "He was better equipped, younger and more agile," Grace reported to Stella. She crowned him with a flower wreath and found him sweet, gay, and quite talkative. Poetry was the main topic of their conversation. There was a need, they agreed, to express oneself fully and not in "the usual and proscribed commercial way." She found his poetry sad. "There was the paradox always with Everett—he was an old friend one moment and a young friend the next, and we were both exploring the world together."[77]

VIII

The Bohemian

1933

NEEDLESS TO SAY, THE EXPERIMENT in higher education did not work. At the end of the second semester Everett received Ds in history, philosophy, and military drill. He did well in geology and received a B in English, which surprised him, since he didn't complete all the assignments. *I have not been very successful with college. I don't belong in the place (U.C.L.A.) but it has been another experience, and anything that happens is of value as an experience, when it's over.*[1] By the end of March, he had the remainder of 1933 and 1934 planned. *In a month or so when it is hot, I am going to shoulder my pack and go up into the Sierras with some rice and oatmeal, a few books, paper and paints. It will be good for me to be on the trail again.* He would end the year in San Francisco. *Next year I expect to spend almost the whole year in the red wastes of the Navajo country, painting industriously.*[2]

Drawing on his experiences during his first three years of wandering, Everett produced his most resonant poem in early May. It was titled "Wilderness Song," and the first stanza covers three different western landscapes.

> *I have been one who loved the wilderness;*
> *Swaggered and softly crept between the mountain peaks;*
> *I listened long to the sea's brave music;*
> *I sang my songs above the shriek of desert winds.**

---

*See appendix A for the whole poem.

Everett had sampled the first landscape, the Sierra Nevada, on foot in 1930. Three years later he set out to explore John Muir's "Range of Light" more extensively, from its southern tip in Sequoia National Park to the more centrally located Yosemite National Park. He knew it would not resemble the desert: more dark greens and light grays, his painterly eye told him.

Ruess left home on May 27, saying good-bye to his mother and her friend Grace Meinen. His father was at work. Waldo, accompanied by his girlfriend of the moment, drove his brother to Three Rivers, at the entrance to Sequoia National Park. Everett sought out the packer who had the concession for the park, and they chatted about possible pack trips into the high country until late at night. Ruess was in search of burros, definitely preferring them now over horses. He bought a black and a gray donkey.

From the 100-plus-degree heat of Three Rivers, Everett and the two burros climbed the four thousand vertical feet of the winding dirt road to the cooler Giant Forest. Knowing that the ranger would not allow his burros in the campground, Everett found a nearby meadow for the donkeys and a hollow between the roots of a giant sequoia tree for his campsite. *It is really as delightful a camp as I've ever had. Deer browsed beside the burros, chipmunks scolded and the wind rustled in the tree tops.* In early June the snow still choked the high country, so his activities were confined to lower elevations. *I am having the time of my life so far. Things have been quite engrossing.*[3]

His emotional instability returned during June and early July. *My health and complexion have greatly improved, and every once in a while I feel ecstatic, but I slip out of such moods quite easily.*[4] He was on a high when he wrote a friend. *I have nothing to lament. More than ever before, I have succeeded in stopping the clock. I need no timepiece, knowing that now is the time to live.*[5] He replied crossly to a question from his family. *No, I am in no danger of a nervous breakdown at present. How about you?*[6]

■

Everett's five years of wandering were spent hopping from one pristine island to another and avoiding the more mundane landscapes. The different units of the national park system were strung along the dusty roads and trails in five western states. Even his nexus, the northern portion of the Navajo reservation, was being considered for national park status. Davis Gulch at the end of his travels was later included in the Glen Canyon National Recreation Area, which is administered and patrolled by the Park Service.

The Roosevelt administration's Depression-era work program had ramped up by 1933, and Sequoia National Park was one of the places where it was most noticeable. June was the busiest month in the park's history, with the establishment of five camps for Emergency Conservation Work (ECW, later to become the CCC, or Civilian Conservation Corps). Thirty-six soldiers had charge of 1,124 workers, and in overall command was Park Superintendent John R. White, who had been in charge of Sequoia since 1920 and would influence park policies for a total of twenty-five years.

Known as the Colonel for his former rank in the military, the lean, red-headed White stood ramrod straight and exercised a benevolent command presence over his troops. His was another orphan park, distant from railroads and populated cities and lacking advertising calling attention to its attractions. These included the landmark Moro Rock, the outsize sequoias, trout fishing, and high country wilderness. The superintendent thought the work hours in the federal program were too short for the healthy young men, who were treated too leniently. But he was pleased the program would focus on protective measures, not development programs as in prior years. For instance, between 1926 and 1930 two hundred cabins and tents were added to the clutter in Giant Forest. White particularly abhorred the dense concentration of crowds, automobiles, asphalt, and wooden structures, and the maze of telephone and power lines strung from trees in Giant Forest. The first limit on accommodations in a national park was imposed on housing in Giant Forest in 1931. "Again and again, citing potential damage to the 'atmosphere' of the parks, White assumed the high moral ground and portrayed prodevelopment forces as tawdry and greedy."[7]

As the summer of 1933 progressed, the activities intensified. A crew from MGM made a movie about a deer named Malibu. July was exceptionally hot, and the campgrounds were filled with transient tourists and many summer-long campers, the latter being families who made a temporary home in the park while their members went looking for work below in the San Joaquin Valley. Trout fishing was the best in years. The cost of lodging and food at the Sequoia Lodge was reduced. A huge dust storm blew up from the valley and obscured views in the park.

There were 1,500 applications in one month for nonexistent jobs in the park.[8] The CCC men didn't know how to work with their hands or tools and had to be taught to use them. Superintendent White thought more could have been accomplished if the military hadn't imposed its distinctive style of discipline, which caused a backlash among the civilian workers. The Californians in two camps were generally more disciplined workers than the Kentuckians and Ohioans in three camps.

The superintendent believed in trails as a way to cure national ills. He had detected a softening of Americans. White thought the energy expended on hiking in the wilderness would substitute for the physical exertion expended performing chores on farms in earlier years. To counteract this weakening trend among Americans, he embarked on an ambitious trail-building program that included the forty-nine-mile High Sierra Trail from Crescent Meadow in Giant Forest to thirteen miles short of the summit of Mount Whitney, the highest point in the continental United States. Begun as a state project in 1915, the John Muir Tail linking Sequoia and Yosemite national parks was completed in 1933. Everett would travel both trails that summer.

If White was an exemplary park superintendent for his time, then Lon Garrison was the prototype of a model park ranger. The Stanford University graduate worked as a Forest Service fire ranger in Alaska before becoming a seasonal ranger in Sequoia in 1932. He wore the prescribed uniform: choke-bore breeches, high-laced field boots, clean and pressed ranger shirt, and hard-brimmed Stetson hat, which was a problem in high winds. "I was the romantic ranger riding through the wilds, the protector of beauty. I was never frightened by this loneliness. The isolation and the impersonal impact of it all somehow was a blessing. It was a fulfilling job," Garrison said.[9]

In those days, rangers were not specialists. Garrison rode the trails on Pico, his thirty-year-old horse. He aided hikers and kept hunters out of the park during hunting season. Garrison wondered at the number of overweight hikers who got into trouble. He rescued tourists from rock ledges and stranded trout from streams and kept notes on wildlife. In campgrounds he was a pleasant, helpful presence, answering all types of questions—those that made sense and those that didn't. He was hired at a salary of $140 a month, but the Roosevelt administration soon cut that by 15 percent. Garrison lived in a tent during the summer months with his wife and newborn baby. "A job? It was a way to be fully alive and to overflow with love," he wrote years later. "It belonged to me; I belonged there. I was the ranger."[10]

With the establishment of the work camps in 1933, there was a feeling of excitement in the park. Garrison guided a crew of CCC employees to Silliman Meadow on a make-work project to test how they reacted to the wilderness. They were scared and didn't let the ranger out of sight. The men he oversaw were honest, tough, and disturbed. They had walked, hitchhiked, and ridden freight trains across the country and had lived the lives of vagabonds and hoboes. Some had been in jail; stealing, they thought, was better than going hungry. Each month each worker received $5 for spending money, and $25 was sent to their home. Most of the enrollees knew how to work,

Garrison said. But they pleaded with him that day at Silliman Meadow: "Please, Mr. Ranger, don't leave us alone out here with the bears."[11]

Everett and the ranger had a love of wilderness in common. Garrison was the type of male friend Everett gravitated toward: mature, intelligent, someone he could talk to, and a person to learn from and respect. It was no accident that Ruess befriended Fritz Loeffler in Mesa Verde and Lon Garrison in Sequoia, both of whom wore uniforms and exuded masculine authority. Ruess would make friends the next summer with another intelligent man who was in a position of authority. All of these road friends were older, and two were married. They thought highly of this young man who appeared briefly in their lives, and they never forgot him.

Everett moved his camp to a new location, under a massive pine tree on the banks of the Marble Fork of the Kaweah River near Lodgepole Campground. By this time the docile gray burro had acquired the name Grandma, and the black donkey was called Betsy. Garrison came over that night and sat by Everett's campfire. Everett liked the ranger immediately. *He enjoys his work immensely, and says it is his choice of all the jobs in the country. He is color blind and doesn't read much, but he knows the woods wonderfully well.* The next day Everett helped Lon erect some signs and had supper in the ranger station. *We ran the gamut of intellectual topics, discussing the philosophical and gastronomical aspects of life.*[12]

Two days later they were searching on foot for damaged trail signs under three feet of snow. They climbed higher, and it began to snow on June 5, not an unusual occurrence in the Sierra Nevada. Lon showed Everett how to tell red from white fir by the needles and how to identify yellow and lodgepole pine trees. They followed some bear tracks. It snowed more heavily at the ten-thousand-foot level, from where they slid on their bottoms down a steep slope to Heather Lake. *The lake was beautiful. Most of it was covered with ice and snow, but there were patches of emerald green, and the red trunks and green boughs of spruce contrasted against the white snow and gray glacial boulders.*[13] After several attempts, they got a fire started and ate beans for lunch, Garrison having forgotten to bring a hook so they could eat fresh trout. They uncovered more buried signs in the afternoon and ate supper again back at the ranger station. Lon guessed Everett was twenty-three years old. The ranger was twenty-nine.

The next day Everett helped Garrison and another ranger erect a lodgepole pine as a flagpole at the summer ranger station. The following day Ruess awakened too late and missed his friend's departure. He tracked Lon to Clover Creek. Everett was desperate for company. Back at Lodgepole he talked with various people in the stores and post office. Then he returned to his campsite, where he read more of *The Golden Ass* by Lucius Apuleius, also titled *Metamorphoses* and thought to be the only ancient Latin novel to survive in its entirety.[14] He cornered Garrison again, asked him questions about trails, and received a curt reply. Perhaps the ranger had had enough of Ruess for a while. He could be a pest. *I may have been too forward with him.*[15]

A few days later Ruess joined Garrison at Cabin Meadow, where they posted "No fishing" signs along the creek. On nearby Dorst Creek, Lon caught twelve fish and threw four small ones back into the water. Two trout were caught simultaneously. To Garrison and others, trout fishing was a religious experience, especially in the southern Sierra Nevada, whose native golden trout was a subspecies of rainbow trout. Garrison described a fishing experience in these waters: "A trout surfaced in a pool as I watched. It flashed like a rainbow or a golden trout. These were mythical creatures of secret places, only rarely seen, except in places like Golden Trout Creek in the Kern."[16] Everett cleaned the rainbows Lon had caught in Dorst Creek, and they spent the night in the log cabin at the meadow.

———————— ■ ————————

There was a reason why 1933 was one of the best fishing years in the history of Sequoia National Park. Trout were a good example of how natural resources were manipulated to conform with national policies. The best way to preserve the national parks, the thinking went in the 1920s, was to make them popular with the public. One way to make them popular was to fill as many lakes and streams as possible with many different varieties of trout so that the daily limit—twenty-five in California—could be caught. "Everybody, of course, wants to 'catch the limit,'" Director Albright said.[17] Although White would reverse the trend toward development in the park, huge numbers of trout were still being planted in 1933. In July 65,000 eastern brook trout and 44,000 rainbow trout were dumped into creeks, rivers, and lakes. The next month 225,000 rainbows were planted in one river. "Fishing in the higher waters of the park has been the best in years throughout the month," White reported to the Park Service director.[18]

Only rainbow and golden trout were native to the southern Sierra Nevada. Eastern brook, cutthroat, steelhead, and Loch Leven trout came from elsewhere. Albright had estimated in 1928 that as many as eight million trout were planted in national parks. Of that number, perhaps only one in ten survived. The older and bigger fish ate the younger and smaller fish. One solution was to plant trout only in so-called barren waters at higher elevations, where there were no older and larger fish and therefore no chance of piscatorial cannibalism. Another solution was to release the fish not as baby fry but as year-old fingerlings raised on beef liver. The larger fish could then defend themselves better, the thinking went.

One of Ranger Garrison's jobs was to plant fish. On one trip he hauled four cans of eastern brook trout to Silliman Lake on two burros. There was no science involved in planting fish. Lon and other rangers used their wrists to gauge if the temperature of the water was suitable. He tried not to overload any one body of water. When he was given his first lessons in planting fish by a veteran ranger in 1932, he had wondered why cutting trees and grazing cattle were prohibited in national parks while "the consumptive use" of fishing was permitted. Writing fifty years later, Garrison said those waters would probably not be planted at the present time. "Just because a stream will grow a fish does not mean that we must put some there."[19]

Lon and Everett hiked to Heather, Aster, and Emerald lakes, about an eleven-mile round trip. Garrison repaired a sign and caught nine trout.[20] There were hints of spring. *The aspen are just leafing. On the mountain slopes, they grow twisted and writhen like tortured snakes. The sunflowers are out, and the snow is melting rapidly. . . . The waterfalls are foaming and plunging down the granite slopes.*[21] Everett hung around the campground and the village, talking to people and killing time until he could leave for the high country. He was reading *South Wind,* a novel by the British author Norman Douglas set on the imaginary island of Nepenthe, off the coast of Italy. Everett found it delightful. On June 17 he set off with his burros on a ten-day outing at the relatively snow-free lower elevations. One night Everett thought he heard the roar of a mountain lion. Whatever it was scared his burros.

He arrived back at Lodgepole Campground on June 27. Lon introduced Everett to two friends, Marshall Mason, a doctor, and Melvin Johnson, a real estate agent. Both lived in San Jose. They hired Everett and his two burros for a four-day pack trip to Pear Lake, where they planned to fish, and the group departed the same day. On the way up the trail, said Everett, they discussed *philosophy, science, religion, work, and suicide.* They camped above Aster Lake the first night and reached Pear Lake the next morning. Everett fell through the ice, and Mason pulled him out. The doctor loaned Everett his fishing pole, and he caught two trout—his first. *It really was fun.*[22]

On the fourth day, Mason, who did not want to climb a mountain, took one of the burros and returned to the campground, where he waited for the other two. Johnson and Ruess, with the second burro and the remaining supplies, climbed 11,204-foot Alta Peak to get a view of Mount Whitney to the east. They camped in Alta Meadows that night and drank tea, listened to coyotes howl, and talked around the campfire. Johnson wrote Everett's parents six years later: "He was a very unusual boy with a great appreciation of the beauty of nature and a rare ability to interpret that beauty in words and drawings.... I enjoyed Everett's companionship on the trail and in camp for the few days that I knew him and he seemed to enjoy being with us. In fact he was trying to find someone to go with him on his trip that summer rather than travel all of that distance alone. I think that he craved companionship at times more than he admitted, though I marveled at his ability to travel alone as he did."[23] Johnson visited Ruess in San Francisco that winter and treated him to a rare restaurant meal.

Melvin and Everett returned to the campground. Over four days the group had caught 125 fish. The San Jose men bought two of Everett's prints for $2 apiece and thanked him for an enjoyable trip. Everett had lunch with Lon, his wife Inger, and their baby, Lars. Everett devoted the next six days, including the July Fourth holiday, to preparing for a longer pack trip. He bought supplies for a month and a pair of $2 spurs as a gift for Garrison. He tried to avoid the holiday crowds by seeking such out-of-the-way places as Beetle Rock, a temporary solution at best.[24] *They came over on my side [of the river] with their gas lamps and radios, and it was like sleeping on a park bench in Pershing Square.*[25] By July 5 it was peaceful again.

Everett was looking for a companion for his next foray into the high country. He couldn't find one. *Most people are thwarted, or think that they are.*[26] Two days later he headed off on the High Sierra Trail bound for the summit of Mount Whitney. *I had to stop and adjust Granny's pack. We went thru swarms of butterflies, and crossed streams at every turn.*[27] His reading matter was the *Arabian Nights,* interspersed with the *Rubaiyat of Omar Khayyam.* Such exotic fare clashed with the reality of nightly swarms of mosquitoes. He slapped frantically at them. He was the first hiker with pack animals to cross the snow-bound Kaweah Gap that year. Everett found some company at Kern Hot Springs. *For a week, I traveled with two boys from Hollywood, packing their stuff on my burros. I killed a rattlesnake in the brush, pulling him out alive by his tail.*[28]

With Ned Frisius and Charley Hixon, who had also attended Hollywood High School, Everett reached the top of 14,505-foot Mount Whitney on July 20. It was a long slog through thin air. They inscribed a reference to the *Arabian Nights* in the summit register that made them laugh. *No doubt coming visitors will be affected by it too.*[29] They ate lunch in the stone summit hut

1. A figure under Bement Arch in Davis Gulch. Photo by Alex L. Fradkin.

2. A young Everett with his toys. Credit: Special Collections Department, J. Willard Marriott Library, University of Utah.

3. Everett molding clay in an art class. Credit: Special Collections Department, J. Willard Marriott Library, University of Utah.

4. A print by Stella Ruess showing Everett feeding a deer at Yosemite National Park in 1923. Credit: Special Collections Department, J. Willard Marriott Library, University of Utah.

5. Waldo, Stella, Everett, and Christopher Ruess at home. Credit: Special
   Collections Department, J. Willard Marriott Library, University of Utah.

6. A thoughtful Everett as a young teenager. Credit: Special Collections
   Department, J. Willard Marriott Library, University of Utah.

7. An expressive Stella Ruess in the family garden. Credit: Special Collections Department, J. Willard Marriott Library, University of Utah.

8. Christopher Ruess: Unitarian minister, salesman, and probation officer.
   Credit: Special Collections Department, J. Willard Marriott Library,
   University of Utah.

9. Everett on the trail, with Curly atop the burro. Credit: Special Collections Department, J. Willard Marriott Library, University of Utah.

10. Curly, Everett, and his burro ascending the West Rim Trail in Zion National Park. Credit: Special Collections Department, J. Willard Marriott Library, University of Utah.

Wild Coastline   Everett Ruess

11. *Wild Coastline,* a block print by Everett most likely depicting Point Lobos. Credit: Special Collections Department, J. Willard Marriott Library, University of Utah.

12. Near Bixby Creek Bridge on the Big Sur Coast. Photo by the author.

13. View of Hopi and Navajo lands from Second Mesa on the Hopi reservation. Photo by the author.

14. The restored Hubbell Trading Post in Ganado, Arizona. Photo by the author.

15. Agathla Peak in Monument Valley served as a navigational aid for Everett. Photo by the author.

16. Once in immaculate condition, the now-decaying Hermit Trail that Everett used descends into the Grand Canyon. Photo by the author.

17. Everett worked on a ranch near what is now the ghost town of Zeniff in the Arizona desert. Photo by the author.

18. A Navajo hogan, the type of shelter Everett frequently sought. Photo by the author.

19. Navajo horses in Canyon del Muerto graze near where one of Everett's horses died. Photo by the author.

20. Ancient Native American ruins at Tonto National Monument. Photo by the author.

21. The ruins of Square Tower House at Mesa Verde National Park, which Everett transformed into a block print. Photo by the author.

22. An oil painting by Everett, most likely of the Sierra Nevada foothills. Credit: Special Collections Department, J. Willard Marriott Library, University of Utah.

23. A block print by Everett titled *Granite Towers.* Credit: Museum of Northern Arizona Archives.

Granite Towers   Everett Ruess

24. The High Sierra Trail in Sequoia National Park and the distant crest of the Sierra Nevada. Photo by the author.

25. Heather Lake in Sequoia National Park. Photo by the author.

26. The campgrounds in national parks, like this one in Yosemite, were crowded during the Depression years. Credit: Yosemite NPS Library.

27. The bear pit at Yosemite National Park provided nightly entertainment for visitors. Credit: Yosemite NPS Library.

28. The Escalante Desert, with the Colorado River forming an arc at the bottom of the photo and Davis Gulch the second indentation on the left of the jagged Escalante River. Credit: Special Collections Department, J. Willard Marriott Library, University of Utah.

29. The Mormon meetinghouse in Escalante, photographed by Dorothea Lange in 1936. Credit: Copyright the Dorothea Lange Collection, Oakland Museum of California, City of Oakland. Gift of Paul S. Taylor.

30. A hiker descends the livestock trail into Davis Gulch at the spot, denoted by a wooden fence, where Everett's two burros were found. Photo by the author.

31. The cave, more properly an overhang, where searchers found a few of Everett's belongings in 1935. Photo by the author.

32. Everett's mother, father, and brother sitting in the family garden in later years. Credit: Special Collections Department, J. Willard Marriott Library, University of Utah.

and lay outside in the hot sun *on the windy edge of eternity,* as Everett aptly described their perch. *Ice green lakes, valleys, canyons, towns, and mountains were spread below us. Clouds scudded by but it did not rain, for a wonder.*[30] The boys parted company the next day.

Nearly two weeks later, having eaten numerous trout caught with a willow pole and insects for bait, Everett was back at his old camping site near Lodgepole Campground, where he arrived via the Mineral King Valley. The disparity between the wilderness and the crowds in the park bothered him, and he wasn't feeling well. His moods had changed rapidly. The previous day Everett had ridden exultantly down the trail singing melodies from Beethoven, Brahms, Rossini, and Sibelius. Reading *Green Mansions* for the third time made him sad that night. Rima's death and Abel's *hallucinations and feverish visions in solitude* depressed him. Everett had just been alone, had experienced hallucinations, and was feverish. He had heard bells when none were present on his recent journey. He had heard similar sounds in the Yosemite backcountry in 1930.[31]

Everett's right hand was badly infected, and he was in great pain. He checked out a book from the park library on applied psychology to learn about mood changes and underwent treatments at the medical clinic for his hand. In a shaky letter to his family written with his left hand, Everett attributed the infection to blood poisoning. He did not specify the cause.[32]

While recuperating, he made friends with a Visalia High School teacher and his family in the campground. They drove him to town to do some shopping, and Everett met their daughter, Doris Gray. *She has black, curly hair, and is not pretty, but she has the animation or the charm that means more than beauty.* Doris was divorced and had a daughter and a boyfriend. She was a piano teacher. Everett and Doris had culture in common and engaged in an animated conversation until 2:30 A.M. *She too enjoys solitude, and scorns the shallow crowds.*[33] Doris was going to Los Angeles soon and asked Everett if he knew any interesting young women she could look up. No, he didn't, said Ruess. The ones he had known had all moved away.

Everett and the family returned to Lodgepole on August 11. A bear had visited his tent, eaten the bacon, and nosed through his papers, declining that particular item of food. Everett was off the next day minus his hunting knife. He tended to lose things. Just before he departed he wrote a letter to his brother, who had just taken a job as a stenographer in the California desert. Everett railed against the pointless life and described the exotica of the mountains, which probably did not make Waldo feel very good. He said he had been up till 2:30 A.M. talking with a girl. *She was very interesting to me*. He wondered what had happened to Waldo's girlfriend who had accompanied the brothers to Three Rivers.[34]

■

Being on the trail was the essence of life for Everett Ruess. He departed in August on a long jaunt to Yosemite National Park via the High Sierra and John Muir trails. The bells on the two burros *jingled harmoniously,* noted the connoisseur of classical music. He camped on a small island surrounded by a bog of meltwater from the nearby snowpack. *Splendid granite towers were above. At its head the creek had flowed under a snowbank. Stars were reflected in the mysterious quiet pool at my feet.* Anton Chekhov was his literary companion of the moment. For a few days he was in the company of a teller of tall tales about the mountains and his grandson. At Rae Lakes he spent an hour burying the trash from previous campers. *How I despise confirmed dudes, tenderfeet, mollycoddles, and sloppy campers.*[35] He slept poorly. *I call sleep temporary death.* His moods changed. He was suddenly filled with joy and then a dreamlike calm enveloped him.[36]

Simply by casting a line into a lake, he had a constant supply of fish. If he was too tired there was always rice or macaroni for dinner. On September 2, the trio topped Granite Pass at 10,677 feet, and a new set of mountains, valleys, and lakes emerged before them in Kings Canyon National Park. Everett's reading matter now consisted of Shakespeare's *Tempest,* a second helping of the *Rubaiyat, The Travels of Marco Polo,* and a book whose message was the certainty of the solitary life, which plunged him into depression. *I set less and less value on human life, as I learn more about it. I admit the reality of pain in the moment, but its opposite is not as strong. Life does not grip me very powerfully in the present, but I hope it will again. I don't like to take a negative attitude, but it seems thrust upon me.* He wrote those lines while camped beside the Lake of the Fallen Moon, where he spent *a woeful, restless night full of evil dreams.*[37]

Ruess maintained a correspondence with his brother and parents on the trail by giving the letters to passersby, who then mailed them when they reached a post office. A reassuring letter to his parents written on September 6 at the Lake of the Fallen Moon was mailed six days later from Bishop, California, on the eastern side of the Sierra Nevada. *On a little promontory nearby, I watch the moving panorama of clouds, the grey mountainsides dotted with trees, and the long, undulating cloud shadows moving over distant forests. A little waterfall rushes musically down from the cliff. The reassuring tinkle of burro bells sounds nearby. I shall probably reach Yosemite by October.*[38]

Everett arrived in the village of Mammoth Lakes on the east side of the mountains on September 17. He purchased a sack of oats for his burros and then walked to the campground at Devils Postpile National Monument. Six Los Angeles hunters hired him to pack them into deer-hunting territory along Silver Creek in the Sierra National Forest. The group of city dwellers shot at anything that moved. They wounded an underage buck that became an illegal kill when one of the hunters clubbed it to death, breaking his gunstock in the process. Everett helped butcher the young deer. They spent the next few days fearful that every noise in the woods indicated a visit from the game warden, meanwhile surreptitiously eating the venison Ruess cooked. There were plenty of wild hunting stories and drunken revelry; a tipsy packer fell into the fire pit. At the end of the week the hunters gave Everett $10, some canned food, a pair of shoes, and a pack of cigarettes.

Alone again, Everett smoked the remaining venison and watched the new moon rise over the mountains. On September 30 he entered Yosemite National Park over Donohue Pass. *Now I am in the Yosemite that I know, and yet it is still new to me.*[39]

There had been some changes since 1930. The High Sierra Camp at Vogelsang Lake was deserted, closed for the season. The Merced Lake camp was similarly shuttered, and the CCC had taken over one of the chain of recreational camps in Little Yosemite Valley. Unlike Sequoia, where Superintendent White was a moderating influence, Yosemite saw the push for development that began in the 1920s continue unabated during the 1930s. At the newly acquired Wawona, a landing field for airplanes was being constructed. Ten thousand campers jammed Yosemite Valley campgrounds on the July Fourth holiday. Campers were remaining longer, and, accordingly, the depredations of the bears were increasing. Despite the planting of 1,041,000 fingerlings that spring, fewer trout were being caught.[40]

Exhausted from hiking twenty miles, Everett watched the moon rise over Half Dome and then went to sleep. The next day he was in the valley after fifty days on the trail from Lodgepole Campground. Ruess had seen no one else on the trail in the past five days. *The broad, peaceful lakes, the tall, shapely aspens, still green in some valleys, and the quiet water in the pools, make it a dreamy, peaceful autumn.*[41]

After a shave, a haircut, and a shower in the village, he was off again for one last swing through Yosemite with Grandma and Betsy. Again he had problems sleeping. Preferring not to endure more *nothingness and tortured dreams,* he went seventy hours without sleep. So he read at night and then put some food, his camera, and a sketch pad in his pack. He felt slightly dizzy while climbing the 10,850-foot Mount Hoffman in the early morning hours. He reached the summit at sunrise. The view was magnificent and uplifting. *A smoky grey light spread along the cloud fringes, and a smoldering orange glowed at the tops of the distant peaks.* The multicolored aspen leaves reminded him of fall on the Kaibab Plateau. He stopped at the Aspen Valley Ranger Station, manned by Wes Visel. "We shared the simple fare of the station, exchanged ideas and ideals for an evening," the ranger recalled. "Our acquaintance was extremely short but I believe our friendship was exceptionally strong because of a kindred interest in the intangible beauties of this world of ours."[42]

Everett fantasized about renting a small artist's garret on a hilltop in San Francisco, attending concerts, and spending a month or so wandering around the city. He sold Grandma and Betsy to the Visalia High School teacher who had befriended him in Sequoia National Park. The teacher gave him a ride to Merced. Ever curious, Everett checked out the gambling scene in the small valley city and then hopped a freight train to Sacramento and another to Roseville. He waited for the Oakland-bound train and then climbed on a flatcar, arriving in the Bay Area that afternoon. He ascended the Berkeley hillside and arrived at the home of a family friend, which had a stunning view of San Francisco Bay.

■

There would be no artist's garret for Everett in San Francisco, just a single room in the Broadway Apartments on Polk Street at Broadway. Ruess had landed in this city at a fortuitous time. The effects of the Depression were not nearly so drastic there as they were in Los Angeles. Also, San Francisco was the cultural capital of the West and the center of visual arts activities west of the Hudson River. Ruess would circulate at the edge of this artistic ferment and be enriched by it for the next five months.

For prints and paintings there were the M. H. de Young Memorial Museum in Golden Gate Park, the California Palace of the Legion of Honor in Lincoln Park, and the War Memorial Museum–Opera House complex in the Civic Center. All of the activities that took place in these ornate structures were supported by public funds and private donations from what was described as a clubby, inbred, provincial, urban elite who derived their largesse from manufactured goods, banking facilities, ships and railroads, agricultural products, and clothing.[43]

Everett immediately sought out two of the beneficiaries of this wealth by his usual method of knocking unannounced on their doors, presenting a pleasing and intelligent presence, and showing his work. He couldn't have found a married couple who ranked higher on the visual arts food chain than Maynard Dixon and Dorothea Lange.

Maynard Dixon was the dominant painterly presence in the city, having bridged the gulf from newspaper, magazine, and advertising illustrator to become an evocative painter of western landscapes and Indians. Masses of clouds forming a boiling cauldron above a sere landscape, with or without the heroic figure of an Indian, was a typical Dixon scene. It was no wonder that the photographer Ansel Adams, younger and just gaining a foothold in the San Francisco art scene, was a friend of this painter of dramatic scenery. Dressed in western attire replete with boots and a ten-gallon hat, the artist was an arresting sight on city streets. Dixon yearned for a simpler West and traveled frequently to such places as Ganado and Kayenta. He had just returned, with his wife and two sons, from a trip to southern Utah when Everett knocked on the door of his studio in the writers' and artists' enclave known as the Monkey Block on Montgomery Street. "Dixon became a feature there, almost a totem of the building," wrote one of Lange's biographers.[44]

Despite their nearly forty years' difference in age, Ruess and Dixon had much in common. They relished wandering by themselves for long periods in the desert wildernesses of the Southwest, living with Indians, and painting. But Dixon was at the apex of the fashionable Bay Area bohemian community, and Everett had yet to be judged worthy of admission. That didn't deter young Ruess from voicing his opinion of the master. *I met Maynard Dixon in his studio, and shall see him again. I liked his work for a long time, and the man himself is interesting. He has been thru much of the Arizona country that I covered and knows some of the same old timers.*[45]

Everett's first week in San Francisco was busy. Besides visiting Dixon, he went to a violin recital by Mischa Elman at the Opera House, saw the movie *The Emperor Jones* (with Paul Robeson in the title role), and obtained a library card. He needed his city clothes and asked his parents to send him his gray suit, gold shorts, orange shirt, blue socks, black shoes, green and red sweater, purple and orange neckties, and anything else that didn't have holes and still fit him. He must have presented a startling image strolling on the streets of San Francisco with his black Stetson perched on top of all that color.

After a period of hot weather, fog settled over the city, as was customary in late October. Everett was reading *The Autobiography of Lincoln Steffens*. Oh, and by the way, he told his parents, Paul Elder's bookstore and gallery at 239 Post Street had taken his mounted prints on consignment. *They seemed pleased to have them.* Placing his art in this San Francisco cultural institution was quite a coup for the gifted amateur printmaker.[46] From sketches or photographs taken in the field and then transferred to India-ink drawings, Everett hand-carved the images on linoleum, which was then mounted on wooden blocks. He or his mother, from whom he learned the technique, or a commercial printer, if the price was right, printed the images.

Everett's efforts at self-expression were diverse. His block prints were his most successful art form. They exceed all of his other output in raw power, simplicity, and technique. The stark, modernistic images are not as derivative as his paintings and poetry. His photographs were of the snapshot variety. Passages in his letters are quite evocative, while his college essays tend to be stiff. He was deeply committed to all these art forms. Eventually he would have had to choose a specialty.*

What Everett had in his favor was youth and artistic commitment. No wonder the Dixons took a liking to this young man who had arrived on the outskirts of Bohemia-by-the-Bay after successfully navigating the wilds of the Sierra Nevada and the Southwest.

It is hard to imagine now how Maynard Dixon dominated the artistic presence of Dorothea Lange in 1933. The social realism she practiced in the mid- to late 1930s had not yet become her forte, while Dixon's romanticism had not yet become passé. They were on the cusps of their respective fames. Dixon was a master of the past. Lange was moving from making portraits of rich San Franciscans to depicting the realities of the present found in the fields and on the streets of the Depression-riddled West. Not only were their artistic visions diverging, but when Everett met them they were in the midst of a trial separation after twelve years of marriage. There was no single home, just their two studios, in which they lived and worked. Their two sons were farmed out to a school in Marin County, where they boarded with local families. Dorothea and Maynard were still a stunning couple who partied

---

*Of course, no one knows how far or in what direction Everett's art would have progressed. His prints are his most popular art form, and some sell in the low thousand dollar range. Donna L. Poulton, associate curator of art of Utah and the West at the University of Utah, said of them: "He certainly understood and has a good sense of composition, form, negative space, and value. He also interprets the inherently modern landscape of the Southwest in very minimal/modern forms in his linocuts. He had a great intellect and a very good eye, but he probably needed more sophisticated tools and certainly more training." She placed him in the "gifted amateur" classification. Donna L. Poulton, personal communication, August 3, 2010. Others voiced the same opinion. The original linocuts are stored at the Utah Historical Society, which has prohibited any further use because of their fragility.

occasionally with such mutual friends as the photographers Ansel Adams, Edward Weston, and Imogen Cunningham and Cunningham's husband, the printmaker Roi Partridge.

With Adams as spokesperson and Imogen Cunningham, Weston, and other Lange friends as members, a loose coalition of Northern California photographers had formed a movement called Group f/64 in honor of the lens opening that provided the greatest depth of field and sharpness outside the studio. They sought to displace the softer, more narrowly focused efforts of the pictorialists.[47] Lange was not invited to join the group, perhaps because in their opinion she had not yet completely emerged from being merely a studio photographer. The group had a show at the de Young museum in late 1932. On the basis of the success of that show, Adams had opened a gallery on Geary Street near Union Square on the eve of Everett's arrival in the city.

Art—photography in particular—would soon diverge, not merely from soft to hard focus but also from portraits and wilderness landscapes to socially relevant subjects. Adams, Weston, Dixon, and Ruess were adherents of the former categories; Lange was of the latter. Everett learned more from Maynard but enjoyed Dorothea's company to a greater extent. He spent an afternoon and an evening with the Dixons and their artist friends shortly after his arrival in the city. *I had a grand time, and it was certainly good to be among friends and artists again.* He ate his first cooked meal in more than a week that night. *I'm beginning to make friends now, and I think I shall enjoy the city more and more.*[48]

Ruess was busy. He hauled his prints around to other galleries, without success. *Ansel Adams waxed very enthusiastic about my black and white work. He could not exhibit it in his gallery, but he gave me a number of suggestions which I am following out. He is going to trade me one of his photographs for one of my prints. The photograph I chose is of a mysterious lake at Kaweah Gap, where I was this July.* Sheer granite walls shelve into a dark lake with ice at the

---

*He chose wisely. Fifty years later Gibbs Smith, who had published a book about Everett, took a photo workshop from Adams in Carmel. The group assembled in Adams's home. Smith asked Adams if he recalled this trade. He didn't. Virginia, Adams's wife, led Smith into the couple's bedroom and showed him the print, whose title the publisher could not remember. Adams then recalled Ruess's visit to his gallery and the trade. Gibbs Smith, personal communication, June 18, 2009. The lake is Precipice Lake. Adams photographed it in 1932 while on a Sierra Club trip that started at the same place in Sequoia National Park where Everett's Sierra

base of the cliff. It is very fantastical.[49] Everett had a number of pending social engagements. He thought it unlikely that he would be in such demand for long. One of his appointments was with Lange, who wanted to photograph him in her studio.

■

As Everett has less than one year to live and has reached full growth, now is a good time to pause and describe his appearance, beginning with what Lange saw through the viewfinder of her camera, how others might have regarded him. It took an unusual interest in the subject for Dorothea Lange to provide portraits free of charge. Eleven negatives survive. Lange was not satisfied with the results of the first session, so there were two sittings.

What Lange saw was someone caught between being a child and a man. Everett's full lips and chubby, unlined face are framed by a black background, white shirt, dark sweater, and trademark black Stetson. She also photographed him hatless and with the hat cutting off part of his face and Everett peeking pixie-like from behind it. Perhaps because he was so unmarked on the surface, there is no hint of an inner Everett, other than a suggestion of an effeminate nature. Was she aware of his inner turmoil? His face was an alabaster mask that cracked slightly around the mouth and eyes when he smiled. When Everett is not smiling like a child in the series of portraits, he is pensive, like an adult. His slitted eyes suggest an exotic origin. There is no hardness in his face, only the softness of innocence that would have been crushed in time—leaving what in its place?

When Everett smiled, he seemed guileless, something that appealed to strangers. In three months he would pass within a block of where I live on the California coast. Had he knocked on my door and explained his mission, I am sure I would have admitted him. He had good manners and startling things to relate about faraway places. I know he would have wanted to be fed and spend the night or nights until he felt the urge to be on the trail again. The least I could have done would have been to provide him a place in the backyard to pitch his tent. The block prints alone, which he carried with him hoping for a sale, would have been worth the price of admission. I bought one a few years ago.

Nevada journey began the next year. A slightly scratched print of *Frozen Lakes and Cliffs, Kaweah Gap, Sierra Nevada* recently sold for $193,000 at a Christie's auction. In the 1930s, however, Adams's photographs did not sell, and he had to abandon his San Francisco studio eight months after opening it.

As for his more quantifiable physical features, Everett weighed 150 pounds, which were distributed over a sturdy five-foot-ten-inch frame. He had brown hair and hazel eyes.

———————■———————

As his parents were due to visit soon, Everett put his $10-a-month room at 2048 Polk Street in order. He had just traded one of his prints to a family friend for a work by the famed nineteenth-century Japanese landscape printer Hiroshige Ando. It was hanging on the wall along with his black Stetson. Three of his prints were also on the walls, and he expected to hang some of his photographs soon. His two kyaks were on the floor along with his Navajo saddle blanket. The table at which he worked was placed between two windows with a view of Polk Street, the recent scene of a children's Halloween parade.[50] The two small Mexican glasses he had purchased, one blue and the other purple, *are like wine for the soul when held up to the light, the colors are so beautiful.*[51] A plumber had loaned him a phonograph, so now he could listen to music in his room. A neon light cast a soft rose glow over the room at night.

He had eaten three cooked meals in the past two weeks. His diet consisted mainly of fruit, bread, and milk. He had developed an unspecified skin condition. A doctor said it was due to the overreaction of his skin glands and not his diet. The visit to the clinic cost $1.65. After his night with the Dixons, he had enjoyed another home-cooked meal and a delightful time with Frances and Charles Schermerhorn, who knew Christopher Ruess through Charles's work as a probation officer for the Marin County Juvenile Court. Charles loaned Everett a volume of nine plays by Eugene O'Neill. Everett's third cooked meal was compliments of his uncle Emerson, with whom he had gone to a concert. This brother of his mother's lived nearby, but Everett did not think he would see much of his busy uncle.

Emerson Knight was one of the outstanding landscape architects in Northern California at the time. When the state acquired Point Lobos in 1933, Knight designed the trails. He also had a hand in plans for the preservation of historic buildings in downtown Monterey. Besides gardens for large estates in San Francisco and on the peninsula, he designed the Mount Tamalpais Amphitheatre in Marin County, where the Mountain Play is performed each year. Knight was a consultant for the National Park Service, the California State Park Commission, the East Bay Regional Park District, and the Save the Redwoods League. A sentence in a paper written for a landscape architecture class at the University of California, Berkeley, indicates a similarity in outlook with his sister and nephew: "He was a romantic in his approach to gardens, taking great pleasure and delight in scents, colors, morning mists and the rustle of leaves." Knight sought, as they did, "the ideal beauty."[52] He also wrote poetry.

There were other outings for Everett. He had gone to the Rimsky-Korsakov opera *The Golden Cockerel* with his high school friend Cornel Lengel, who had inherited some money and was living the bohemian life in a picturesque shack with no bath on Telegraph Hill—the artist's garret Everett had imagined for himself. He had also seen the puppet play *Dr. Faust* performed by Perry Dilley, obtaining tickets for both performances by trading his prints.

Everett's immersion in the arts continued unabated. *The other day I had perhaps the best Art lesson I ever had; a lesson in simplicity from Maynard Dixon. That time I really did learn something, I think, and I have been trying to apply what I learned. The main thing Maynard did was to make me see what is meaningless in a picture, and have the strength to eliminate it; and see what was significant, and how to stress it. This he showed me with little scraps of black and white paper, placed over my drawings.* The Dixons were thinking of renting a house in the Cow Hollow area of San Francisco and bringing their two sons home from Marin County. Everett thought if he helped them move he might be offered a room.[53] The Dixons moved into the rented Victorian on Gough Street in early 1934. No invitation to join them in their new home was forthcoming. Everett accompanied Dorothea to Berkeley to hear the illustrator and artist Rockwell Kent lecture and show his work.

Everett made use of every moment. He was reading Nikolai Gogol's *Taras Bulba;* James Branch Cabell's *Jurgen: A Comedy of Justice,* whose protagonist journeys through imaginary realms seducing women, including the Devil's wife; and the poems of Robinson Jeffers and Edna St. Vincent Millay. He had attended a San Francisco Opera production of Wagner's *Tristan und Isolde,* paying $1 for standing room. *To feel the full beauty of the music and the voices, I sat on the floor with my back to the wall and closed my eyes. The final song of Isolde mourning Tristan's death always seems to me the finest thing in music when I am hearing it.*[54]

Always thinking ahead, Everett was planning to take a trip up the coast to the redwoods in Del Norte County. He thought he might leave the city sometime after January. Then he would be off again in March or April for a full year in his beloved desert. He didn't plan beyond 1934.

His parents visited him in San Francisco in mid-November. Everett was having a hard time, Christopher thought, suffering a mild case of poison oak, being physically weak, and having a touch of the flu. The three Ruesses made the rounds, visiting old friends. On another day Everett, Stella, and

Maynard Dixon had lunch, after which they went to an exhibit of Dixon's paintings at Gump's, a luxury outlet for art and department store items on Post Street. The drive and the short visit were like a honeymoon for Stella and Christopher, who now rarely left Los Angeles.

The visit brought father and son closer together. Everett had been asking himself a series of questions lately, and while he could supply answers to most of them himself, he very much wanted his father's input. He sent Christopher a list of twenty-three questions. Six days later, on December 10, he received the answers. The son was attempting to find himself, the father to guide him through life. The result is a rare glimpse into a meaningful exchange between a parent and a child, and an example for other parents and children.

Everett was progressing toward a delicate balance between life and death, and the coming year would determine the outcome. Two of his questions illustrated his quandary. His father handled them in a compassionate manner.

First, Everett asked about life. *Is passage from the sensual to the intellectual to the spiritual a correct progression of growth, and if so, should that growth be hastened?*

Why not live in all three at the same time? Why such sharp demarcations? A house has a foundation, a first story, and a second story. Why not all three at the same time? "Nor flesh helps spirit more now than spirit flesh" or the like is a saying of Browning's. The Greeks separated flesh and spirit. We moderns tend not to do so, but to respect all parts of creation, each in its place.

Then Everett asked about death. *Is there any fulfillment that endures as such, besides death?*

I doubt if death fulfills. It seems to end but I doubt that it ends much. Not one's influence or the influence of one's work. Perhaps even the echoes of your voice may go on forever. Some instrument might pick them up years or ages hence. Beauty is an ultimate fulfillment, as is goodness, as is truth. These are ends in themselves, and are for the sake of life. Many things are worth while that are not enduring. Eternity is just made of todays. Glorify the hour.*

Everett, the college dropout, and Christopher, the lapsed minister and county probation officer, were not ordinary people, and they proved their extraordinariness in this exchange. The dialogue demonstrates the intelli-

---

*See appendix B for the entire father and son dialogue.

gence each possessed and the intimacy and trust they shared, momentarily. It satisfied Everett's inquiring mind, and he thanked his father in a formal manner. *I was very pleased with your carefully considered replies to my questions, and I think you have answered them very well.*[55]

———————————■———————————

Everett spent time with the Schermerhorns at their home across the bay in the village of San Anselmo, Marin County, and with Charles on excursions up and down the coast. One Sunday Ruess went with Charles to a church where a man described as a Socialist Methodist spoke. Socialism was also being discussed at the Ruesses' Los Angeles Unitarian church, and Christopher had recommended some books on the subject to Everett. The onetime Socialist and left-leaning Democratic gubernatorial candidate and author Upton Sinclair was roiling the political waters of California at the time. How could anyone be concerned with beauty and art when the world was headed toward fascism, asked the author of one of the books his father mentioned.[56] Christopher asked his son for his reaction.

He could not change who he was, Everett remarked. *I naturally say that he is wrong, because if I agreed with him, I would contradict my whole life. . . . So, instead, during this last year, I have continued to seek beauty and friendship, and I think that I have really brought some beauty and delight into the lives of others, and that is at least something.*[57] To his brother he said he was proud of the way he had conducted his life. *In short, I often feel in a conquering mood, and I am proud of my life, for I believe that I have really lived life at its most intense, and that I shall continue to do so.* At the end of that paragraph he mentioned he had met a *girl with whom I am intimate.*[58]

The adolescent attempted to match his brother's interest in women by overemphasizing his relationships with the opposite sex. The only woman Everett was involved with besides Dorothea Lange in San Francisco was Frances Schermerhorn, the mysterious "Frances" in previous books about Ruess who was thought to be his one known girlfriend. She was, in fact, twenty-seven years old when she met Everett, the mother of a four-year-old son, and married for five years to Charles. A native of Nebraska, she had not attended college and was listed in the 1930 census as a homemaker. The family lived on Meadowcroft Drive in a middle-class neighborhood in San Anselmo. Frances and Everett shared a love of music and little else.[59]

He invited her to his apartment to listen to *the most heart-rending symphony you ever heard,* tempting her with Roquefort cheese, which he could ill afford, a new painting to view, and two things he wanted to read to her.

He pleaded with her: don't refuse, for he must see her. Don't despair, for he was trying not to. Everett ended another note with *sleep sweetly tonight*. He wished her *the most blithe and serene Christmas* anyone could desire.[60] The youth was expressing his deep yearning for a meaningful friendship. He may have been in a manic phase of his illness.

The dark times returned. Nine days after he wrote his brother about his conquering mood and newfound intimacy, Everett felt unstable. He attributed that to being nineteen and sensitive. *I have been discovering new moods, new lows, new and disturbing variations in myself and my feelings for individuals, and people as a whole. On the other hand, there is a lot of fun in me yet, and I have had some unusually gay times that weren't feverishly so. But for the most part there has been an undercurrent of resentment or unrest.* Turmoil prevailed. He could find no outlet for his feelings. *Various turnings, twistings, and recoils* left him dizzy. Everett thought he was *straying from normalcy*. He seemed to be *part of a somewhat symmetrical scheme which I seem to see dimly.*[61]

There was a break in Everett's correspondence with Frances Schermerhorn until May, when he wrote her a stilted letter of apology and explanation from Kayenta. *I was sorry, though, that our intimacy, like many things that are and will be, had to die with a dying fall. I do not greatly mind endings, for my life is made up of them, but sometimes they come too soon or too late, and sometimes they leave a feeling of regret as of an old mistake or an indirect futility.*[62]

—————◼—————

Everett gathered his scattered persona together. After a Christmas with family friends in Oakland, he went to another concert with Uncle Emerson. *There are things in Wagner that always make me feel like flying.*[63] He took Dorothea to a concert by Roland Hayes, the first African American concert singer to receive widespread acclaim. He traded his block prints for photographs from William E. Dassonville, a well-known San Francisco landscape and portrait photographer.

On the last day of the year, Everett went for a long walk across San Francisco after a rainstorm had cleared the air. *I watched the clouds shifting on the skyline, the stevedores loading tons of copper on a freighter, the gulls wheeling over the bay, the clear, wet grass on hill slopes, the shacks and slums of the poor, and the mansions of the rich. I paused for about a quarter of an hour to admire the trunk of a symmetrically towering old eucalyptus on Russian Hill. I never saw more vivid or more beautiful coloring in a eucalyptus before.*[64]

IX

Vanished

1934

AS THE YEAR—HIS LAST—BEGAN IN SAN FRANCISCO, Everett was pleased with the direction in which his life was unfolding and didn't believe the lack of a college education would be a hindrance, as his father thought it might be. He valued his freedom and what it had taught him. Furthermore, he preferred the vitality of San Francisco over the staleness of Los Angeles. He was cherishing his time in San Francisco, knowing there would never be another period like it.[1] He had recently placed some prints in one gallery, from which he didn't expect much profit. He had had no success at Paul Elder's gallery. Everett had checked once and found they hadn't displayed his prints. Ruess had dinner twice in January at the Schermerhorns', the second time at their new and larger home.

Everett began hitchhiking north along the coast in early February, stopping for a week near Tomales in western Marin County at the sheep ranch of Khan Alam Khan, an Afghan with a German wife and a rotating number of foster children.[2] Called Khan Ali by neighboring ranchers, he was thought to have been a professional wrestler once because of his cauliflower ears. Everett had been introduced to the rancher by Charles Schermerhorn, who assigned children to foster homes as a juvenile probation officer.

Ruess left vivid descriptions of coastal ranch lands in the rainy season. *The ranch is on the ridge of a vast hill, looking down upon the sea. Lines of lacy eucalyptus and twisted cypress break the wind. On the slopes are large rocks and into their crevices are fitted the laurel trees, their crests shorn by the winds.* One evening he took a walk. *I walked mile after mile, over vast rolling hills, down canyons with rushing streams. At sunset I started back to the ranch, but I had started a bigger circle than I thought, and walked for an hour or two until I topped a rise and heard the roar of surf and the bleating of sheep and saw the lights of home.*[3]

He studied the people as he journeyed north and didn't find much to recommend them. *Most of the people are living the super simple life, and have no energy for thinking.* At Rockport on coastal Highway 1, Ruess stopped at what had been a flourishing lumber camp. *There are rows and rows of empty houses and disused machinery.*[4] He spent the night with a caretaker, and in the morning they speared salmon in the nearby creek. It was a short walk to the ocean. *The sea has been gloriously beautiful these stormy days; grey green combers rolling in—white foam reaching over the dark beaches. The surf crashes against the cliffs, leaps into the air, and slowly, gracefully subsides into the sea. At other places, there are long strips of foam racing in ahead of the combers far out to sea. Sometimes on the dark stormy sea the hidden sun shines thru and makes an unearthly radiance. Other times the grey waves glisten like new metal under the crests when they topple.*[5]

Beautiful prose, emanating from word pictures embedded in his mind, transferred instantaneously to his pen, and not rewritten. The description of the winter ocean balances Everett's superficial social commentary.*

After traveling through the redwoods as far north as Crescent City, he returned to San Francisco on February 26. Everett took a stroll that day and purchased inexpensive tickets to the noted Shakespearean actor Walter Hampden's performances of *Macbeth* and *Hamlet*. Three candles burned that night in his apartment while he listened to Beethoven's Fifth Symphony. *The city seemed senselessly hideous and squalid when I reentered it today, after the clean spaciousness of green hills and blue seas. But it was good to see and hear from my old friends. I know some fine people in this city.*[6]

Everett counted Maynard Dixon and Dorothea Lange among such friends. On his last Sunday in San Francisco the three of them drove to Khan Alam's

---

*This letter and others demonstrate his ability to write lucid prose on the first draft. His spelling and word choice were excellent. I taught nonfiction writing at the University of California, Berkeley, and at Stanford University, and I would have given Everett an A on this first exercise. Most of the students I taught did not have his command of English or his expressive skills.

ranch. *I sold her on his profile.*[7] Then they returned to the Dixons' new home. The last page of the letter describing the outing was adorned with the writing and drawings of the Dixons' eleven-year-old son, who wrote, "Maynard Dixon makes very good drawings." He signed *Danny Dixon* under his words and drawings of airplanes, a house, and a steamship.

Everett sold a painting, allowing him to purchase a ticket on the coastal steamer *Emma Alexander,* which would arrive in Los Angeles Harbor on March 7. Could someone in his family please meet him with a car? *I will have a good deal of luggage.*[8] In this manner Everett arrived home after wandering through California for nine months.

■

Everett spent most of March and early April preparing for what he referred to as his last trip.[9] He reached his twentieth birthday during this interlude and was facing an uncertain future. With some of his classical music–loving friends, Everett drove to the Covina home of Alec W. Anderson, who had several thousand records.[10] This group, which included Edward Gardiner and Bill Jacobs, spent a few days in Anderson's home, almost constantly listening to music. J. S. Bach was Ruess's favorite composer, Anderson said. Ruess recited his poems, large chunks of the *Rubaiyat of Omar Khayyam,* and a poem by the English poet Ernest Dowson.* He spoke to Anderson of his quest for beauty and his love of the desert. He felt he was wasting his time in Los Angeles. Before leaving, Everett offered Alec his choice of one of his block prints, and Anderson chose *Canyon de los Muertos,* which Everett said was his favorite. Anderson hinted that he would like to visit Kayenta. Everett didn't think that was a good idea, stating that Carmel was more suitable for someone not used to the rough life.

Back on the streets of Los Angeles, Everett witnessed a typical scene of that era. *A few nights ago I went to a Young Communist League demonstration. There were posters with captions like "We Can't Eat Battleships," and sound talk about the stupidity of armament, and the wretched condition of the lower classes. But in about five minutes, the Red Squad came with six men, who leaped out*

---

*The Dowson poem, "Non sum qualis eram bonae sub regno Cynarae," whose title is a quote from Horace's *Odes,* was his best-known work. The last line of all four stanzas of the poem is: "I have been faithful to thee, Cynara! In my fashion." That line was the inspiration for the Cole Porter song "Always True to You in My Fashion," from *Kiss Me, Kate.*

of a car, laid about with their clubs, snatched the posters from the boys and tore them up, seized all the papers, kicked the girls in the legs, and chased the boys and girls for several blocks, trying to separate the group. Such are Free Speech and Free Assemblage in America.[11] The Los Angeles Police Department formed the Red Squad in 1933 to deal with Communists and other radicals, such as striking labor union members. It was authorized to use excessive force and didn't hesitate to do so, as Everett's eyewitness account confirms.

It was time for Everett to make arrangements with his brother to leave Los Angeles. Waldo would be driving his 1929 Ford coupe from near Indio, where he was working for the Metropolitan Water District of Southern California. Camp Berdoo was twelve miles east of Indio and at an altitude of 1,900 feet, where it was cooler than in the nearby Coachella Valley. Still, the camp's summer temperatures averaged between 110 and 120 degrees. When he had time, Waldo went swimming with fellow workers or riding in his car with a girl from Indio. He chatted on the teletype with a female operator in Banning and wondered how his girlfriend in Los Angeles, who had accompanied the brothers to Sequoia National Park, was doing.* He sent what money he could afford, which wasn't much, to his parents and brother. When Waldo agreed to drive Everett to Kayenta after some initial reservations about what the rough roads might do to his car, Everett voiced his appreciation. *You are surely a good brother to me.*[12]

They left Camp Berdoo on April 12, arriving at the Colorado River in the early-morning hours of the next day. After a short sleep, they were off again, stopping briefly in Flagstaff for supplies for Everett. On the road from Tuba City to Kayenta they had three flat tires and got stuck in the sand once. The brothers stopped to talk to some Navajo who were sitting around a fire in front of their hogan. The Indians couldn't speak English and the brothers couldn't speak Navajo, so all communication was in sign language. The Ruesses traded two grapefruits, which the Indians were not familiar with, for some squaw bread. At Kayenta, Waldo regretted he didn't have more time to see Monument Valley. "I don't blame Everett for being crazy about that country. It did not seem to me that the Navajos were especially hospitable or friendly, nor did the traders seem to be."[13] Waldo dropped his brother off where he could negotiate for a burro. It was the last time anyone in his family saw Everett.

---

*A search of the Ruess family photos at the University of Utah reveals that a veritable United Nations of girlfriends posed with Waldo in the various countries he lived in, worked in, and visited. He is smiling in very few of the pictures.

Ruess was back in familiar territory. *The country here is all that I could wish it to be, and I am happy again.* Burros were scarce around Kayenta, and language was a barrier, so Everett hiked with a pack to nearby Dinnehotso, where the trader bargained with the Indians for two burros for him. Everett named the pack burro Leopard and the saddle donkey Cockleburrs. They promptly disappeared, but he found them the next day with all his equipment intact.

Everett left Kayenta on May 3 and headed toward Chinle on the same route he took in 1931. He plunged into the Canyon de Chelly for the third time and experienced alternately vast calms and intense furies. *Once more I am roaring drunk with the lust of life and adventure and unbearable beauty. . . . And yet, there is always an undercurrent of restlessness and wild longing. . . . Alone I shoulder the sky and hurl my defiance and shout the song of the conqueror to the four winds, earth, sea, sun, moon, and stars. I live!* This time there was no Curly to accompany him, and he signed the letter to Bill Jacobs with a simple *Everett.*[14] To their mutual friend and music lover Edward Gardiner, Everett wrote that he had been alone in the canyon for five days and had nearly been gored by a wild bull. Gyrating shadows of buzzards circled above and *strange, sad winds* swept down the canyon. *One way and another, I have been flirting pretty heavily with Death, the old clown.*[15]

It was all so familiar, this farewell trip. Farewell to a phase in his life, or farewell to life itself? His words and actions became more repetitive and frenzied. He rode up into the Lukachukai Mountains, where he had been ill in 1932. He received a letter from Frances Schermerhorn. *I enjoyed your letter, and I know I did not mistake myself when first I liked you. We did have some moments of beauty together, didn't we?* In the distance he could see Shiprock in the moonlight. It was *a ghostly galleon in a sea of sand.*[16] He turned back toward Kayenta. *I shall never forget coming down the Lukachukai Mountains at dusk, with the blood red moon falling thru the pine branches as I descended.*[17]

Back in Kayenta, Everett stayed with Lee Bradley. *He is a tall, commanding figure of a man, half white, and combining the best qualities of both races.*[18] Bradley had the government mail contract and worked as a translator, extra, and bit part player for many John Ford movies shot in Monument Valley. Bradley and his wife lived in a rambling adobe house. For pets they had a baby prairie dog, a goat, rabbits, and the father or grandfather of Curly. While at Kayenta, Everett heard of the death of the trader José Garcia, who had befriended him the previous month at the Chilchinbeto Trading Post on the road to Chinle. *José's kindness and courtesy almost brought the tears to my eyes, for there is something very fine about him, and I have not met many of his kind in this country.*[19] Garcia died when the wheel of a truck came off, and he was buried under its load. The trader was one of two good friends Ruess had had on the reservation, the other having departed because of an unnamed misfortune.

The loss of two friends and the accumulation of what Everett perceived as ill treatment from white traders prompted a rant against the latter. *Living in the midst of such utter and overpowering beauty as nearly kills a sensitive person by its piercing glory, they are deaf, dumb, and blind to it all. Behind bars in their dirty, dingy, ill-lighted trading posts, they think of nothing but money.* Everett cited the example of his recent purchase of a beautiful Navajo bracelet with three turquoise stones with a rich, green luster. All the trader could think of was its price. *He saw it only as merchandise.* Everett expected a lot in terms of hospitality and information from the traders, who were in business, after all. At the same time, Everett's criticisms of the Navajo had mellowed. *They are so childlike and simple and friendly when left alone. I have often stayed with the Navajos; I've known the best of them, and they are fine people.*[20]

Before leaving and heading north through Monument Valley and then west to Navajo Mountain, Everett noted the appearance of a major archeological expedition in Kayenta and the young men who were part of it. He intended to visit them in their camp after he returned. Everett reshod his burros at the Oljato Trading Post in preparation for the rough trail and wild country to the west. This was a new part of the region for him.

From Oljato, a steep trail led out of Copper Canyon. *A vast expanse of broken country lay between the mesas. Far north was the silent, nearly empty canyon of the San Juan, with a vivid green strip of willows. Opposite me the mile-wide canyon was banded with blue green, grey blue, a delicate purple, surmounted by dull vermillion, which grew more vivid until at the rim of the mesa the color was almost blindingly intense.*[21]

Ruess almost lost Leopard. *Near the rim it was almost a scramble, and Leopard, whom I was packing, in attempting to claw his way over a steep place, lost his balance and fell over backwards. He turned two backward somersaults and a side roll, landing with his feet waving, about six inches from the yawning gulf. I pulled him to his feet. He was a bit groggy at first; he had lost a little fur and the pack was scratched.* Everett was attached to his beasts of burden. *It is hard not to be sentimental about my burros; they are such droll, friendly creatures.*[22]

From the steep pass between the two mesas, the trail followed the trough of Piute Canyon, then rose to the cool of War God Spring at the 8,200-foot level of the south slope of Navajo Mountain. Here there was a marshy hollow, and a trickle of water ran through the aspen trees. Two bands of Navajo horses, each with a bell mare, grazed nearby. Their bells had a deeper resonance than the tinkling burro bell. *The beauty of this place is perfect of its kind; I could ask for nothing more.* Everett's reading matter on the mountain sacred to the Navajo was varied. He read *A Dreamer's Tales* by the Irish fantasy writer Lord Dunsany and copies of the *Manchester Guardian* his parents had sent him, with their distressing news of Germany and other foreign countries preparing for war. The view was toward Davis Gulch and other canyons he would soon visit to the west. It was a rough and inhospitable country—the ultimate desert wilderness—full of sandstone domes and towers, with gashes of vermillion canyons cutting through the sage-green tops of mesas. *The beauty of this country is becoming a part of me. I feel more detached from life and somehow gentler.*[23]

For the next two days Ruess and the two burros plodded along a rough trail hacked through the canyon country. *It was tremendously dramatic, to stride down steep sandhills in shadowed canyons only a dozen feet wide at the bottom with towering walls above.*[24] At the Navajo Mountain Trading Post he met the trader Ray Dunn, who would leave his imprint in Davis Gulch and play a minor role in the search for Ruess. Everett reached Rainbow Lodge on June 30, where he found the people friendly. Descending the trail three nights later to avoid the heat of daylight hours, Everett reached Rainbow Bridge National Monument and its giant arch. He signed the guest register on July 3, the 1,891st person to do so. Ruess inscribed the route of his sixteen-day journey on the register. He then headed south to Kayenta with the idea of joining the expedition he had seen forming there earlier in the summer.

———■———

Everett became a lowly member of the Rainbow Bridge–Monument Valley Expedition on July 9. The purpose of this civilian campaign, organized with military precision in the manner of the great nineteenth-century expeditions, was to provide the scientific justification for—meaning archeological importance of—a huge new national park encompassing some three thousand square miles. The idea for a Navajoland National Park arose in two minds: Wetherill's in Kayenta and Albright's in Washington, D.C. Both had concerns about protecting artifacts and scenery. Wetherill's trading post and guest facilities would also gain business, and Albright was interested in acquiring new park lands. An internal Park Service assessment of Navajoland in 1931 stated: "This proposed national park would have great interest to the American public because of its unusual features of ethnology and archeology, as well as because of its unique and remarkable scenic qualities."[25]

Wetherill, Albright, and regional Park Service officials looked over the proposed national park in 1932 and liked what they saw. The new park would be modeled on Canyon de Chelly National Monument: the Navajo would continue to live on the land, and the federal government would protect the ruins. The idea floundered when the government's stock reduction program proved to be an economic disaster to the Indians, with whom federal land use programs fell out of favor.

But the Navajo had not yet voiced their opposition in the summer of 1934, when the second of six scientific expeditions was sent into the field. The first expedition was hailed by *Science* magazine as "the largest and in some respects the best equipped scientific party thus far sent into the southwestern United States."[26] Students, faculty members, and staff of various schools were recruited with advertisements, such as the one placed in the University of California alumni magazine: "Wanted: Ten Explorers." Seventy-five volunteers responded on both coasts, overwhelming the organizers. Most had to pay their own travel and food expenses, between $300 and $400 per person, no small feat in the midst of the Depression.[27] Some worked at menial chores to reduce their costs. By the time the expeditions ended, more than thirty colleges and universities were represented on their rolls.

The expeditions were organized by Ansel F. Hall, the first ranger who specialized as a naturalist at Yosemite, who was now in charge of all interpretive activities in national parks and had offices on the UC Berkeley campus. Hall, a friend of Wetherill's, was also involved in the Boy Scout movement. He was a shrewd promoter and a romantic idealist with organizing skills, all necessary talents to get such an expedition into the field. Travel was by foot, horse, and pack train, boats on the San Juan and Colorado rivers, airplanes (from which photographs were taken for mapping purposes), and a fleet of trucks and wooden station wagons donated by the Ford Motor Company, which profited from the resulting publicity. The territory was so vast and unknown that the first expedition, in 1933, was reduced to the status of a reconnaissance venture.

Specific archeological objectives were more carefully defined when the second expedition was launched in 1934, again with an enthusiastic response. A headline in the *New York Times* on the day before Everett joined the expedition declared: "Huge Wild West Region Suggested for a Park." The story gave the impression that this section of the country was both wild and weird.*

---

*"Huge Wild West Region Suggested for a Park," *New York Times,* July 8, 1934. The story is a good indication of how the East regarded the West at that time. It begins:

Everett's burros and cooking and climbing skills were in demand. Lyndon L. Hargrave of the Museum of Northern Arizona in Flagstaff was in charge of the archeological work, and Everett had met him in 1931 at the Mesa Ranch School's summer camp in Flagstaff. Ruess was assigned to a small crew headed by H. Claiborne ("Clay") Lockett. Their job was to excavate Woodchuck Cave, a major find in the Tsegi Canyon system. Clay Lockett's family had ranched in the Flagstaff area since 1881, and his father had been a state senator from Coconino County. Clay graduated from the University of Arizona and was employed as an ethnologist by the Flagstaff museum. He was also an artist. Lockett joined Fritz Loeffler at Mesa Verde and Lon Garrison at Sequoia in Everett's male pantheon.

Woodchuck Cave in Water Lily Canyon had been "discovered," in Hargrave's words, the previous summer, "but because of its forbidding position apparently never before had been investigated by scientists." On a Sunday lark "some of the more daring" members of the 1933 expedition worked out two routes to the cave, which was six hundred feet above the floor of the canyon. The steeper pitches had "hand-and-toe holds pecked into the cliff, thus showing the trails to have been used by natives in prehistoric times."[28] One of the workers said, "It took about an hour to get up there from where our camp was, and it was a slightly scary climb, the last part because part of it had fallen away and you had to go up part of it on these sort of steps."[29] An alternative route for pack trains with supplies crossed Skeleton Mesa and then bridged gaps with piled branches called horse and burro ladders. The cave was a shallow arch seventy feet wide whose overhang had a maximum depth of thirty feet. It was thought to be a burial site sometime during the Basketmaker II era, from 800 to 1100 C.E.

The attractions of the expedition for Everett were multiple: the opportunities to spend time with young men who were knowledgeable about the ancient Native American presence that so fascinated him, to draw and paint scenes of great drama and beauty, to climb and descend from dangerous heights, and to be fed (but receive no pay).

"The Wild West is still not entirely tamed nor wholly familiar, even after all these years of discovery by jealous writers of travel literature. A tract has almost escaped notice out on the Utah-Arizona border which, from tales told by some of the few white men who have seen any of it, is so weird and so full of glimpses of prehistoric America and of the evolution of the earth's crust that it is being suggested as a new national park."

The work at Woodchuck Cave was far more interesting than the chores he had performed during the first two weeks of his employment. There was a magnificent view, discoveries were made every day, and Everett was having *great fun* with Lockett, *a grizzled young chap of 28, widely experienced, and a magnificent humorist. He is an ethnologist and something of an artist as well.* They examined and discussed each other's paintings and then went back to work. *This cave is in the Navajo sandstone a few feet under the rim. About three hundred feet below and some eighty feet back under, is Twin Caves cliff dwelling, but this cave is far more interesting. The culture here goes back to the first quarter of the Christian era, and presents many unsolved problems. . . . We have been in the cave four days now. There is a very precarious way down the face of the cliff with footholds in the stone, hundreds of years old. The only other way is the horse ladder, six miles up the canyon. We came that way with pack burros, passing the carcass of a horse that slipped. . . . We have found twelve burials here, with two fairly well preserved mummies. One mystery lies in the fact that all of the skeletons are headless, tho there are two lower jaws. Evidently the graves were robbed, perhaps by the Pueblo I people, but it is a difficult problem to ascertain the facts.*[30]

It took nineteen years to assemble the facts, partly because Lockett went to work for the Bureau of Indian Affairs shortly after sifting the ruins of Woodchuck Cave and the museum did not publish his findings until 1953. The body parts of twenty humans, ranging in age from newborn infants to adults over fifty years old, and their associated artifacts were dated as far back as 200 C.E. All the adult skeletons were headless, a desecration attributed to later ancient Indians because valuable jewelry that would have interested more contemporary grave robbers was not disturbed.[31]

Another gruesome sight was the headless body of a well-preserved mummy that had been wrapped in a rabbit fur robe. His legs were drawn up toward his chest, and two severed feet lay on top of his body. A stone pipe was nearby, as was a necklace of five hundred lignite coal beads strung on a cord of yucca fiber. In a circular pit lay the bones of a young woman and two infants, one with a single bead on its chest. Perhaps the three of them had died during childbirth. The robes of infants were woven with a softer-textured rabbit fur than those of the headless adults. A fire in the rear of the cave had consumed some bodies and artifacts. Ancient woodchuck bones gave the cave its name.[32]

While working and camped in the cave for two weeks, Everett and Clay got to know each other quite well, Lockett said. Everett's climbs were beyond daring. "I know that Everett was always anxious to get into situations which provided thrills and excitement. When these situations arose he would think about them, write about them, or often paint them. One time in camp he stood out on the edge of a 400 foot cliff during a rain storm and did a water color sketch of a waterfall. I remember this very clearly because I personally was scared to death just watching him perched on the edge of the cliff."[33]

It was Lockett's theory, later voiced to Everett's father, that "some place while climbing a cliff, either for a thrill or investigating some Indian ruin or something similar, that he may possibly have fallen to death." He didn't think Everett would ever have separated himself from his burros. "I understand that the burros were actually found and I feel sure that if he were alive he would still be looking for those burros for I remember very distinctly that he loved those traveling companions of his."[34] Lockett returned to Flagstaff before the expedition ended and began to work on the material he had collected from the cave.

One of the other members of the 1934 expedition recalled Everett. Vernon DeMars was an unemployed architect who had studied at the University of California, Berkeley, and had been working for Ansel Hall when he joined the expedition. He had a passion for Indian dances and an ability to document the ruins in drawings. He and Everett later traveled together through Indian lands. DeMars described Everett as someone who would have fitted right in with the flower children of the 1960s. "We got kind of acquainted. He had a burro and all his cooking equipment with him."*

For Everett, the six weeks with the expedition had been a fascinating experience. *The last night's work was done by firelight. Huge shadows played on the orange wall of the cave, which reached upwards into the darkness. Outside, rain hissed down, and once we heard wild geese honking as they flew south.*[35] After he left the expedition in mid-August, Everett paused briefly in Kayenta for the last time before heading south over Black Mesa to the Hopi reservation. He was in a hurry to see the Snake Dance.

———— ■ ————

---

*Vernon DeMars, "A Life in Architecture," Regional Oral History Office, University of California, Berkeley, 1992. DeMars, who died in 2005 at the age of ninety-seven, was a professor emeritus of architecture at the University of California, Berkeley. He designed many notable projects, including Capitol Towers in Sacramento, the Golden Gateway Redevelopment Project along San Francisco's Embarcadero, and the student center complex on the UC Berkeley campus. He also codesigned Wurster Hall, which houses the university's College of Environmental Design. He was twenty-six years old when he accompanied Everett.

Traversing Black Mesa from north to south was an ordeal. *I had only four days to cross more than one hundred miles of trackless wilderness, in order to reach Hotevilla in time. I rode up from the desert floor to the rim of Black Mesa by moonlight, camping in the pines. Then I beat my way southward, steering by the sun, and following a canyon as far as was practical. The whole country slopes southward, and there are no landmarks of any kind, and there was hardly any water. I did not see a human being until the third night. After that I passed a number of Navajo camps, beat my way through thru the timber and the high sage until I reached Dinnebito (Navajo Water) Wash, and rode into the pueblo at daybreak of the dance.*[36] Members of the expedition had preceded him by automobile. Everett painted the Hopi village while children clustered around him, *some helping and some hindering,* and watched the Snake Dance.* Also present at the dance were Oliver La Farge, an anthropologist and the author of the novel *Laughing Boy,* and the niece of Kaiser Wilhelm II.

At Hotevilla on Third Mesa, where he acquired a Hopi bowl for his mother, Everett met DeMars, and they traveled to the Hopi village of Mishongnovi on Second Mesa, where they spent the night in a kiva watching the Indians practice the Buffalo and Antelope Dances. Then they hitched a ride with a Hopi silversmith to Gallup to watch the intertribal dances. Everett learned Indian songs and acquired a Navajo woven saddle blanket. On September 1 he returned alone to Mishongnovi, *where my Hopi friends painted me up and had me in their Antelope Dance. I was the only white person there.*[37] He didn't try to take any photographs of the Hopi dances because that would have been like *taking a picture of communion in some church.*[38]

Reunited with his burros, Everett headed toward the trading post at Cameron. Along the way he lost Leopard and the packs he was carrying in a fall into the Little Colorado Canyon but replaced him immediately with a larger burro. *Chocolate is tentatively the name of Cockleburrs' new companion. He is young, strong, and good natured, inexperienced, but bound to learn from*

---

*Randall Henderson, who first brought Ruess's story to a wider audience as the publisher of *Desert Magazine,* attended the Snake Dance five years later. The snakes' fangs and poison sacs were intact. A few Hopi dancers and snake handlers had been bitten, but with no evident harm. Henderson sat next to a doctor from the U.S. Public Health Service who wanted to see if the participants were bitten and what medicine they used. "No white man, to my knowledge, knows the answer for sure. And the snake priests will not tell," Henderson wrote in *On Desert Trails: Today and Yesterday* (Los Angeles: Westernlore Press, 1961), 228.

his experienced comrade. Everett bought him for $9 from a Navajo woman, who threw in a currycomb as part of the deal. Ruess replaced his lost kyaks with boxes he painted with Anasazi designs. *Their like has never been known, I'm sure.*[39] He arrived at Desert View on the rim of the Grand Canyon on September 9, killing two rattlesnakes along the way.

Leaving his burros with an artist friend at Desert View, Everett hitch-hiked to Flagstaff and spent three or four days with Clay Lockett and his wife in their small cabin. It was fall. *The San Francisco peaks soar high in the afternoon light. The slopes are golden with yellowing aspen.* The light also drew his attention in Oak Creek Canyon. *I painted a couple of striking effects of brilliantly lighted buttes against inky storm skies. Also a massive tower, calmly beautiful under shadowy clouds.*[40] He had used the last of his poison ivy medicine in Tsegi Canyon and asked his mother to send more to him at the Grand Canyon. He said it could be obtained in a Los Angeles drugstore.[41] What remained of the medicine his mother sent was found in Cottonwood Gulch in 1957.

To a young man he had met the previous summer in the Sierra Nevada who had gone on to college, Everett related his nonacademic experiences in 1934. *In my wanderings this year I have taken more chances and had more and wilder adventures than ever before. And what magnificent country I have seen—wild, tremendous wasteland stretches, lost mesas, blue mountains rearing upward from the vermillion sands of the desert, canyons five feet wide at the bottom and hundreds of feet deep, cloudbursts roaring down unnamed canyons, and hundreds of houses of the cliff dwellers, abandoned a thousand years ago.*[42]

Everett returned to Desert View and wrote his parents that he had sold enough paintings and prints that they could discontinue sending his $15 monthly allowance. He was proud of himself for having shod both burros. *It was some battle, and none of us came off without a few bruises.* He plunged into the Grand Canyon for a brief stay at Indian Garden, a small oasis below the south rim. *Autumn is here with a sharp tang in the air, but below in the canyon I have been enjoying a second summer. The cottonwoods are just beginning to be touched with yellow and orange. Down into the canyon again!*[43]

He crossed the canyon for the last time. It was not an easy trip. His burro Chocolatero, formerly Chocolate, was the cause of two misadventures. The donkey would not cross the bridge over the Colorado River at Phantom Ranch and had to be dragged across by a burro belonging to a packer, leaving a bloody trail behind. Another time Chocolatero stirred up a nest of bees, which stung Everett multiple times. He lost the use of his hands, and his eyes were sealed shut for three or four days.

Everett passed through Kanab and then paused a few miles north at Cave Lakes, where he sold a couple of pictures to Charlie Plumb, the artist who drew the *Ella Cinders* comic strip, a variant of the Cinderella story that was made into a movie in 1926. Plumb had a reputation as something of a vagrant and had once retreated to a Pacific island to draw. *He is drunk or blotto at least half the time.*[44] Amazingly to Everett, the cartoonist worked three months a year and received $1,500 twice a month for drawing the strip. Riding on, Ruess encountered an early season snowstorm on the Paunsaugunt Plateau, just west of Bryce Canyon National Park. He entered the park. *The fantastic beauty of this place certainly has not been exaggerated. It was worth the long trip and the rough trails.*[45]

In the park he met the ranger Maurice Cope, who invited Everett to his winter home in nearby Tropic. After two days looking around Bryce, Everett descended to Cope's house in the Mormon village just east of the national park. *I enjoyed riding down from Bryce Canyon, thru the grotesque and colorful formation.* There were nine children in the Cope family. Their father went to work in the park in 1925 and after holding a number of temporary positions became its first permanent employee in 1933. Cope and his family lived in the park during the summer months. They were one of five families in Tropic that had indoor plumbing. Everett slept in the barn.

It was Cope who noted that Everett was armed and had plenty of ammunition, most probably for his .25-caliber pistol.[46] He also made the professional assessment that Everett was in "good health," his burros were in "fair shape," and everything was "very favorable" for his projected journey. Ruess outlined his plans to Cope: he would proceed south from Escalante and then follow the west side of the Colorado River over Smoky Mountain to the settlement and post office at Marble Canyon.[47] From there he might continue south to the Navajo reservation, where his journey had commenced that year. He outlined other options to his parents. If he crossed the Colorado at Hole-in-the-Rock, he might travel down the east side of the river and then head south to the reservation. A crossing would not be risky. *The water is very low this year.* He might even go in an entirely new direction and head north to the small settlement of Boulder, Utah.

For five days Everett had *great fun* with the Cope family in Tropic. *This morning I rode out with one of the boys to look for a cow. We rode all over the hills and stopped at an orchard to load up with apples. Then I went to church, my first time in a Mormon church. It was an interesting experience, and about my first time in church since I was in San Francisco. In one class we had quite a talk about crime, economics, juvenile court, etc. A frank discussion of the national cri-*

sis. One of them said that the war & turmoil prophecies of one of their Mormon saints would be fulfilled next year.

The twenty-year-old Everett engaged in apple fights with children. That night, and extending into the early-morning hours, *we amused ourselves with some Navajos who are camped nearby.* The Indians' long black hair and bandanas frightened the children, who hid behind an outhouse. On another night Everett went to a dance with the Copes' daughter Rhea and son Gene. He was introduced to other teenagers. Everett danced and visited with Lenora Hall, who later wrote a history of the area. To his brother he confided he thought it was a good thing he hadn't fallen in love with a Mormon girl. *I've become a little too different from most of the rest of the world.*[48] From Tropic he mailed his malfunctioning Kodak camera to his parents.

In a sense, Everett was the Pied Piper of youthful innocence and freedom without the dire consequences visited upon others in the German legend. He emerged in the role in the small villages of southern Utah. The presence of this playful boy-man attracted the attention of Tropic's young people during the five days he spent with the Cope family. "We waved goodbye as Ruess led his two burros from Cope's yard," Lenora Hall recalled.[49]

———— ■ ————

The road from Tropic to Escalante did not follow the more direct route of the current State Highway 12 but rather looped north to Widtsoe, a dying farming settlement that, along with Escalante, would be photographed in 1936 for the federal government by Dorothea Lange. As at Zeniff, Arizona, the lack of water was the main problem.

Everett spent a night with two Navajo eating mutton, drinking coffee, and singing Indian songs. *The songs of the Navajo express for me something that no other songs do.* The dirt road jogged right at Widtsoe, followed what is now Forest Highway 17, and climbed Escalante Canyon. It peaked in the pine and aspen forest at the 9,300-foot level of the Escalante Rim, passing between Table and Aquarius Plateaus. The Forest Service maintained a telephone at the summit of the pass for stranded travelers. *My camp is on the very point of the divide, with the country falling away to the blue horizon on the east and the west.*[50] To the east, the direction in which Everett was headed, a magnificent panorama of near-vacant, serrated lands unfolded, the last extensive terrain to be explored and named in the continental United States. From left to right were the Waterpocket Fold, the Henry Mountains, and Navajo Mountain. The road descended Main Canyon beside Birch Creek and five miles west of Escalante joined what would become the state highway in 1958. Everett spent the night at a ranch in Upper Valley and ate with the family who lived there. "We thought he was a real nice boy, but kind of foolish to take off alone like that," said the rancher.[51]

Escalante was a classic Mormon outpost on Utah's southern border.[52] It acted as a filter for the more inhabited regions of the Kingdom of Zion to the north. Navajo who wished to trade were usually the only people who arrived there, mostly from the south. The wrinkled and arid landscape, incised by deep canyons and fast-running seasonal streams, was one of the most impregnable terrains in the country. The canyonlands were, in effect, a natural barrier behind which the inhabitants of Escalante lived and practiced their particular brand of religion and moral beliefs with little interference from the outside world.

The Mormon village, settled in 1875, was named after a Catholic priest, Father Silvestre Vélez de Escalante, whose overland journey of discovery one hundred years earlier passed to the south of what would become Escalante. The Mormons adopted the village pattern of rural settlement, favoring a centralized village with corrals and stockyards surrounded by irrigated fields. In this manner no land was wasted on scattered developments, and a tight, homogenous community of like-minded people was encouraged. When Everett passed through, a large number of the nearly two hundred families had the same last names. The town averaged nearly six children per family.

The wide streets were laid out along the four compass points, drinking and irrigation water flowed in open ditches along the streets, the cottonwood trees provided shade, and the sandstone homes bespoke a certain permanence particular in the West to Utah. The village remained an isolated frontier settlement through the first half of the twentieth century. It was sixty-five miles from the county seat in Panguitch and ninety miles from the closest railroad. There was no law in Escalante. "The Depression didn't affect us much," said a resident, "because we never had much before the Depression."[53] Clothing was homemade, and most food was raised locally.*

––––––

*Dorothea Lange visited Escalante in March 1936 to take photographs for the Works Progress Administration. In her field notes she jotted down facts and quotes from the inhabitants, such as that Escalante had a population of 1,200 and "People just been sittin' here waitin' and hopin'" and the town had had "one depression after another." The latter quote was attributed to the Mormon bishop Harvey C. Bailey, who would join the search for Everett. Lange took three photos of Bailey in a suit and tie. She also photographed barns, houses, the Mormon church, and the

Escalante was not completely sealed off from the outside world, however. There was a picture show twice a week. Cattle and sheep raising was the only business, and it had fallen on hard times during the Depression. There was a severe drought in 1934 and a steep decline in prices for livestock. The Forest Service attempted to cut back on grazing. The local stockmen resisted strenuously. They didn't like outsiders meddling in their affairs. For the previous twenty years they had petitioned to have every forest ranger removed.

———————■———————

One day in early November a strange apparition—astride a donkey, with its feet almost touching the ground, and leading another burro—rode into Escalante. The dirt streets were deep in dust that drought year, but irrigation water still flowed in the open ditches, besides which shade trees mitigated the fierce summer heat. It was autumn, the barns were crammed with hay, and the smell of burning leaves suffused the village.

The rider passed the Star Amusement Hall, where he would see a movie in a few days, and the small cluster of businesses at the junction of Main and Center streets. The white sandstone Mormon meetinghouse, the red brick schoolhouse, and the substantial brick residences on the corners of the rectangular street grid were the most noticeable structures. There were also smaller log cabins and shacks.

Everett was an outsider riding a beast of burden and a painter and a poet, all of which qualified him as an alien, albeit a harmless one. He had no practical occupation or any visible means of economic support, except for some pictures he was trying to sell to people who couldn't afford them. "Peddlers found their way over Table Cliff from time to time, but probably no one had ever come to Escalante before with a stock of watercolors and block prints," wrote a Utah historian.[54] The anachronistic sight riveted all who witnessed it, and word soon spread of the stranger's presence.

Ruess saw himself as different from others, and he was not unmindful of the impression he made on this extremely religious population. He was a living image risen from the pages of the Bible. His entrance into Escalante was the beginning of the myth of a Christ-like presence floating through the desert wilderness who was eventually impaled upon a metaphorical cross,

—————

store. She noted there were no WPA projects in Escalante. There was no mention of Everett in her notes. Field notes for March 26–27, 1936, Dorothea Lange Collection, Oakland Museum of California.

by either his own or someone else's actions. Regardless of the manner of his immolation, he would achieve a legendary status. That image and the fact that he disappeared not far away are the reasons why his myth has lodged securely and endured in Utah. Sancho Panza and Jesus Christ rode donkeys, he reminded his brother in his last letter, *so I'm not the only one.*[55]

Everett had much to be happy about. He was financially secure for the first time during his five years of wanderings. He had insisted that his parents not mail him his monthly stipend and instead sent them $10, suggesting that $5 be spent on something they really wanted. *Let this be the first install-ment on that nickel I promised you when I made my first million.*[56] Stella and Christopher used the money to frame his watercolors, twenty of which he mailed from Escalante. *It has been fun to have plenty of spending money, and be able to celebrate and make presents whenever I want to. . . . This has been a full, rich year. I have left no strange or delightful thing undone that I wanted to.*[57]

But the dark side of life still trailed Everett. The prospect of death remained a constant in his thinking. He was obsessed by the romantic possibilities of his demise and the tangible relics and bones of the ancient Anasazi Indians. In both Tropic and Escalante, and in Los Angeles before he left for Kayenta, he viewed the movie *Death Takes a Holiday.* He had also seen the play on which the movie was based. In both dramatizations, Death, wanting to expe-rience life, suspends his usual activities for three days and discovers love. The four viewings of the drama, the last just before he disappeared, must have humanized the specter of Death in Everett's mind.

Christopher Ruess saw similarities between the lines in the play and his son's words. "Makes one feel sad," Christopher confided to his journal two years after Everett's disappearance. "Seems too much like echoes in Everett's diary." He wrote down quotes from the play that were similar to his son's thinking: "I've known too much and seen too much." "Has it ever occurred to you that death may be only more simpler than life, and infinitely more kind?" "The shadowy places of the imagination are her home." "'Good-bye, my friends,' says Death in leaving after being human for a while, 'Remember that there is only a moment of shadow between your life and mine. And when I call you, come bravely through that shadow, and you shall find me only your familiar friend.'"

The former Unitarian minister wrote an observation in his diary that applied not only to his son but to all teenagers. The idea he expressed does more than anything else to demythologize the pervasive fable that Everett Ruess was a saint-like western Thoreau. He was much more. He was a human being, and a young one at that, who had experienced greater extremes than most teenagers—or adults, for that matter. His life has real meaning and relevance for our time because there are other seekers like Everett who need to be understood before they harm themselves and others. Christopher Ruess's admission was both a warning and a guide for all parents: "The older person does not realize the soul-flights of the adolescent. I think we all poorly understood Everett."*

In Escalante, Everett played the Pied Piper role again, and the town's boys loved it. *I have had plenty of fun with the boys of this town riding horses, hunting for arrowheads, and the like.*[58] "We were with him all the time when we weren't sleeping or doing something," said a resident who recalled the few days Everett spent in Escalante.[59] He seemed like a big brother to them. Everett camped under the cottonwoods and near an irrigation ditch in a field adjacent to the village. Norm Christiansen, who was twelve years old then, trailed him everywhere. "We talked about Indians and where he had been and what he had seen, and in those days everybody ate venison year round, and we'd take venison over and slice it off and roast it on sticks. It always tasted better over there than anywhere else. He was a great guy and had a good way with people, especially with young people. Really likable."[60]

Everett's last night in Escalante was peaceful. *Tonight I have been sitting by the fire with two of my friends, eating roast venison and baked potatoes. The burro bell is tinkling merrily nearby as Chocolatero crops the alfalfa.*[61]

Two young men, Melvin Alvey and his brother, talked with Everett on his way out of town on November 12. They didn't think he was properly equipped to be out in the high desert for six weeks in the winter. Everett had never overwintered in the wilderness. The nearest he came to spending part of a winter in the desert was in December of 1931, when he had the comforts of the Reynoldses' home and other nearby accommodations, including a hotel, to retreat to. And Roosevelt, Arizona, was hundreds of miles to the south and at a lower altitude.

The brothers eyed Everett's equipment. "Well, you're traveling pretty light," Melvin said.

I don't need very much. Everett said he was planning to be back by Christmas.

---

*Christopher Ruess, diary entry, April 3, 1936. Christopher typed selected diary entries and mailed them to Waldo in China, which is how they survived after Stella burned his original journals. This revealing entry is on page 2 of the March 29 to April 11, 1936, extract sent to Waldo.

Alvey didn't think he had enough food for that length of time, and he could see no stove or tent. He observed years later, "Worst time of the season to be going down to that desert. Cold. That's cold weather for a man to go down there to write and draw pictures at that time of the year."[62]

Everett and his two burros headed south on the road to Hole-in-the-Rock. He felt liberated from the stifling constraints of civilization, even the minimal form found in Escalante. In the desert he was surrounded by the beauty of nature and his most treasured possessions: his Navajo saddle blankets and silver bracelet with three turquoise stones, items that would never be recovered. Everett had informed Waldo that he didn't want to return to the cities. *Even from your scant description, I know that I could not bear the routine and humdrum of the life that you are forced to lead. I don't think I could ever settle down. I have known too much of the depths of life already, and I would prefer anything to an anticlimax.* If he didn't return to the city, what was the alternative? *Do you blame me then for staying here where I feel that I belong and am at one with the world around me.*[63] Everett was caught in a vise between the ideal and the practical worlds, a hurtful but not unusual position for someone just emerging from their teens. He was trapped by the completeness of his life up to that moment and its looming diminishment.

A week after leaving Escalante, Ruess spent a couple of days with two sheepherders.[64] They answered his questions about ancient Indian ruins in the vicinity of their camp at the head of Soda Gulch, not far from Davis Gulch. They offered him a leg of mutton. He declined it, stating that he preferred to travel light. That was the last reported sighting of Everett Ruess. Then he vanished, completely.

X

The Search

1935

THE STAGE NEEDS TO BE SET FOR WHAT FOLLOWS. The Escalante Desert was not a wilderness in the strict sense of the word. It was the winter range for cattle and sheep, and the ranchers and hired hands who tended those animals roamed across it, as did the rustlers who preyed upon them, and the bands of Indians who traded for goods in the small Mormon communities and hunted for deer on the Kaiparowits Plateau. For more than 130 years, a road has bisected the desert from north to south. It was suitable for horses and wagons at first and then high-clearance automobiles and pickup trucks equipped with four-wheel drive in more recent years. Two criteria for wilderness areas are that they be roadless and "untrammeled."[1] The Escalante Desert has been neither since 1879.

In an ill-conceived plan, 230 people heeded the call of the Church of Jesus Christ of Latter-Day Saints and set out in 1879 to establish a colony in southeastern Utah to serve as a Mormon outpost. They built a wagon road south from Escalante that paralleled the plateau. The sixty-mile track was called the Hole-in-the-Rock Trail and ended in a crack in the wall of Glen Canyon, through which a trail was blasted to the Colorado River. From there they crossed the river and eventually made their way to near Bluff, Utah. The effort became part of Mormon pioneer mythology despite the abandonment of the route a few years later. But local ranchers continued to use it, with stops along the way.

Forty miles south of Escalante is Fortymile Spring, a water source, and nearby is Dance Hall Rock, a large Navajo sandstone formation with a natural amphitheater used by the road builders to dance their jigs. The road from Escalante to the spring was relatively easy going for the pioneers and those who followed. But then the country becomes more broken, and the road dips into and out of canyon creases. It was in just such a wrinkle in the landscape that a truck carrying Boy Scouts on a camping trip rolled over and killed thirteen scouts in 1963.

Soda Gulch and Soda Springs, the latter also known as Soda Seep, were water sources located forty-nine miles down the trail from Escalante. At fifty miles there was another spring and the Bailey ranch cabin, present in the 1930s and 1940s but later destroyed by fire. Fiftymile Creek trickles down Soda Gulch, whose name is a local designation that does not appear on U.S. Geological Survey maps. The creek empties into the Escalante River.

Separated from Soda Gulch by a ridge to the east of the road is a narrow slot canyon, the beginnings of Davis Gulch. This gulch is accessible from the old stock trail about halfway down its north side. The rim of Glen Canyon, from which there is a view of Lake Powell today, is ten miles farther down the road.

The history of the Colorado River corridor, now buried under the waters of the reservoir, also negated a wilderness designation. Scores of gold miners hacked trails and roads into the steep canyon to make access to the river easier. Tons of equipment, including the makings of a thirty-eight-foot-long, double-decked gold dredge, were hauled to the bottom of the Mormon trail. With the possibility of large-scale industrial development looming, thought was given to building a railroad across Glen Canyon, but that never happened. There was a one-room stone trading post at the foot of the trail on the north bank of the river. It was abandoned in 1901 when the miners departed. One of the traders noted in a diary that he had been busy but had gone twenty-five days without seeing another white man.

A ten-foot-long boat, its frame covered with galvanized sheet metal taken from an advertising sign and made watertight with tar, served as a ferry and "carried a good many passengers across the river at this point," wrote a historian of the region.[2] The sign bore a date of 1915. Sometimes as many as twenty-five or thirty Navajo, Piute, and Ute, gathered in separate tribal groups, camped on one side of the river or the other waiting for a ride. They carried hand-woven blankets, animal hides, and wool north and returned with store-bought goods and strings of horses. The crude ferry was still in use in 1939.

Then there were the footnotes of history that occurred before and after Everett's disappearance. A posse trailed a rustler into the Escalante desert, found him eating dinner with two cowboys, and shot him when he made a run for it. The rustler, a stranger, died a short time later in the Escalante jail, a converted granary. Beginning on December 6, 1934, a man was camped at the end of the Hole-in-the-Rock Trail, but he never saw Everett.

A young man who was one year older than Everett was thought to be lost in the same general area at approximately the same time. Dan Thrapp became entangled in the maze of canyons at the junction of the Colorado and San Juan Rivers while on an ambitious horseback trip from Green River, Utah, to Winslow, Arizona. Like Everett, he had dropped out of college and was fascinated by the cliff dwellings and their ancient occupants. He had been working for a New York Museum of Natural History expedition in Wyoming and had taken a leave of absence. Thrapp was overdue by two months, and his parents had notified the authorities. Airplane and horseback searches, dispatched by the *Deseret News* in Salt Lake City, were undertaken, and the newspaper coverage far exceeded what Ruess received at the same time. Thrapp had managed to stretch his two-week supply of food and was in no particular trouble. He built a raft and crossed the Colorado River a number of times. The young man heard about the searches and emerged from the wilderness wondering why there was such a fuss.*

—————————————■—————————————

Stella wrote Everett a three-page Christmas letter with news from home and mailed it to "Everett Ruess, Escalante Rim, Utah" on December 22.[3] That

---

*I knew Dan Thrapp at the *Los Angeles Times,* where he was the religion editor in the late 1960s and early 1970s. I had no idea of his earlier remarkable life of adventure. He got a journalism degree and went to work for United Press International in Argentina. He crossed the Andes by mule to enlist as a private in the U.S. Army. During World War II, Thrapp rose to the rank of captain and ran pack strings over the Burma Hump into China. He was awarded four battle stars. After the war he worked for United Press in England, Italy, Africa, and Greece, and while at the *Times* he wrote books about the Apache wars in Arizona. He was a quiet, unassuming man when I knew him. Most of my information about Thrapp comes from Scott Thybony, who is working on a book about three simultaneous searches in southern Utah centering on Thrapp, which also mentions Ruess and Clint Palmer, a murderer; and from "Dan L. Thrapp, 80, Chronicler of West," *New York Times,* May 4, 1994.

was the address on his November 11 letter to his parents mailed from the village of Escalante. The news covered various matters.

Everett's paternal grandfather had died peacefully in his sleep, and Waldo and all the grandchildren except Everett—she noted pointedly—had been present for the funeral service in Los Angeles. Christopher read passages from Walt Whitman and a free-verse poem he had written. "It was unusual and beautiful," Stella said.

Waldo was about to depart for China to work as a secretary for a Christian missionary organization, leaving her with no sons near home for the first time. "I hope you won't often be so far from civilization that we can get no word to you." There had been an open house at their home to celebrate Waldo's birthday and imminent departure, and many of his brother's friends had attended. They had signed Waldo's and the family's guest books. For Everett, Stella inscribed, "Seek beauty! Create beauty!" She asked, "Does that sound Everettian?" For Waldo, Stella wrote, "Follow the gleam!" For her daughter Christella, who had died twenty-six years previously, she wrote, "Glorify the hour!" They had also recorded songs and poems, including Everett's "Morning in L.A. Harbor" and a portion of "Wilderness Song," on a record. Then Waldo departed on a Norwegian freighter bound for Shanghai on a nonstop voyage.

Four days before Christmas Stella had danced to the song "The Spirit of Christmas"—pizzicato, she specified—at the beautifully decorated home of the president of the Los Angeles chapter of the National League of American Pen Women. She signed the letter "Happy Christmas Day from Mother!"

On February 2, 1935, the unopened letter was mailed from Escalante to the Ruess family home, now at 836 N. Kingsley Drive, with Everett's name and address crossed out with X's, as if he no longer existed. The envelope was marked *Unknown* and *Return to sender.* Obviously he was missing.

Christopher had to work. Stella took charge of locating her son. She began by notifying authorities at post offices, Utah and Arizona law enforcement offices, national forests, newspapers, radio stations, trading posts, and Indian reservations that Everett was missing. She sent a letter on February 7 to Mildred Allen, the Escalante postmistress who had been in contact with Everett in November and had returned the Christmas letter to his parents.[4] The February 14 daily bulletin of the Southwest Region of the Forest Service carried the following notice: "Missing Man: Everett Ruess, age 20. Travels with pack outfit of two burros. 'Explores,' makes watercolor sketches. . . ." A reporter picked up the information from a Forest Service official. The first press account of Everett's disappearance ran on the same day in the

Los Angeles Evening Herald. On February 16, the *Los Angeles Times* carried a four-paragraph item headlined "Artist Lost in Wilds of South Utah." Working through prominent men he knew from his work and his church, Christopher got word to National Park Service and Bureau of Indian Affairs personnel and the Army Air Corps. March Air Force Base near Riverside, California, was alerted, and pilots on training flights looked for a speck on the desert floor.

An Indian trader said he had seen Everett the previous year with two burros on the road. Such a sight, he noted, was "very, very" unusual. Bureau of Indian Affairs officials on the Navajo, Hopi, and Piute reservations said there had been no sightings of Everett nor any talk of him among the Indians. Local sheriffs responded similarly. Stella sent thirty letters on February 22 to other people, including friends of Everett. None had heard from him recently.

Stella and Christopher's long siege of uncertainty and grief began that month, as did the searches that employed such diverse means as airplanes and spiritualists and have continued intermittently to this writing, with the momentary belief in 2009 that Everett's bones had been found and identified by modern science.

━━━━━━ ■ ━━━━━━

Gail Bailey had been tending his sheep in the desert when Ruess was in Escalante in November. He descended Davis Gulch in mid-February to check grazing conditions. He saw two burros in a brush corral and some equipment: two halters, two kyaks, and a pack saddle. He didn't recall seeing a riding saddle.[5] "It wasn't much of an outfit," said Bailey, who didn't know who the owner was.[6] The camp seemed abandoned, but the donkeys appeared to be in good shape to Bailey. He left the burros in Davis Gulch and returned to Escalante with a halter. He was later questioned by the sheriff and the county attorney.[7]

When it was determined Everett might be missing, Escalante was alerted. Informal search parties consisting of one, two, or a handful of men who could spare the time departed almost daily. Much of the activity was directed by H. Jennings Allen, the former postmaster, whose wife now held that position. Allen was newly elected to the position of county commissioner. He and Bailey headed a search party that included three other Escalante residents familiar with the desert. They departed on March 3.[8]

Leaving the road, the searchers dropped into Willow and Soda canyons, where they found nothing. They entered Davis Gulch via the precipitous stock trail, dismounting and leading their horses down the slickrock. Almost immediately upon reaching the canyon floor, they spotted Everett's two burros, Cockleburrs and Chocolatero.* The donkeys were standing within a near-perfect natural corral formed by the steep sides of the canyon and a brush fence. The canyon bottom in their immediate vicinity was denuded of vegetation. The burros seemed scrawny to these men. The difference in the two descriptions of their physical condition may have been due to the fact that both were undersized to begin with. They were confined within a large space, only part of which had been grazed. The fact that there was still feed was demonstrated when Bailey drove his rams into the gulch a few weeks later.

One of the searchers carved his name and the date on a panel containing the abstract designs of Anasazi drawings and a more recent inscription, *NEMO 1934*.[9] The search party attached no significance to this enigmatic inscription but did note other clues to Everett's presence in the canyon. They discovered a collection of pottery shards under an overhang on the north wall, halfway between the inscriptions and the corral. Scattered about were condensed milk cans and candy wrappers, and there were indications of a bedroll having been laid out on the dry ground of the natural shelter. Everett had obviously camped there.

Tracks of his size-nine boots were found in the upper and lower parts of the canyon, suggesting he had been searching for ruins. More tracks led to the foot of Fifty-Mile Mountain. There were also tracks near the bottom of Davis Gulch, where there were patches of quicksand. The first thought of the original searchers—and perhaps the best guess as to Ruess's fate—was that Everett had been sucked into the quicksand.

Its lethal properties were demonstrated years later by a documentary filmmaker. A granddaughter of Dorothea Lange, Dyanna Taylor, traipsed through the Escalante River canyons with a crew filming *Vanished!*[†] She

_____

*Bailey's account, newspaper reports, photographs of the burros being led from Davis Gulch, reports by Park Service rangers, correspondence to and from the Ruess family, C. Gregory Crampton's reports, and W. L. Rusho's interviews with members of the search party testified to the presence of the burros in Davis Gulch. This would become a key issue seventy-five years later in the attempt to validate the supposed discovery of Ruess's bones.

†After Dorothea Lange and Maynard Dixon divorced in 1935, Lange married Paul Taylor, a professor of economics at the University of California, Berkeley. Taylor helped turn the photographer's attention toward the plight of migrant laborers. Dyanna Taylor was one of their grandchildren. She remembers her grandmother quoting Everett's question "Does the soul need wilderness?" Lange speculated

nearly vanished. Laughing at first, Taylor and a crew member stepped into a patch of quicksand. Their laughter quickly turned to panic. Fortunately, others were present and laboriously hauled them out, minus their shoes. The near disaster was filmed and is part of the documentary. Everett had been alone, and there would have been no one to pull him out. John Wetherill thought Everett was capable of taking care of himself in the desert "unless he had met with an accident."[10] Wetherill didn't specify what type of accident he meant.

The burros resisted being led up the slickrock trail, so each had to be hitched to two saddle horses and pulled. Bailey's uncle, Harvey C. Bailey, the town's Mormon bishop and one of the searchers, took the burros and the equipment that had been recovered to his mountain sheep camp.

Six days after the search began, it began to snow in the desert—and it kept snowing. The drought was broken, and Everett's trail grew more obscure.

———— ∎ ————

Everything of value belonging to Ruess was missing. This included money, Navajo blankets, the silver Navajo bracelet with three pieces of turquoise, clothing, food, utensils, camping gear, riding saddle, gun, ammunition, books, sketching and painting materials, and his 1934 journal. The missing objects raised questions: Did he hide them somewhere? Did he take them with him, wherever he went? Was he murdered and then robbed? Did he perish accidentally and then some person or persons helped themselves to his belongings?

While conducting an archeological survey in 1957 of what would soon be covered by Lake Powell, researchers found tin and aluminum pots and pans, plates, spoons, cups, a knife, a canteen, glass jars, and tin cans. They also found a package of razor blades and some medicine that had been purchased from the Owl Drug Company in Los Angeles. Everett shaved, and he had asked his mother in September 1934 to send him Eopa Poison Oak Preventative & Curative, stating that it could be obtained from a drugstore.[11] The mentholatum in the medicine was a soothing agent used for skin care. "Could this have been the last camp of Everett Ruess?" one of the anthropologists asked.[12]

The wife of Robert H. Lister of the University of Colorado, who had been in charge of the three-man field party that included Edson B. Alvey of Escalante,

———

about what happened to Everett, and her musings caught the attention of her grandchildren. Dyanna climbed mountains, and a cousin sought outdoor adventures. Dyanna Taylor, personal communication, November 12, 2010.

later added details left out of the original terse message Bob Lister sent to the anthropology professor Jesse D. Jennings of the University of Utah:

> One day the fellows climbed into an alcove in Cottonwood [Gulch] for lunch. They spotted something shiny sticking out from under a rock. It turned out to be a flannel-covered canteen of the 1930s vintage and some eating utensils. All had been purposefully smashed and hidden under rocks. More telling were several tubes of dried oil pigment of the sort artists use and another of mentholatum with a label reading *Owl Drug Co., Los Angeles, Calif.* Immediately they searched for human remains but found none.
>
> Bob suspected that they had found some of Ruess's things, that he may have been killed there, and that the animals were driven over to Davis Gulch to throw any searchers off the track.
>
> I don't know if the wranglers were present then or not, but they surely knew about the find. One was an Alvey. . . . Bob turned all this material over to the sheriff in Escalante, who asked him not to tell any of the locals, but the "secret" was out.
>
> Bob never heard anything more about the matter but felt that the sheriff was not going to do anything. He saw Escalante as a village full of suspicions but not willing to stir up trouble over a mystery a quarter of a century old.[13]

Although the archeological survey was not focused on such peripheral discoveries, Jennings, who was in overall charge of it, told Lister: "As part of the 'romance' of the region your find is of great importance."[14]

Cottonwood Gulch was less than three miles south of the head of Davis Gulch. It drained directly into what was then the Colorado River and is now Lake Powell. The southerly, or left, arm of Cottonwood Gulch is now known as Reflection Canyon. There were pictographs and ancient granaries in Cottonwood Gulch, indicating a sporadic agricultural presence. The steps to one granary were extremely risky, and anyone climbing to it would have had to rappel down.

The researchers gave the camping equipment to the Garfield County sheriff in Panguitch (not Escalante, as Mrs. Lister thought), along with their account of where they had found it and what it might represent. This was old news. The sheriff, who was about to leave office, did nothing. Waldo Ruess was told about the items and wrote the new sheriff in 1960. Some were shipped to Los Angeles. "My mother and I do not feel we can say anything definite regarding them," Waldo told the sheriff, "but she thinks the spoons look identical to some we have, or had, around the house. She thinks further that he did have a canteen like the one you have sent us."[15] Cottonwood Gulch was outside the area where the searches had concentrated.

———■———

Eventually every ethnic and religious group that lived in or worked in or traveled through the region either was blamed or fingered another party or faction for Everett's alleged murder. Innocent until proven guilty did not apply; rather, its opposite did, although no one was ever legally charged with harming Everett. Proof was lacking in all cases; innuendo was rife; personal opinions were aired; scores were settled; and since there was no body, and thus little chance of prosecution, known braggarts claimed the deed, and there were a number of unverified deathbed confessions in southern Utah. A lot of people sought their fifteen minutes of fame by faking a connection to Everett.

Among the prospective searchers were publicity seekers and opportunists. Two claimed the rank of captain. For a fee, a retired Los Angeles captain of police detectives offered his services, as did a Utah gold miner by the name of Captain Neal Johnson, who said he got his rank in the Mexican air force. There was a lengthy correspondence between Johnson and Christopher. Johnson said he needed $45 to keep Navajo scouts in the field for six days. Christopher sent him the money. Johnson submitted the following report: "One chief told me today, 'Picture man heap savvy wild mountains. OK.'"[16] Johnson said he could get no further information and made excuses for not doing more. Ruess was warned off Johnson by Mormons and knowledgeable guides, who either disliked his lifestyle or had never heard of him. Christopher asked for his money back, but Johnson was a likable rogue, and Christopher did not want to rule out any chance of locating his son. He told Johnson he doubted the miner's veracity but believed there was good in every man.

Johnson sent Ruess a clipping from the *Salt Lake Tribune* indicating his involvement in the search. He said he was going on a secret expedition organized by the newspaper and asked for $25 to buy trinkets for the Indians. Christopher sent him the money. Johnson believed that Everett was alive, which was exactly what his parents wanted to hear, and living with Navajo. It was a measure of Christopher's charity, or desperation, that he allowed Johnson to spend a week in their Los Angeles home. Johnson slept in Everett's bed, visited Christopher's office, had dinner with the Ruesses' friends, and talked with Stella for two or three hours. Christopher, sensing Johnson was broke, gave him $2. "I can't make him out," Ruess wrote Waldo in China.

"He may never have sent any Indians in at all—a peculiar character. We are financing him no further."[17]

In April, Donal Jolley, the chief ranger of Zion National Park, wrote the only official report on Ruess's disappearance, with input from the ranger Maurice Cope of Bryce Canyon National Park and H. Jennings Allen of Escalante. Jolley titled the one-and-a-half-page Department of the Interior document, which he sent to the director of the Park Service, "Report on Search for Everett Ruess Who Is Supposedly Lost near the Colorado River." Jolley knew Ruess personally from the youth's 1931 visit to Zion. His report covered a number of possibilities but did not settle on any one. Ruess didn't care for publicity, Jolley wrote, and only wanted to be alone in the wilderness, "where he could take care of himself anywhere, unless he met with foul play or an accident."[18]

Neither the Park Service nor any other federal or state agency nor the local sheriff's office participated in any of the searches, which were carried out by private citizens and clubs. Everett had fallen through a crack in the jurisdictional landscape and was missing in the vast public domain.

There were theories about where he was, however. Since Ruess supposedly spoke the Navajo language fluently and had said he was interested in living with the Indians, at least for a time, the thinking went, he could have left his burros in Davis Gulch and proceeded alone or with Navajo companions across the Colorado River to the reservation. There was a crossing at Hole-in-the-Rock the Navajo used. Winter was the low-water time of year in the era of no big dams upstream, and that winter had seen very little rainfall. Jolley pointed out that there was a canoe at the crossing, and there was always the ferry.

One reason why voluntarily leaving his burros and crossing the river to spend a long time with the Navajo made no sense is that Everett cared for his burros. He could have arranged to leave the donkeys in Escalante if his plan was to travel without them. The conjecture that Everett drowned while crossing the river also made no sense, given the low water, the means to cross the river (canoe and ferry), and the fact that he was a strong swimmer.

The foul play theory centered on rustlers, with two locals as suspects. In order to discourage rustlers, ranchers had spread a rumor that a federal agent was in the vicinity. This theory supposed that the rustlers had mistaken Everett for the agent and killed him when he surprised them in the act of stealing cattle. Randall Henderson, the publisher of *Desert Magazine* and the first book about Everett, was a leading proponent of the rustler–mistaken agent theory. He first heard it discussed around a fire by two Escalante men while on a camping trip near Davis Gulch in 1951.[19]

The rumors and factions focusing on this theory in Escalante were insidious and intense. Tribal bonds and tribal rivalries both cemented and fractured the isolated settlement. "It is rather like a big family or a tribe capable of inspiring intense attachment and loyalty, but also rivalry, resentment, and a desire to escape," wrote one chronicler.[20] Everett's disappearance became a lifetime-defining event. People told stories to gain or deflect attention, to harm or defend their neighbors, and to trick or confuse the out-of-town media. Of course, no one knew who or what killed Everett, this being impossible to discern.

Keith Ridelle and Joe Pollock were petty crooks and rustlers. Both had been charged in the 1920s and 1930s with various minor crimes, but neither had gone to jail until Pollock was convicted of rustling in 1936 and spent a couple of years in the Utah State Penitentiary. They were both hard men, but, as one of their defenders said, "Lots of rough boys don't kill people." They lived in Escalante, so they were not likely to be shot by locals for their transgressions, as had happened to an earlier rustler.

Pollock and Ridelle, the former married to the latter's sister, were both feared and liked. Where their neighbors lined up on their probable culpability for Everett's disappearance depended on how these neighbors regarded them: were they small-time rustlers who sought meat during hard times, as others were known to do, or did they head an interstate rustling operation that wouldn't hesitate to kill an inquisitive agent and dump his body in the Colorado River, as was alleged by some? Gail Bailey was convinced they had disposed of Ruess in the latter manner. A third rustler, the actual triggerman, was also supposedly involved. Sides were also taken on whether Ridelle's drunken confession of Ruess's murder years later to Norm Christiansen was valid or the ravings of a known braggart. Local opinion tended toward the second interpretation.*

Waldo Ruess thought rustlers had killed his brother. When he visited Escalante in 1964, he entered the home of one of them. The man, not identi-

---

*The guide Ken Sleight lived in Escalante after World War II and headed the Chamber of Commerce during the 1960s. He told Diane Orr: "Everyone down there will tell you exactly what you want to hear, and if they don't know it, concoct it. They've done that before with other things." Another resident, Melvin Alvey, said: "There was too many different stories after it was over with. Everyone told their idea and their opinion. All you knew was the stories they were telling, and there was plenty of them." Outtakes from Orr's documentary *Lost Forever* (Beecher Films, 2000).

fied by Ruess, was sick and lying on a couch. His words before Waldo had a chance to say anything were: "I didn't kill your brother."[21] There was an unfounded variation of the rustler theory that lifted the blame entirely from locals and placed it on outsiders: Everett was shot while poaching cattle.*

———————■———————

Since no public agency or elected official—such as the state attorney general or the local sheriff—would become involved, the Associated Civic Clubs of Southern Utah organized a search for Everett. The volunteers decided to concentrate their efforts on Davis Gulch and the tracks found by the earlier search party. A wagonload of supplies was dispatched to Dance Hall Rock, and nine riders, each leading a pack animal, followed on May 30. When it was determined the wagon could go farther, Soda Seep became the base camp. Daily reports were carried back to Escalante, where they were phoned to the *Salt Lake Tribune* and published as news stories.

The clubs' major discoveries were made on June 2 and 8. They found *NEMO 1934* carved with a knife on the wall of the canyon near the stock trail and another *NEMO 1934* incised on the doorstep of an Anasazi ruin perched on a ledge near LaGorce Arch. Four pieces of Anasazi pottery were sitting on a nearby rock. There were size-nine tracks in the lower portion of the gorge. "The direction of these tracks led the searchers to believe that Ruess may have worked his way through many of the gorges along Escalante Creek," the *Tribune* reported, thus reinforcing the quicksand theory.

The searchers thought *Nemo* might have been an Indian word and decided

———————

*I give no credence to this theory, which blames Ruess for his own death and takes the onus off others. Debora Threedy, a professor at the University of Utah law school who has written and performed dramas about Ruess, was told by a neighbor that he was present at the deathbed confession of a man, whom he would not identify, who said he and a couple of other men had killed Everett because he had poached one of their cows. Threedy has a summer home in Torrey, Utah, on the other side of Boulder Mountain from Escalante. The desert south of Escalante is a winter range for Torrey cattle. Threedy, personal communication, June 1, 2009.

There have been a number of so-called confessions of the murder. Paul Nelson, who wrote a master's thesis about the region and Ruess, worked for a guide service in the 1990s. On three different occasions around a campfire, he heard third- and fourth-generation ranchers repeat a similar version of this story. Nelson, personal communication, May 18, 2009. See the last chapter for an explanation of how memory can twist facts, or consider the "fifteen minutes of fame" syndrome.

to contact Ruess's parents to determine its exact meaning. The Ruesses received a telegram asking if the word *NEMO* had meant anything to Everett. It certainly did.*

Nemo was Everett's personal signature and perhaps his farewell note. It was as if he had nothing else to live for, knew he was going away, and wanted to leave a sign that would proclaim his presence and resonate through the years. What better word than the cryptic *Nemo,* associated most prominently with T. E. Lawrence's translation of Homer's *Odyssey* and Jules Verne's *Twenty Thousand Leagues under the Sea?* Everett had read both classics and absorbed their messages. The date added punctuation and identified Everett as the sign maker. His signature made people think and imagine, the goal of any writer or artist.[22] It helped establish his myth. Along with his obsession with *Death Takes a Holiday,* it was the best indication of Everett's state of mind at the time of his disappearance.†

Odysseus and Lawrence spoke to young Ruess of the romance of adventure and wandering in the desert. It took the Greek hero Odysseus, or Ulysses as he was known to the Romans, ten years to return home from the Trojan War. His family didn't know if he was dead, missing, or lost. The word *odyssey* is now applied to epic wanderings, thanks to this tale. From the land of the lotus eaters, where his crewmen were beguiled, Odysseus journeyed to the land of the cruel Cyclopes. He and his men were trapped in a cave by the one-eyed giant Polyphemus, who began devouring the crewmen two by two. The giant asked the wily Odysseus his name. "No man," he replied. He later blinded Polyphemus, who roared his distress. When the neighboring Cyclopes asked who was harming him, Polyphemus told them,

------

*Stella replied by telegram to the query on June 5: "Everett read in desert Greek poem Odyssey translated by Lawrence of Arabian desert. Here Odysseus Greek word for nobody. Nemo being Latin word for nobody. Odysseus trapped by man-eating giant in cave saves life by trick of calling himself Nemo. Everett dislikes writing own name in public places." Stella Ruess to Ray C. Carr, June 5, 1935.

†The March search party may have seen these inscriptions, but they missed their significance. The *Salt Lake Tribune,* depending on the June search party's reports for its stories, used the words *carved* and *cut* repeatedly and stated that the letters were made with a knife. When W. L. Rusho visited Davis Gulch in the early 1980s he said the words were inscribed in charcoal. Neither type of inscription is visible now, having been covered from time to time by Lake Powell. Ruess was following a well-established western tradition of leaving a mark of some type on a stone surface to commemorate his presence.

"No man," and they dismissed his complaints. (In the Latin translation of the *Odyssey,* the Greek word becomes *nemo,* variously rendered as *no man, no one,* or *nobody.* Thus, *nemo* represents personal negation.) Odysseus and his men then escaped from the cave by clinging to the bellies of the giant's sheep. Everett was familiar with the story as far back as his school days in Indiana.

T. E. Lawrence, who was known to the world as Lawrence of Arabia, had led the Arabs in desert warfare against the Turks during World War I and had become the model in Everett's time of the lone, literate hero who adapted to local customs in the desert wilderness. He related his Arabian adventures in *The Seven Pillars of Wisdom,* which Everett had also read. Lawrence was versed in Greek, was familiar with warfare, as was Odysseus, could relate to the dangers of an extended journey, and had a lifelong interest in Homer's poem. His translation of the epic work was published in 1932 and fed Everett's ever-active imagination.[23] Lawrence died in a motorcycle accident two weeks before the civic clubs launched their search for Everett.

With a bow to the *Odyssey,* Jules Verne bestowed the name of Captain Nemo on the enigmatic commander of the submarine *Nautilus* in his novel *Twenty Thousand Leagues under the Sea,* a well-worn copy of which Everett possessed. The name reflects "his withdrawal from society: he is the romantic outcast, the 'nameless one,'" noted two authorities on the novel.[24] Nemo undertakes an underwater odyssey in the form of a self-imposed exile and wanders the depths of the world's seas experiencing the deaths of his crewmen, strange sights, and near disasters. For publishing purposes in nineteenth-century Europe, Verne created a character with an indeterminate background, a no man in other words, who would not offend any reader's nationalistic sensibilities. Nemo achieved underwater what he could not on land: complete freedom from governmental constraints and a personal independence that must have been appealing to Everett. A biographer of Verne's wrote: "The quest of the masterless man for a perfect freedom would fascinate Verne to the end of his creative life."* The novel ends with the narrator, a professor of natural science, stating that if Nemo's disappearance into a

---

*Peter Costello, *Jules Verne* (New York: Charles Scribner's Sons, 1978), 143–44. Characters named Nemo appear in countless other works of the imagination, including Charles Dickens's *Bleak House. Finding Nemo* was a popular animated 2003 Pixar film starring a fish searching for his son, Nemo, who is capable of taking care of himself.

maelstrom was strange, it was also sublime. He posed the question found in Ecclesiastes: "Who can fathom the abyss?"[25]

The searchers concluded Everett had not crossed the Colorado River. They returned to their ranches on June 9 for the hay harvest and to move their livestock to summer ranges. They promised further searches. Extreme summer temperatures soon descended on Davis Gulch.

———■———

Stella was beginning to believe in early June that Everett was dead, but Christopher thought he was living with the Navajo. "I vaguely suspect that he is playing a whimsical game with himself, of disappearing from civilization and being lost in a savage tribe, as Ulysses was." He added, "Very likely he has been thinking of himself as an Odysseus." The former Harvard Divinity School student and Unitarian minister compared Everett to Jesus, who cried on the cross, "It is finished." Living to eighty, Christopher said, would have added nothing to the life of Everett Ruess or Jesus Christ.[26]

On borrowed money and accrued vacation time, Stella and Christopher set off on June 21 on a two-week pilgrimage. They didn't expect to find Everett, since others had diligently searched for him, but they wanted to meet the people who had had contact with him, experience the landscapes he had passed through, and hopefully come to some determination of his fate. They removed the rumble seat from their two-seater Ford, which they had christened Waldetta in honor of their son in China, to add more storage space for two cots, bedding, camping equipment, and food. After the Ford overheated on the first day in the Mojave Desert, they lowered their speed on the flats to between 35 and 40 mph and reduced it further when ascending hills on Highway 66. At night they slept either in the open or in auto camps, paying a reduced rate of $1 for a cabin since they supplied their own bedding. They took no written note of Depression-era traffic heading west in 1935, perhaps because of their preoccupation with what was ahead of them. Grief must have been a third passenger in that little vehicle, but it showed up rarely in their written accounts of the journey.[27]

They crossed the rapidly filling Lake Mead on a ferry shortly before the road on top of Hoover Dam was opened to traffic and had the bolts on the car tightened in expectation of rough roads ahead at the Ford agency in Kingman, Arizona. At the Grand Canyon they visited the Desert View Watchtower built by the Fred Harvey Company in 1933. The five-story structure mimicked smaller Anasazi watchtowers. It offered the widest possible view of the canyon, and its ground floor resembled a Hopi kiva, with which

Everett was familiar. He had been a daily visitor to the watchtower the previous year and had been in the Antelope Clan kiva on Second Mesa.

Christopher and Stella's next stop was the Cameron Trading Post on the south bank of the Little Colorado River, where they talked with the trader, Hubert Richardson. He had written Christopher in late February that Everett had stopped at the trading post with two boys in a car loaded down with household goods and paid a small grocery bill in 1934. Everett had also picked up a registered letter forwarded from the Marble Canyon post office.[28] At Kayenta the Ruesses stopped to talk with John Wetherill and his wife Louisa, "good friends of Everett," Stella noted. Stella was impressed with the way Louisa casually flicked the cigarette she was smoking in a graceful arc into the fireplace. Wetherill said he had mapped out for Everett the cliff dwellings in and around Davis Gulch that were worth exploring. He thought the young man took chances that none of the archeologists he had worked with on numerous expeditions had taken and had probably died in a climbing accident. He discounted the theory that Everett was living among the Indians. Surely he would have heard a rumor within the past six months about such a thing.

On Wetherill's advice, the Ruesses turned off the paved road and headed north on a dirt track to the Navajo Mountain Trading Post to talk with Ray Dunn, who may have heard of a white man living with the Indians. Not knowing the backcountry method of deflating tires to deal with deep sand, the two city dwellers got stuck in a dry riverbed for five hours on a hot summer afternoon. Using their camping plates as shovels, a blanket as a wheelbarrow, and stray boards for traction, the middle-aged couple finally got turned around and headed back to Red Lake.

It was a remote land without the conveniences of a city. They ran out of gas and oil and could find no place with compressed air for their tires or grease for their wheels. Gas hit a high of 40¢ a gallon but was usually half that amount. The couple were "down almost to the primitive" in terms of automobile needs, but "our little Ford always carried us safely through." Water for bathing was a luxury. They rather romantically viewed Indians bathing naked at a trading post as "children of nature." They also encountered numerous Navajo begging or drunk at trading posts. The Ruesses photographed a small group of burros, noting the decline of the breed: "The noble burros of Sancho Panza and Everett Ruess doth pass away." And always there was The Question: "Stella was game for talking to all possible persons and asking whether they knew Everett. Many did, for he and his burros were distinct and since he has been lost everybody has read of it in the newspapers, and they have discussed it."

One day they got lost and encountered a Hopi Indian in a suit with a red sweatband around his head and four beaded necklaces around his neck. This strange figure was buying a sheep from a Navajo. He was Edmund Nequatewa, who worked as an ethnologist, translator, and folklorist for the Museum of Northern Arizona in Flagstaff.[29] He thought it unlikely that Everett was living with any Native Americans, and he was unfamiliar with any of the names Neal Johnson had given the Ruesses of Indians he had consulted. Nequatewa's guess was that Everett had been the victim of a white prospector who sought his possessions. After making inquiries, he repeated this theory in a subsequent letter to the Ruesses.

With an ailing fan belt, the Ruesses coasted down a long incline and slowly made their way across the Navajo Bridge to the Marble Canyon lodge and trading post operated by Buck and Florence Lowrey. Buck, born David Crockett Lowrey in Tennessee, was the county sheriff, and Florence was the postmistress who ran the Marble Canyon post office, to which Everett had directed his mail be sent. Florence had returned the mail, alerting the Ruesses—along with Mrs. Allen at Escalante—that their son was missing. It was a hectic time for the Lowreys and their children. Their gas station had just been robbed by three men who had also wounded the attendant. Buck was off with a posse of nearly forty men. This group captured the three bandits, one a hitchhiker and the other two escaped convicts from Wyoming.

After having a new fan belt installed at Marble Canyon, the Ruesses were off to Zion National Park and a visit with Ranger Jolley and his family. Zion is a sheltered place, away from the buffeting of desert heat and wind. Everett's presence surrounded them there: the photograph of Everett, Curly, and his "good adopted friends" on the mantel of the Jolley residence; Everett's watercolors on the walls; the places where he had camped and climbed and where Stella imagined her son had "declaimed some well-loved lines to the surrounding vermillion cliffs." She felt Everett's spirit more acutely in Zion than anywhere else. Stella and Christopher camped in the canyon, and she wept for most of the nighttime hours. "I felt so poignantly this haunting beauty that Everett loved, and the keen poison oak suffering that he had endured in this canyon." She climbed the short Weeping Rock Trail to the alcove where a seep of water emerged and composed a few lines of poetry. Then Stella said she didn't need to weep again.

Grief was put away, and the journey that was taking its emotional toll sped up. The next day they were at Bryce Canyon National Park, where they met an artist who had known Everett at the Otis Art Institute and a couple who were convinced he was somewhere on the Navajo reservation. The Ruesses visited the Cope family, whose thirteen-year-old son gave them a tour of the park and pointed out Navajo Mountain in the distance, which had "meant so much to Everett for its Indian mysteries." It was a chilly night at the nine-thousand-foot level, where they camped among the pine and Douglas fir trees.

The following day they drove eastward to Tropic, where they photographed the hall where the dance was held and the Copes' winter residence. Then they were on their way to Escalante, where H. Jennings Allen met them and invited them to spend the night in his home. They talked with the Mormon bishop and some of the searchers. There were no new revelations, just a chance to make the acquaintance of some of the people who had just been names to them and get a quick look at the village and surrounding canyonlands where Everett was last seen alive. The next day Allen drove them partway down the Hole-in-the-Rock Road. "We wished that we could fly," wrote Stella, who would return in thirteen years and descend into Davis Gulch for one last close encounter with her son.[30]

They said good-bye to the Allens and drove to Panguitch for a banquet with the civic clubs and interviews with a reporter from the *Deseret News* and the local newspaper. They were, for a short time, celebrities. Stella and Christopher headed home on July 1, pausing at a snug cabin in Cedar Breaks National Monument "to read and write and ponder our strange adventurings."

A few days after the Ruesses returned home, Christopher wrote the Wetherills a summation of their conclusions. He cited Everett's affinity with the Navajo, believing that his son had been accepted by them and spoke their language more fluently than most Navajo. His son's disappearance could be explained by "either Mr. Wetherill's theory that Everett took too great risks and lost his life trying to investigate some cliff dwellings near Davis Gulch, the lower Escalante, or else that Everett went Navajo, that he is now for a time an Indian among Indians, and hence not known as a white man among them would be."[31] The probation officer noted that there was "a strong urge in youth in the high teens" to disappear.[32]

Then reality intruded. The Ruesses were shocked to read that a charred body, thought to be Caucasian, had been found in Gallup, New Mexico. This news would be the first of many "discoveries" of the remains of Everett Ruess, a grim constant throughout the years. Christopher wrote the chief of the Gallup police on July 13, giving the details of Everett's disappearance and asking for more information. The body was so badly burned that only part of the skull, including the teeth, remained, the chief replied. An intensely hot fire had consumed the flesh and other bones. Stella asked the College of Dentistry at the University of Southern California to send her Everett's dental records. They were forwarded to Gallup.

Among other things, the records showed that in 1932 and 1933 two gold inlays and gold foil had been placed on teeth on the lower jaw. There was a missing molar on the right side of the upper jaw. On August 1, the chief wrote Stella that the estimated height of the body was five feet, eleven inches, approximately Everett's height, but there were no missing teeth nor any sign of melted inlays. He didn't believe the body was Everett's and returned the records.[33] The dental records would surface again as a decisive part of the puzzle surrounding the discovery of the bones in 2009.

———■———

As the summer waned, Christopher began to agree with Stella that Everett "has finished his course." He confided in his ministerial manner to his diary: "He lived and perhaps he has died for his God—Beauty. He dared much. He carried his life on his sleeve. He endured hardships as a good soldier of his Cross. He drank the cup of the joy of life to the bottom. He lived gloriously."[34]

There was one last search in August. It had all the trappings of the journalist Henry Stanley's setting out in search of a lost explorer by the name of David Livingstone in Africa, except the major characters in 1935 had different names, and the stand-in for Stanley, the journalist John U. Terrell, never had the opportunity to utter the salutation "Everett Ruess, I presume." Terrell practiced the "Front Page" school of Chicago journalism. In 1931, when Ben Hecht's play of the same name was made into a successful movie, Terrell was identified as one of the two star contributors to *Midweek* magazine seen dining frequently at Schlogl's, a German-American restaurant frequented by Chicago literati and newspapermen. By August 1935, he had moved to the *Salt Lake Tribune,* the non-Mormon alternative to the church-owned *Deseret News.**

———

*Terrell was a prolific writer who produced colorful prose. He was employed by the *San Francisco Chronicle* when he wrote an unattributed April 1941 story with problematic details about two convicts who were supposedly the first to successfully escape from Alcatraz and were now living in South America. The story displayed the writer's version of history rather than the reality of the event. Terrell, who had worked as a cowboy in his youth, went on to write more than forty

The *Tribune's* search was by automobile and horses. Shortly after it ended, the newspaper ran a series of four stories written by Terrell, the first beginning on page one in late August. All the stories were burdened with frequent references to the "Tribune expedition." Nothing new had been found, but the series contained a lot of background about Everett and his disappearance. Terrell concluded that he had not crossed the Colorado River and was killed by "a renegade bad man or Indian" in or near Davis Gulch. The reporter was aided in the search by Neal Johnson and a Navajo tracker named Dougeye. They had talked with every conceivable source of information in northern Arizona and ridden into Davis Gulch from the Navajo reservation. Terrell finished the series: "'But some day,' we said, 'pieces of his outfit will turn up. Then we would take the trail again.'"[35] That day never arrived for Terrell.

Christopher and Terrell corresponded as the series ended. Christopher offered to donate a small sum of money for a state-sanctioned search and asked Terrell if the *Tribune* was interested in publishing a book written by Stella that would serve as a memorial for Everett. He said they had found during the June trip that Everett had become "a sort of legend or romance" for many of the people who lived in southern Utah.[36] Prodded by the *Tribune,* Utah's attorney general made vague promises about a criminal investigation that never materialized, and the book proposal did not fit the newspaper's function.

The significance of the *Tribune's* effort was not what it uncovered but rather the fact that for the first time the story of Everett's disappearance was told consecutively in one serialized account. The series established the bedrock for the mystery that propelled Everett into the myth-laden ranks of the missing. That the writer Wallace Stegner was a young English instructor at the University of Utah at the time the series appeared was an added bonus, as he would draw additional attention to Ruess in seven years.

The first official notice that Everett was missing appeared in the September 4, 1935, "Daily Police Bulletin," a publication of the Los Angeles Police Department. The bulletin featured a "Missing Person (Long Standing)" announcement accompanied by a photograph of Everett by Dorothea Lange.

---

books, many about the history and Native Americans of the American West. In a book with the subtitle "Reminiscences of a Distinguished Western Historian," he wrote a fictional account, based on his 1935 search for Ruess, of a young Los Angeles artist named Roger Call who is murdered by a drunken Navajo. Terrell, *Bunkhouse Papers* (New York: Dial Press, 1971), 181–200.

EVERETT RUESS, 836 North Kingsley Drive, Los Angeles, Calif., left this city in April, 1934, last wrote parents from S.E. Utah, at Escalante, November 11, 1934. Last seen by sheepherder near Davis Gulch, where Escalante and Colorado River meet, November 19, 1934. Traveled with a pack burro, using kyaks with bright Indian decorations, and with saddle burro.

Description: Age 21, 5 ft. 10 in., 150–160 lbs., brown hair, hazel eyes, tall and thin, tanned skin, one tooth (upper right) missing; wears Stetson sombrero; walks long strides like Indian, speaks the Navajo Indian language; occupation artist and writer.

This boy does water colors; is interested in Indian caves, cliff dwellers, etc.; said to be very friendly with Indians and whites in these remote settlements.

In February, 1935, this boy's two burros, halter, etc., were found by a searching party, in vicinity of Escalante; these burros appeared to be in starved condition and positive identification of them was made by the Escalante citizens who knew Everett and the burros.

Also it is reported that Everett inscribed the word "Nemo" on several cliffs in the above vicinity, which may be a clue to tracing him, in that particular district.

Information for Capt. Allen, Missing Persons Detail, L.A. Police Dept.

The *Los Angeles Times* ran a brief story in mid-October stating that there "may" be another search and quoting Christopher.[37] No search occurred. By the end of the year, Christopher was divided in his thinking, writing a friend: "No further word of Everett after 7 searches. It may be he is wandering like old Ulysses, whom he loved. He did not wait, for years, but Sang his song early."[38] Christopher was informed in January that Utah governor Henry H. Blood, who had written the Ruesses a letter praising their patience in May, would not authorize state funds to be spent in a search because he would have to do the same in similar cases, such as that of a Standard Oil Company plane missing over the Great Salt Lake at the time. Also, winter had descended on the canyonlands, said the secretary of the civic clubs, and further searches were impossible.[39]

■

Everett's disappearance took an emotional toll on his family. A large outpouring of sympathy and suggestions from friends and strangers combined with sightings of Everett in distant places added to the burden of losing a son and a brother. From China, Waldo commiserated with his parents. Life must be a nightmare for them. If they couldn't aid the searchers for lack of money, what about asking a well-to-do relative for a loan? Waldo suggested making a book out of Everett's letters. He didn't see the need to return home because his brother might surface any day.[40]

The crisis bred introspection. Waldo wondered about his own tendencies toward wandering. Why did he keep driving himself farther and farther away from home, first to the California desert, then to Shanghai, and now to a new job in Hankow? He was depressed and felt like he was "gradually breaking down." They had lost one family member. "It begins to look to me as if you are practically losing me," Waldo told his father. There were similarities between Everett and him. "I am afraid that you have two 'strange' sons rather than just one." Waldo craved human affection and love but said he had had little of either in his life. "I wonder where these things were inherited from—what throwback it is?" At the age of twenty-six, Waldo supplied the answer to his question in a damning indictment of his parents' lack of demonstrable love.

> Even the love in our family has been rather impersonal. I think you and mother rather repressed outward affection towards Everett and me when we were young, except for occasional or more-or-less matter-of-fact kisses. That is the English way, I imagine. Consequently I think both of us have had rather strange ideas (exaggerated ideas, perhaps) of love and affection, the lack of them, etc. I don't mean to be condemning you. You are the way you are because of the way you were brought up in your early lives and neither of you knew anything about love or the ways of love when you first came to each other when you were married. Without love life doesn't seem to be worth much to me. You have a kind of love for me and want to do everything you can for me, but it is not enough; it in itself is not enough to draw me home.[41]

Christopher's response was an explanation under the duress of the loss of one son and the possible alienation of the other. He had been hurt by his son's criticisms. He reasoned, comforted, and lashed back in a very different type of dialogue from the one he had engaged in with Everett in December 1933.

They had been "chary" with their advice, he said, because they thought their sons would be too greatly influenced by them. Waldo was encouraged to live his own life, although Christopher thought it was foolish to believe "that any lad of twenty to twenty-five can do that" in a wise manner. They missed Waldo greatly, "the more so now that Everett is not here, whether he be living or not." Waldo had squandered the opportunity for a college education, his secretarial job was not very important, he had made a mistake living in a foreign country, and he was too dazzled by the rich and famous.

Christopher laid most of the blame on Stella.

> I was away from home too much, and both you and Everett too much
> modeled your notion of life from a woman's life, your Mother's. She
> has had an idyllic life, is still a girl in looks and joys, few women have so
> charmed a married life. She has always done just about as she pleased, has
> incarnated happiness. She did not have to suffer, to labor, to do what she
> did not like to do. You have got the silly notion that a man can live that
> way. Everett did too. He may have paid for it with his life.

Everett hung over them like a spectral presence, a beacon that illuminated
the discussion, and a shining example of how life should be ideally lived.

> The world is full of miserable people breaking their hearts to be what they
> are not—living lives of maladjustment, non-adjustment, false fronts, make
> believe. Everett beat us all in that—he was for what is real—he saw through
> the sham. If he lives, he will mature, I believe, and learn to like women,
> learn to tolerate civilization, but still realize that all this sham is sham.

Christopher had one final thought in that revealing letter. Perhaps his
youngest son was better off dead. "Everett may have really fulfilled his life
living it as he did (if he is dead)."[42]

Waldo repeated his suggestion that Everett's photographs, artwork, and
writings should be compiled into a book, stating that it was a task his mother
would enjoy. His parents began gathering material for publication that fall.

They dreamed of Everett. Christopher visualized him as a skeleton. To
Stella he appeared as a healthy young man in a sweater adorned with Indian
symbols who strode into the kitchen and announced, "Well, here I am."[43]

Their Christmas card that terrible year celebrated Everett. Stella's drawing of a burro's shoe was inspired by the real burro shoe Everett had sent
Bill Jacobs. The text was Everett's wilderness poem. Stella wrote on one
card: "Everett's disappearance is still a mystery, but we thought our friends
would like this sample of his writing. He wrote very happy letters and there
is no proof of his death."[44] Christopher now doubted that Everett was living
among the Indians. Of his brother's possible fate, Waldo said: "As many of
his poems and writings lead one to think might happen sometime, he has
undoubtedly driven himself beyond his physical endurance and died, beautifully and alone in the desert."[45]

XI

Healing
1936–2008

THE TREMENDOUS OUTPOURING OF SYMPATHY for Stella and Christopher was fed by newspaper accounts and radio reports, by word of mouth, telephone, and telegraph, and by the letters, remembrances, and Christmas cards mailed by Everett's parents to alert people and agencies to his disappearance. Their many communications were dispatched to seek information, to send an indirect message to Everett if he was still alive, and to make known the worth of their son. What resulted was a testimony to Everett himself, the esteem in which his parents were held, and the ongoing drama of the story. The responses reached the extremes of sightings of Everett in distant places and mystics employing various occult devices to find him.

One of the first individuals to reply to an alert was Maynard Dixon. "That is certainly distressing news," he wrote. "But wanderers like Everett have disappearing habits, and he may yet show up." "Mrs. D," meaning Dorothea Lange, was on a photo assignment for the government. Lange had had no recent letters from their son, her husband said. When she returned in a few days, she would send them portraits of Everett that could be used for identification purposes.[1]

Edward Weston sent a penny postcard with a few lines handwritten on the back: "Your remembrance reached me in Santa Fe. I don't forget Everett—it was kind of you to include me as one of his friends. The way of his going, I feel, is the way I would like to depart—close to the soil. But he was so young."[2]

The editor who read "little Everett's" submissions to the *American Indian* magazine during his Valparaiso years recalled that he "wrote himself into his every line. And it was not difficult for me to read, and understand him." That he had set out on such difficult adventures just a few years later was hard to imagine. "His high-hearted dreams seemed but a foundation for future building, instead of something that he was momentarily apparently expecting to test out—and in his own way. He has achieved—he has conquered—be sure of that."[3]

Lawrence Janssens, a friend who hadn't heard from Everett for a while, was worried and then relieved to hear from his parents that Everett might still be alive and living among the Indians. Lawrence had heard disturbing rumors. "The idea that he could be dead left a great gap in the circle of my friends." Everett had led a dangerous yet rewarding life, Janssens remarked. "Even though he has overreached himself in his adventuring, he has had more pure enjoyment out of his life than the average person. I know of no one else who obtained what he wanted out of life to such an extent as Everett did. If he is dead, at least he has lived, and lived fully."[4]

To those people he met on the trail, Everett was not easily forgotten, because of his distinctive appearance, enthusiasm, artistic talents, and intellectual curiosity. Alan Booth and Perc Warren of Plattsburg, New York, had been on a camping trip through the national parks in the summer of 1931 when they stopped at the Grand Canyon and camped with Everett for one night. The next day the three boys had explored the canyon. "I can remember how happy he seemed and interested that we should see as much as possible of the Grand Canyon," Booth recalled. He was sure that Everett had found much happiness in life.[5]

At the Warren Trading Post on the Navajo reservation, Harry Nurnburger recalled various discussions he had had with Everett. It was difficult to express his feelings in a letter. He just wanted the Ruesses to know that he was "glad" to have known Everett.[6] From Roosevelt, Arizona, Eleanor Reynolds, with whose family Everett had enjoyed many meals and evenings, wrote: "It had been so gratifying to meet a youngster whose ideals were big and beautiful and not cramped by civilization's stupid customs."[7] Fritz Loeffler, the Park Service ranger at Mesa Verde, was hopeful: "I can't help but think and certainly hope that he is alive somewhere because I know he was experienced in taking care of himself under trying conditions—Utah has much wild virgin country."[8] A Mill Valley, California, couple recalled meeting Everett in the backcountry of Sequoia National Park in the summer of 1933. "Your son was a very interesting lad and he loved many of the things I do in my prosaic way without his ability of expression," wrote the husband.[9] Ranger Lon Garrison remembered Everett and his feelings toward his parents. "He was very strongly an individual; seemed to care very little for the ordinary conventions, in fact was quite impatient with them; had a keen love of life and the outdoors. From the fact that he told me somewhat of the problems confronting you two, I judged that he felt a normal affection for his home, although being nineteen, he was rather critical of his parents' judgment."[10] Another ranger in Sequoia National Park, Bill Atwood, had given Everett information for his trip to Mount Whitney in 1933 and checked on him periodically. "In my memory Everett stands out among the crowd for his pleasant and friendly personality and his exceptional love and appreciation of the beauties of nature."[11]

The letters from relatives, friends, and acquaintances focused on giving his parents emotional support and remembering Everett. Stella's brother Emerson, the San Francisco landscape architect, recited the Unitarian mantra: "One thing you can be glad for is that you steadily encouraged Everett along the path he chose and that he was allowed freedom in the pursuit of his dreams, his ideals, work, and play. For his years he has had much expression."[12] Words were inadequate to express her sorrow, wrote a friend from Palisades Park, New Jersey, who thanked Stella for the Christmas cards she had sent over the years. "The memory of the happy days with you and your boys will always stay with me as a wonderful, precious friendship."[13] Anna Gast, the mother of Everett's Valparaiso friend Harold, hoped that Everett was safe with the Indians. "The Little Flower [Saint Therese] will return him back to you. I have great love and faith in her. I'm going to make a novena in her honor for Everett's safe return."[14]

Consolation came in many different forms. "Is it not possible that his desert life may have affected his mind so that he would temporarily lose his memory?" wrote a friend. "It would be a sad sad loss not only to you but to the world to have his clear young voice stilled at this time."[15] From Santa Barbara came a letter from a woman who was about to be discharged from a hospital after her fourth operation. She wrote on her back with a magazine held on her knee for support: "Keep up your hope and faith. God will not fail you."[16] A Pasadena woman wrote that a friend's daughter had disappeared for a time and had returned without experiencing any of the dreadful things one would expect under such circumstances. A close friend told Stella that Everett was "unequivocally" safe and that he possessed "a fullness of unique sensitiveness to existence not given to many."[17] Whatever the outcome, said another good friend, "he saw beauty as we in the valley never have."[18] Day after day more messages arrived. "What a soul—what a power to expose his lofty thoughts that boy had! There seems a prophecy of fate in his wistful word-pictures," said a friend.[19]

More prosaically worded letters were addressed to Stella from the National League of American Pen Women, the Order of Bookfellows, and the Western Women's Clubs. For Christopher there was correspondence from a referee at the Los Angeles Juvenile Court, the director of the State Bureau of Juvenile Research, and a probation department colleague in San Francisco, who urged him to save "face time" with him and his wife at the next conference.

Then there were the people who had sighted Everett or had mystical insights. In most cases the Ruesses responded, demonstrating their desperation. These people mostly parroted what had already been printed or some variation of it. The ever-unreliable Neal Johnson had been in Phoenix and seen a young man who looked like Everett. The would-be Everett had told Johnson to wait and said he would be back in a few minutes, but he never returned. Christopher didn't put much stock in this story, stating that Johnson "dreams when he is awake." But he couldn't dismiss it entirely, because he wished it were true.[20] Stella and Christopher drove to Prescott, Arizona, to meet a gold miner whose teeth were "a couple of snags" but who wrote poetry and painted. He had lived among the Indians. Tony, as he was known, was not Everett.[21] By far the most tantalizing sighting was by Burton Bowen, with whom Christopher corresponded from 1939 to 1953. In May 1935 an Everett look-alike registered in a federal transient camp for the homeless in Florida as Evertt Rulan, according to Bowen, who said he had befriended the man.[22] Bowen didn't realize until September 1938, when he read an article in *Desert Magazine,* who Everett was and that he had been missing. Bowen passed on bits of information to the Ruesses that were supposedly known only to him about their son. For instance, this Everett said he had hitchhiked from Arizona with his dog Curly. "Everett" and "Curly" were inseparable at Disston Lodge in Bunnell, Flager County, Bowen said. The man, who seemed about twenty-three, dressed in the same rough clothes as Everett and carried a four-by-six-inch sketchbook in which were inserted two photographs of Everett and his burros. This Everett remained in the camp for one week and then disappeared. The information intrigued Christopher enough that he alerted the insurance company that was paying a small annuity on a life insurance policy in Everett's name to investigate. Christopher said he would return the money if Bowen's story proved true. The insurance company did not think Bowen had enough information to identify the man as Everett. The correspondence between the two men continued when Bowen moved to Veterans Administration hospitals in Bath, New York, and West Los Angeles. At times he sounded just barely plausible.

Christopher tended to handle the sightings; Stella dealt with the mystics. Some information they received fell between these two categories. A handwriting analysis by a San Diego woman with the title of *doctor* before her name revealed that a May 1934 letter indicated Everett may have suffered an accident, committed suicide, or simply disappeared. He was torn by conflicting urges, tendencies, and desires, the analyst said. Depression followed his elation. By holding an envelope containing one of Everett's letters, a psychic found a love motif involving a dark, young woman—perhaps an Indian. He had not died and would be found soon. A horoscope cast in Berkeley revealed death by drowning. Such a death was written in the stars at the time of his birth and was inevitable, the astrologer said. Everett's parents were assured he had not suffered. A Salt Lake City mailman, to whom the Ruesses donated $2 for his efforts, devised Everett's Cycle-Graph. This type of numerically determined graph, developed by H. Spencer Lewis of the Rosicrucian Order, uses a concept similar to biorhythms. The circles and swirls serve as a guide for charting life activities in accordance with "vibratory conditions" emanating from a birth date. The years 1929 to 1936 were a negative phase for Everett. Things picked up after then.

Caradonna Bittel made the most consistent effort to provide a spiritual solution. Ten years after his disappearance she was convinced Everett was still alive and would return one day. Bittel said that the susceptible youth had come under the influence of the Mormons and had been sent on some type of extended mission. She had known Everett through her daughter, who had also attended the Otis Art Institute and Hollywood High School. Her daughter's friends would gather in their home and have serious discussions. Everett was "as curious as a cat," she said, and was always asking questions about "Infinity and God's ways."[23] Everett had twice visited her and her daughter in their Los Angeles home two years after his disappearance. There was no way they could have been mistaken about his identity. He had acted differently and talked about returning to Mexico.[24]

Bittel chided him: "Everett Ruess!"

He replied, "Is that who I am?"

He did not recall prior visits to their home. Bittel thought he had stumbled on some Mormon secret and been hit on the head and made to disappear, a tactic she called "imposed amnesia." He was living on a mountain near Mexico City whose name began with a T, but she could not remember its entire name. She didn't know his fate, other than that "he was on some hidden secret occult path that he was mighty careful not to expose."[25]

The Ruesses wanted to spread Everett's words and art to as wide an audience as possible. They established a poetry prize in his honor and sought to have a book published.

After an investigation that involved contacting four principals in the search for Everett, the Mutual Life Insurance Company of New York and the Ruesses agreed to settle a $1,000 policy on Everett with a $56.40 annual annuity to his parents for as long as they lived.[26] When sufficient funds accumulated, writing and artistic prizes would be awarded to children. If Everett was alive, his parents would surrender all the payments.[27]

At first the idea was to offer the prizes to schoolchildren in Utah, but when that proved to be impractical, the geographical boundaries were narrowed to Los Angeles High School and the genre was limited to poetry. The first awards were given out in June 1938. Approximately thirty people signed the guest book at the ceremony, including Everett's former creative writing teacher, Snow Longley Housh. The next June another batch of awards was conferred, sixteen cash prizes and honorable mentions. Housh published the winners in student verse anthologies covering those school years.

Getting a book published, as Waldo had suggested, was far more difficult than endowing a poetry prize. Stella took the lead and began working on the project in March 1936. Its initial title was *The Wilderness Journal*. To both parents the totality of Everett's output was deeper and richer than they had originally suspected. The handwritten material was edited, copied by hand by Stella, rough-typed by Christopher, and typed in final manuscript form by a professional typist. They changed the title to *Youth Is for Adventure*. The 277-page manuscript was divided into five parts and lacked coherence.

They sent the manuscript to a New York literary agent, who circulated it to East Coast publishers in 1937. A Houghton Mifflin editor thought "the writings are too random and monotonous."* A Los Angeles acquaintance, the writer Hamlin Garland, could see why the manuscript interested the

---

*Margaret A. Jackson to Miss F. M. Holly, June 14, 1937. The literary firm was F. M. Holly, at 156 Park Avenue, which also offered translation and typing services. Flora Holly had the distinction two years after opening her agency in 1905 of turning down a manuscript of short stories submitted by Gertrude Stein. She did not think they would sell a sufficient number of copies. Holly charged the Ruesses $10 to read and evaluate their manuscript. She thought it had an excellent chance of selling, but that proved not to be the case with East Coast publishers.

Ruesses, but it didn't interest him. More had to be written about Everett's disappearance, he said, and his writings needed to be edited further so "they were more easily understood by the reader."[28] The agent returned the manuscript.

In early 1938 the Ruesses sent out another round of letters asking if the recipients had seen Everett, with the notation at the top: "Confidential: not for publicity or publication." On the assumption that Everett was still alive and living under an assumed name, they urged a quiet approach so as not to force him deeper into obscurity. "We are not at all interested in urging him to come home," they wrote. "We are not interested in telling the world he is found. We feel that he has a right to live his own life in his own way to his own ends."[29] But have him write his parents, they urged, because he appears in their dreams and words every day. The publisher of the *San Juan Record* in Monticello, Utah, replied: "But let us think that wherever he is—in the seen or unseen realms—that when the time is right he will reveal himself."[30]

There were times when Everett was not a constant presence in their lives. Stella gave a tea party for the Camp Fire Girls in her garden. The women wore long white gowns, and the chairs were arranged in a circle. The garden had an Oriental motif, with a teahouse and a fish pond. Tall shoots of bamboo, carefully tended beds of shrubs and flowers, and neatly edged paths gave a sense of ordered peace within the teeming city. The verse by the English poet Thomas Edward Brown on the card announcing the tea established the tone for the setting. It began, "A garden is a lovesome thing." Another year Stella hosted eighteen garden parties, one of which was a full-moon festival held in her Shangri-La garden. It featured poetry readings, healings, and impersonations of Lincoln and Washington. The guest speaker was the editor of the New Age Press, and an Oriental dancer performed under lights that made the garden look like a fairyland.

———— ■ ————

Other than John Terrell's series of articles in the *Salt Lake Tribune,* there had been only minor snippets of coverage in newspapers about Everett's disappearance. Randall Henderson, a magazine publisher, loved the desert and actively promoted its charms while managing to avoid its darker aspects. He was the first in "the band of mythologizers who keep Ruess's memory alive."[31]

While attending the University of Southern California, Henderson began his journalism career as a cub reporter at the *Los Angeles Times.* He followed the advice of the sports editor, who envied the freedom of owning a country newspaper. Henderson then worked on newspapers in rural Arizona and the southern California desert, where he conceived the idea for *Desert Magazine*. The magazine began life in November 1937 in El Centro, California, with six hundred subscribers and grew to thirty thousand readers under Henderson. He romanticized the desert, abandoning objective coverage for what he called "interpretive reporting." Henderson found a kindred, romantic spirit and a way to increase circulation in the story of Everett Ruess.

He was unaware of Ruess until Hugh Lacy began submitting articles about him and sending his letters to the magazine in 1938. Lacy had held a variety of jobs, including professional boxer, before taking up writing and becoming a senior editor for the Works Progress Administration in Los Angeles. He was a friend of the Ruess family, which sought the publication of Everett's work in the magazine in order to reach out to him, if he was still alive, and to encourage the artistic talents of other youths. The family gave the letters to Lacy, who approached Henderson. To Henderson, the material was fascinating, and it eventually increased his circulation threefold. Stella and Christopher had found their ideal writer and publisher at last. The readers of the magazine also loved the desert and its odd denizens.

Everett was introduced to readers in the September 1938 issue in an article by Lacy titled "Say That I Kept My Dream." Lacy wrote, "He was one of the earth's oddlings—one of the wandering few who deny restraint and scorn inhibition." The last sentence concluded, "He kept his dream."[32] Given the time—the Depression edging into World War II—the description of a free spirit caught readers' attention.

The magazine's rollout of the Everett saga continued through every monthly issue in 1939. Henderson ran letters from Ruess to his friends and family and short selections from his diaries. The youth's prints and photographs accompanied some selections. Henderson also published letters to his magazine in response to this material. One reader sent a poem that ended: "Some call him fool—I think he knew / His trail led to some rendezvous." Henderson was pleased with the series. It had received "much favorable comment," and readers continued to order the initial September issue.[33] The climax to the yearlong drumbeat was a second story by Lacy, "What Became of Everett Ruess?" It ran in the December 1939 issue. Lacy held out hope to readers that Everett might still be alive. He cited reports of supposed sightings of Everett in such diverse places as Monterrey, Mexico, and Moab, Utah. Everett's disappearance remained a riddle "as unreadable as the wilderness that swallowed him."[34]

Midway through 1939, Christopher suggested a book, and Henderson was immediately receptive to the idea. "Of course, such a book must be a work of art, and I assure you that if I find it practicable to go ahead, it will be attractive in format—something we will all be proud to have," he promised.[35] The material published in the magazine and additional words and illustrations were compiled and appeared in book form in October 1940 as *On Desert Trails with Everett Ruess*.[36] A cheaper, slightly smaller edition was published in 1950. In this manner the astonishing afterlife of Everett Ruess, which would extend through 2009 and beyond, was launched.

The Ruesses were flooded with responses to the book. Christopher compiled the contents of nearly one hundred letters on thirty-two single-spaced, tightly packed typewritten pages. Nearly all were effusive in their praise. "His was the pantheistic impulse of a youth thirsting for poetry and beauty, joy and emotion," wrote one Hollywood correspondent.[37] Waldo, who by this time was working in the American embassy in Chungking, China, gave a copy of the book to Nelson Trusler Johnson. The ambassador, who was laboring under wartime conditions in the provisional Chinese capital, still had the time to read it. Ambassador Johnson said he was particularly struck by the series of questions Everett asked his father in the fall of 1933 and the answers that Christopher had furnished. He regretted he had not asked his father similar questions.[38] A psychologist who taught at UCLA wondered if Everett had placed himself in a position where his only choice was either death or disappearance: "But I would say that perhaps he saw his own critical situation—of coming to terms with reality or going under—and he felt unequal to the task. And so his death—if so it was, or his disappearance into an Indian community—was his way of 'going out' while still unthreatened."[39]

———■———

The Ruesses had been fortunate to find a committed publisher like Henderson. They were even luckier to obtain an early evaluation of their son's life and work from Wallace Stegner, which had a multiplying effect. Stegner would become the premier chronicler of the American West in the twentieth century, and his novels and nonfiction works would reach national audiences. *Mormon Country* was Stegner's first nonfiction book, and he wrote it quickly. It followed on the heels of the four novels he produced between 1937 and 1941. Educated through high school and his undergraduate years in Salt Lake City and working as an English instructor at the University of Utah from 1934 to 1937, Stegner was familiar with who Ruess was. Homesick for Salt Lake, he made a quick trip back to Utah from Harvard University in the summer of 1941 to gather material for the book. *Mormon Country* avoided the self-congratulatory tones of the Mormons and the jeremiads of outside writers. The book was published in 1942 and survives in print as a paperback to this day.

The chapter "Artist in Residence" includes a nine-page description of Everett's last journey and disappearance, the searches for him, and conjectures about what might have happened. Stegner concludes: "It is just possible that the loss of identity is the price of immortality. Because Everett Ruess is immortal, as all romantic and adventurous dreams are immortal. He is, and will be for a long time, Artist in Residence in the San Juan country."[40]

Stegner found Everett lacking in some respects. He was "not a good writer" and only "a mediocre painter," but "he was learning." He described Everett as making his way through the Southwest "chanting his barbarous adolescent yawp into the teeth of the world." On balance, however, Stegner admired the fact that Ruess was a seeker.

> There are also the spiritual and artistic athletes who die young. Everett Ruess was one of those, a callow romantic, an adolescent esthete, an atavistic wanderer of the wastelands, but one of the few who died—if he died— with the dream intact.
>
> What Everett Ruess was after was beauty, and he conceived beauty in pretty romantic terms. We might be inclined to laugh at the extravagance of his beauty-worship if there were not something almost magnificent in his single-minded dedication to it. Esthetics as a parlor affectation is ludicrous and sometimes a little obscene; as a way of life it sometimes attains dignity. If we laugh at Everett Ruess we shall have to laugh at John Muir, because there was little difference between them except age. . . .
>
> The peculiar thing about Everett Ruess was that he went out and did the things he dreamed about, not simply for a two-weeks' vacation in the civilized and trimmed wonderlands, but for months and years in the very midst of wonder.[41]

Waldo Ruess sent Stegner a copy of *On Desert Trails* in 1981 after the two met briefly at a function at the University of California, Santa Barbara. Stegner said he had had very little to work with at the time he wrote *Mormon Country* other than Terrell's newspaper stories and Everett's biographic information and quotations culled from various press accounts. He was pleased "to have my recollection of the romantic, tragic Everett Ruess story revived." With the dual perspectives of passing years and *On Desert Trails,* which he called "a classic of its kind," Stegner commented to Waldo on the book and the life:

It is the original lone nature-lover's journal, the original adventure of a sensitive young man into country then known only to a few Indians and a few Mormons in the oasis towns. He made the most of his opportunities. The images that his writings are full of come from an early and uncluttered time. The adventures he went out on were really adventures, not tourist trips. He saw the country close-up and by his own efforts.*

Stegner was a catalyst. He had taught Edward Abbey in the creative writing program at Stanford University and had frequent contact with the writer N. Scott Momaday at Stanford. When Abbey recorded his impressions about working as a seasonal ranger in Arches National Monument in southern Utah, he dwelt on the strangeness of the desert in the chapter "Episodes and Visions" in his classic *Desert Solitaire*.[42] The desert was all-pervasive and intangible. It lured people into "futile but fascinating" quests for "the great, unimaginable" treasures it seemed to promise. He could understand why Ruess "kept going deeper and deeper into the canyon country, until one day he lost the thread of the labyrinth": he was searching for a treasure that "has no name and has never been seen."[43] Abbey portrayed the life-and-death qualities of the desert in another work. "In the desert one comes in direct confrontation with the bones of existence, the bare incomprehensible absolute *is-ness* of being. Like a temporary rebirth of childhood, when all was new and wonderful."[44] Abbey wrote Waldo Ruess that his brother was "the kind of active romantic which many of us would have wanted to be in our youth."[45]

Principally a poet at Stanford, N. Scott Momaday sought Stegner's advice on fiction writing. His novel *House Made of Dawn* won a Pulitzer Prize. He was one of the few westerners who bridged the poetic and fictional subcultures of the literary, academic, and American Indian worlds of the West.

---

*Wallace Stegner to Waldo Ruess, July 30, 1981. As was his habit in later years, Waldo then flooded his correspondent with a series of long letters sprinkled with many an *entre-nous* and including his own lengthy biographic information. Waldo didn't like the New Mexico author John Nichols's introduction to the 1983 Gibbs Smith book *Everett Ruess: A Vagabond for Beauty* and asked Stegner to reconsider declining the publisher's initial request that he write the introduction. Stegner had refused because he was writing a novel at the time. Waldo objected to Nichols's description of Everett as an "oddling." The editor thought Nichols's modern voice was needed to balance the book's sentimentality. Waldo Ruess to Wallace Stegner, April 28, 1983.

The Native American author was mainly attuned to Everett's mythic status. "From the time of the Greeks, at least, we have been baffled and disturbed and fascinated by the passing of young men," Momaday wrote. "Everett Ruess took up the dark trail and followed it steadily in the direction of myth. And his achievement is the achievement of myth." Momaday found it intriguing that by dropping hints of death and disappearance into his letters, like crumbs of bread along a path, Ruess had contributed to the making of his own legend. The author dealt with myths and oral traditions in his works and could recognize another mythmaker.

In Everett, Momaday also perceived a budding talent, someone who was wrestling with the sublime (*ineffable* was Momaday's word) but hadn't quite arrived there yet. "The descriptive elements in his writing are often strong and lyrical. The composition of the block prints is generally impressive, and the stark features in the landscape—monoliths and trees, especially—are rendered with a fine dramatic force." What was most important, however, was the fact that Everett had disappeared—not partially, but totally—which enabled the mythmaking process to begin.

To Momaday, Everett was intensely alive, supremely alone, and sensitive to beauty. A cross between a mountain man and an Eagle Scout, he fit the stereotype of the physically capable, artistically talented, lone young man cut down by his own obsessions and blind fate before his promise was fully realized. In death he melts into the landscape, becomes one with it, and achieves a communion with the wilderness that could never have been accomplished had he lived. His story is picked up, magnified, and passed from hand to hand and mouth to mouth, gaining a certain mystique in the process. Others are inspired at home, or to push their bodies to extremes in desert wildernesses and scribble *Nemo* on rocks in an attempt to become one with the myth.[46]

━━━■━━━

As the myth of Everett Ruess spread, Stella descended into Davis Gulch. It was a journey of farewell, for there were no more searches scheduled or discoveries to be made. Her guide was Harry Aleson. He had been gassed in World War I, was adrift between the two world wars, and didn't really catch hold until he began rowing and hiking through the canyon country in the 1940s. He then began guiding paying guests on trips and conducting his own off-season explorations of Glen Canyon and the Escalante River drainage. Since 1938, when he had read Lacy's first story in *Desert Magazine*, he had pondered Everett's disappearance. Aleson was highly idiosyncratic—a desert character, in other words. He didn't pay income taxes and fed his guests gourmet meals while restricting himself to baby food because of his war wounds.

In August 1946 he descended the steps notched in the sandstone and used by Everett and others to enter Davis Gulch, walked downstream, and spotted the ruin on whose doorstep Ruess had scratched *NEMO 1934*. Like others, he was caught by the saga and felt sympathy for Ruess's parents. He was also adept at creating publicity for his trips, and one way to get space in newspapers would be to invite Stella and Christopher Ruess on a special expedition that would include a side excursion into Davis Gulch. Because of his work, Christopher couldn't make the trip in April 1948, but Stella could.[47] She and a friend drove from Los Angeles to Richfield, Utah. Aleson met them there with another man, then drove the party of four to Escalante. Stella spent the night with Mildred and H. Jennings Allen, and the group headed south in the early-morning hours on the Hole-in-the-Rock Road.

They spent the night in the Bailey cabin at the fifty-mile mark. Aleson cooked a tasty dinner of pork and pineapple. Stella chose to sleep outside in her sleeping bag atop an air mattress. She was besieged by mosquitoes, but the Big Dipper was extremely clear in the desert sky. The sixty-eight-year-old woman and her three companions began hiking at 8 A.M. over the red rock that rose and fell in gentle swells along the ridge separating Fiftymile Creek and Davis Gulch. She noted the bushes, grasses, and wildflowers and the Henry Mountains, Navajo Mountain, and the Kaiparowits Plateau, all familiar landmarks to her younger son.

The party descended to Davis Gulch on the stock trail and ate sandwiches and drank juice from cans in the shade of willows and box elders. They struggled down canyon through the thick undergrowth to a point opposite LaGorce Arch where there was a sharp bend in the creek and a large overhang. Indian pictographs and the signatures of Aleson and some members of the first search party were inscribed on the wall. Stella and her friend added their names.[48]

They slogged "like elephants in the jungle" through the thick tangle of vegetation, wading across the creek numerous times in the wool socks and high gym shoes with thick soles that Aleson had provided as footwear. They avoided the quicksand. Finally, they spotted a ruin on a ledge—the Moqui House, in the terminology of the time. Aleson tested the toeholds and determined that Stella could make the ascent. He followed, instructing her where to put her feet. She braced her hands against the walls on either side of the primitive ladder and climbed, finally reaching the fifteen-foot-wide shelf. Stella said, "I felt pretty shaky because I thought it would be much harder getting down." There were dim pictographs on the wall. The one room with no roof and four-foot-high walls was the size of a small bathroom. Two steps led up to the entrance. On one of them *NEMO 1934* was scratched.

This ancient ruin was as close as Stella could get to her dead son. "Mrs. Ruess sat in near-silence, while the two talked in hushed voices for nearly an hour," Aleson wrote of Stella and himself in his third-person account for the newspaper. To the guide, Stella was "the bravest of courageous women." She helped herself to two shards of pottery as they left and made it down with no problems.

The day had been long and the four were exhausted, so they camped where they had eaten lunch. Each had a sandwich and an orange for dinner. Aleson loaned Stella his sleeping bag, and she loaned him her sweatshirt. He made a fire that burned all night. They all sat around the small source of warmth until 11:30 P.M. talking about Everett. Aleson "discredits every theory except that Everett fell from a cliff," Stella noted.

In the morning they had a half-sandwich and another orange apiece before beginning the climb out of the gulch and the hike along the ridge. Aleson estimated their round-trip distance as eighteen miles. They drank water from pools in the rocks. Stella was exhausted. Mrs. Allen's bathtub and rubbing alcohol felt very good that night.

Stella spent the next day visiting Escalante residents who had met Everett or searched for him. Escalante seemed a drab town to her. The saddle on her borrowed horse slipped, and she was thrown to the ground. She felt dizzy. Aleson gave her some ammonia to smell. Stella spent another night at the Allens' and then departed on the mail truck for Richfield the next day. The following day she was driven to Fruita, where she had lunch with Dr. Arthur L. Inglesby in his log cabin. Inglesby had searched Davis Gulch in 1937 and found *Nemo* scratched in four or five places. His theory was that Everett had been marooned on a ledge and starved to death.

———————— ■ ————————

In 1952 the *Los Angeles Times* published a long story that began: "Mystery haunts the name of Everett Ruess." At the end of the article his parents were said to believe their son had drowned while attempting to swim the Colorado River or might still be alive and "trying to 'reach the end of the horizon.'"[49] The story contained no new information. Its most striking feature is the photograph of Stella and Christopher Ruess taken in the family home at 531 N. Ardmore Avenue.[50] Christopher is sitting in a chair and holding one of Everett's paintings in his hand, tilted just enough so the spires of the can-yonland buttes are visible. Stella is perched on the arm of the chair, with her right arm around Christopher's shoulder. They are both gazing to the left of the photographer, probably where the reporter was stationed to serve as their visual target. Both are seventy-three, according to the story. They seemed to have reached an accord with each other. I would describe them as dignified, handsome, and burdened with great sorrow.

Christopher Ruess devoted the remainder of his life to good works. At the age of seventy, Ruess, as he put it, had retired not *from* the county probation department in 1949, but rather *to* three worthwhile causes: the Los Angeles County Committee on the Aging; the American Institute of Family Relations, which he served as director of Maturity and Later Years; and the First Unitarian Church, for which he did various chores. His social security and county retirement pensions allowed Stella and Christopher to live a genteel life.[51] He died in 1954. In order to make out her will, in 1959 Stella began the process of proving Everett was dead and had left no issue. A certificate of death was granted in 1961. Stella died in 1964. The bulk of her small estate went to Waldo, who, along with his wife and children, was living in the family home on Ardmore Avenue.

Waldo would live to the age of ninety-eight, dying in 2007 and bequeathing his huge collection of Ruess materials to the University of Utah library. He too was a wanderer, but had lived a different type of life.

The older brother returned to the United States in 1946 under clouded circumstances and national headlines after working as a clerk for the State Department in embassies in China, Japan, northern Africa, and the Soviet Union. Thirty-five years old and unmarried, Waldo had escorted an actress from the Moscow State Theater to her home after a party in May 1946. He attempted to kiss her, and she screamed and jumped from the car, attracting the attention of the police. Ruess was allowed to return to his hotel. A few weeks later a Russian naval lieutenant was arrested for spying by FBI agents in Portland, Oregon. Waldo was then charged with "hooliganism." He claimed diplomatic immunity and moved into the American embassy, but the Russian authorities would not issue him an exit visa. After a monthlong standoff, the alleged spy was released and Ruess was allowed to return to the United States, but his career with the State Department was over.[52]

Back in the United States, Ruess traveled widely and held various jobs. He married a Spanish woman, Conchita, in 1957. After Stella died, Waldo and his family moved to Santa Barbara because the Los Angeles smog bothered Conchita. The couple had four children: Everett's two nieces and two nephews. Waldo became fixated on his brother's life and fate. He began thinking about a trip to southern Utah in 1960, believing that the Cottonwood Gulch area had not been thoroughly searched. He asked Randall Henderson if he knew a guide by the name of Ken Sleight.

Sleight operated Wonderland Expeditions out of Escalante in 1964. Like his mentor Harry Aleson, he was his own person, carving out an environmental niche for himself in a region known for its inhabitants' development instincts. He was a friend of Ed Abbey, who incorporated some of his characteristics into the lapsed-Mormon renegade Seldom Seen Smith in the novel *The Monkey Wrench Gang*. Sleight regarded the canyon country as Everett had: "It's God's creation and you feel that sense of beauty for beauty's sake."[53]

Waldo and Sleight began to correspond in 1963. Sleight had thought a lot about Everett's fate. He had been in Davis Gulch and the surrounding area numerous times. "I have sat around the campfire telling the story of Everett," he said.[54] Would Waldo like to take a trip with him sometime? He usually spent either half a day or a whole day in Davis Gulch.

Waldo joined a Sleight expedition from May 10 to 16, 1964. They had "deep discussions" about Everett's disappearance during those days. Waldo thought rustlers had killed his brother. Sleight believed Everett had drowned while crossing the Colorado River at Hole-in-the-Rock while on his way to the reservation with Navajo Indians.[55] They discussed placing a memorial plaque on the wall of LaGorce Arch and beginning a campaign to rename it Ruess Arch.[56]

In the 1960s Sleight came across a *NEMO* in red paint next to an Anasazi ruin in lower Grand Gulch, forty miles east of Davis Gulch. Since then, time has worn the paint away to the point that it is almost indistinguishable. Sleight theorizes that this was one of a number of copycat *Nemo*s scattered throughout the Southwest.[57] This questionable *NEMO* was used as a collaborating clue in the supposed discovery of Ruess's bones in 2009.

Waldo returned to Escalante in May 1985, where a ceremony attended by some twenty people marked the unveiling of a plaque honoring Everett on Dance Hall Rock.[58] He, Pat Jenks, who had given Everett a ride in his truck in 1931, and the editor W. L. Rusho gave talks that night around a campfire. It was a moving experience for Waldo, who, as one of his children said at his memorial service in 2007, "was left in the shadows behind his brother's accomplishments and his parents' grief over losing a second child."*

---

*Michele Ruess, "Waldo Ruess," memorial service eulogy, September 15, 2007. There was a note of bitterness directed at Everett in this eulogy: "Everett was exploring the California coastline and Utah and Arizona during the Depression years. My grandfather lost his job during the Depression and my father was the one

As the years unfolded, a number of false alarms emanated from the vast, convoluted canyonlands of northern Arizona and southern Utah that produced an unusual number of rumors. They concerned old bones suspected of belonging to Everett Ruess and others. The Navajo trader Gladwell Richardson said people simply vanished on the reservation. By 1941, Ruess's disappearance was nearly forgotten when suspicion fell on two Navajo, Jack Crank and John Chief, who admitted killing an elderly white man in Monument Valley. The Office of Indian Affairs on the reservation said there were rumors about the involvement of Crank in the death of a young man around the time that Ruess disappeared, rumors that proved not to be true.[59]

An elderly Piute woman came into Richardson's Inscription House Trading Post in 1941 and told a story of some Piute who had seen bleached bones and tattered clothing on a sandbar in the canyon of the San Juan River. Ruess was Richardson's first thought, and he offered a reward for the artifacts. Months passed, and then in 1942 a Piute named Toby Owl brought in several metal buttons, a rusted belt buckle, and a rusted long-barreled Colt .44-caliber revolver. All the artifacts came from the late nineteenth century.[60] Richardson dropped the matter until after World War II, writing an interested party in 1947: "In our opinion Ruess was murdered. Could have been by either whites or Indians. I know of more than a score of such cases occurring during the last 25 years."[61]

On a Colorado River trip in 1950, Harry Aleson stopped at a canyon on the right bank fifteen air miles from Davis Gulch to see where a human femur had been found ten years previously near a dry waterfall by Norman Nevills, another river guide. Nevills had taken the bone to his Mexican Hat, Utah, home, where it had remained for a few years. It was then transported to Missouri by Hugh Cutler, a botanist whose plant collecting centered in the Southwest. "Could this have been from a white man of 21?" Aleson asked Stella Ruess in 1950. He said he would check it out, but nothing came of it.[62]

Six years later Aleson contacted Stella about a skeleton found on the Colorado River below Hite, Utah. The skeleton was sitting in an upright position with its back against the canyon wall. Its head was missing. A loaded rifle lay across its lap. Aleson had volunteered to go to the site with the sheriff

---

supporting Everett and his parents by working day and night jobs. I think it is safe to say that Everett's art and poetry and essays would be of much smaller quantity if he had not had such a supportive brother."

to make sure it was not Everett. Seven days later he wrote Stella that the skeleton was not Everett's, and he apologized for prematurely writing the original letter containing the gruesome details.[63]

After the deaths of Christopher and Stella, Waldo became the repository of dashed hopes. Stan Jones was passionate about Lake Powell, calling himself the "original, systematic Lake Powell explorer." He wrote guidebooks covering the region and produced maps for boaters. Jones read everything available about Everett. He wrote Waldo in 1975: "I have reason to believe that the remains of your brother have been found." He first wanted to confirm the discovery and then "break the story; not only will it serve to ease the pain your family has suffered as a result of the inconclusive end to your brother's life and life story, but the subject will be news, too."[64] To prepare to write the story, Jones asked Ruess to send him clippings, photos, and letters as soon as possible. The material they contained would serve as background. He offered to furnish references. But the skeletons, one in Davis Gulch and the other nearby, turned out to be Native Americans in shallow graves.

Waldo became curious in 1985 about a skeleton found in a boat in Emery Kolb's garage at the Grand Canyon after the photographer and river runner died in 1976. The skeleton was that of a male, 19 or 20 years old, approximately six feet tall and well muscled. Norm Tessman of the Sharlot Hall Museum in Prescott, Arizona, said it predated Everett and did not fit the description of Glen Hyde, who had disappeared with his wife, Bessie, while on a honeymoon river trip through the Grand Canyon in 1928. Tessman said, however, that he had heard of a skeleton found in Davis Gulch by climbers a few years previously and would be in touch with Waldo if anything developed. The skeleton turned out to be a female Native American's.[65]

Ruess heard in 1988 of a California boater who had found a skeleton in Davis Gulch in the 1970s. The skeleton had 1920s-vintage clothing and was wedged in a crevice. The boater turned over a sample of the bones to a Park Service worker at the Rainbow Bridge Marina. "Please don't get your hopes too high," Ruess was advised. "Tourists constantly turn in Anasazi Indian remains that wash out of sandy hillsides throughout canyon country." The Park Service lost the bones before they could be analyzed.[66]

———————■———————

The mythologizing of Everett Ruess continued. He was the subject of nonfiction books dating back to 1940, two television documentaries, a play, a novel, and a country-western song. A species of dinosaur was given his name, and references to Ruess have spread throughout that most modern means of communication, the Internet.[67] The Southern Utah Wilderness Alliance used the silhouette of a photo of Everett leading his two burros as its brand. The image was prominently placed on its publications and stationery until objections were raised that it resembled a prospector leading his burros on a quest to destroy the wilderness.

Gibbs Smith, who headed the Utah chapter of the Sierra Club for a time, published book after book of Everett's letters and journals edited by W. L. Rusho. Smith first heard of Everett from Edward Abbey. Some of these books were repetitious or derivative of Henderson's efforts. First published in 1983, *Everett Ruess: A Vagabond for Beauty* was Smith's best-selling book and brought Everett to the attention of a wider audience. Through these books Ruess's "romantic and adventurous dreams" (in the words of Wallace Stegner) became known.[68] The classic shape of the tale and the mystery of the ending attracted readers mainly devoted to the West and outdoor activities. No book or other medium, however, stitched his life together in a meaningful manner. The result was that Ruess was portrayed in fragments.

In more recent years Everett Ruess has been featured in such high-end magazines as *Backpacker, Outside,* and *National Geographic Adventure,* which specialize in outdoor heroes, extreme journeys, and best-of and how-to and where-to-go and what-to-buy articles. These magazines carried advertisements for the expensive clothes and equipment needed to accomplish exotic wilderness adventures that Everett had achieved by the simplest and least expensive means. The hottest outdoor magazine writers of their time appropriated Everett. Rob Schultheis listed Ruess before Amelia Earhart in an article in *Backpacker* about mysterious disappearances. Jon Krakauer of *Outside* inserted Everett into his book about Christopher McCandless. David Roberts, a consulting editor for *National Geographic Adventure,* wrote a featured article about Everett for the magazine's premier issue in 1999.

XII

Resurrection

2009

THE MANNER OF EVERETT'S FLEETING RESURRECTION assumed the form of a Tony Hillerman mystery in 2009. I have wondered how Everett would have regarded these goings-on, and I can only conclude that his innocence and otherworldliness would have placed them beyond the means of his comprehension. For this is very much a story of our times and the inhabited world, which Everett shunned.

David Roberts was the most recent in the trajectory of journalists and authors fascinated by Ruess. A prolific and eminently readable writer who sought adventurous assignments, Roberts had written over twenty books about climbing, exploring, and the Southwest and articles for *National Geographic Adventure, National Geographic,* the *Atlantic Monthly,* and *Smithsonian* magazines. His writings about the Southwest were admired for their accessibility and suspected by some for their shadings of facts with respect to Ruess.[1]

After narrating the story of Everett's disappearance, Roberts transported the reader on a contemporary search for Everett in his first article on the subject in 1999. He spotted a mound of rocks on a plateau just to the east of Davis Gulch. "Addled with the heat" and wondering *"What if?"* Roberts began to dig, then stopped.[2] At the time, he preferred to leave Everett's disappearance a tantalizing mystery, but that would change. Curious, W. L. "Bud" Rusho, who had edited books of Everett's writings, and his family dug up the mound and found nothing. Rusho notified Roberts but received no reply.[3]

Roberts wrote a story for *National Geographic Adventure*'s April–May 2009 tenth anniversary issue about the discovery of Ruess's bones seventy-five years after he disappeared. That issue was labeled a "Special Collection Edition." The highly promoted story was titled "Finding Everett Ruess" and touted on the cover as "The Mystery of Everett Ruess: Solved." The editor of the magazine said that Roberts had written about "an American cult legend."[4]

I viewed the news with immediate skepticism. Many partial bodies, skeletons, and bones unearthed over the years have been attributed to Ruess and then determined to be someone else. A Salt Lake City television station had recently linked the bones of an elderly Navajo to Ruess. The stakes were huge. Finding Everett's bones, and especially his missing 1934 journal, would be akin in the Southwest to locating Amelia Earhart's airplane with her flight log intact. Roberts sensed it would be an "explosive and spectacular" story, and it truly was, although not in the manner he originally envisioned.[5]

■

Word began seeping out of southern Utah in the summer of 2008 that Ruess's bones had been found by a Navajo in Chinle Wash, some one hundred trail miles east of Davis Gulch. The *San Juan Record* ran an article headlined "Another Chapter in the Mystery of Everett Ruess" in early July. Armed with a metal detector and a story told by his grandfather and passed down to him via his sister, Denny Bellson had searched along Chinle Wash and Comb Ridge in the Navajo reservation south of the San Juan River. He had found some human bones and artifacts in a crevice burial site.[6]

The story, as it had evolved over seventy-five years within the family, was that his grandfather, Aneth Nez, had witnessed a white boy with two burros attacked by three Utes and beaten to death in Chinle Wash. Nez had then descended from the ridge and carried the bloody body, saddle, and other items from the wash to the burial site in spite of the Navajo fear of contact with the dead. The other items included a belt with silver studs, bits of turquoise and numerous beads, a Liberty Dime button dated 1912, and buttons stamped *Mountaineer* dating to between 1900 and 1935 and traced to the Mormon-owned ZCMI department store. Nez did not undergo a curing ceremony for touching the blood until 1971, when he was diagnosed with cancer.

Bellson notified the FBI office in nearby Monticello, Utah, of his find. Special Agent Rachel Boisselle was skeptical, since he had contacted her earlier that summer about what turned out to be the burial site of an Anasazi woman and child. Boisselle, two Navajo criminal investigators, Sheriff Mike Lacy of San Juan County, and Lacy's three teenage sons visited Bellson's most recent find. They determined, after some rooting around, that it was a Native American burial site.

Roberts, Bellson, and friends of both who lived in nearby Bluff, Utah, and were involved in uncovering and photographing the bones and artifacts were not convinced by the opinion of the law enforcement officials. Neither was Ron Maldonado, the supervisory archeologist in the Cultural Resource Compliance Section of the Navajo Nation. Maldonado, who was not a Native American but was married to a Navajo, had been told about the discovery of the bones by Roberts. He believed the bones and artifacts belonged to a young white man, most probably Ruess. Citing Nez's story, which Maldonado and Roberts equated with Navajo oral traditions, the tribal archeologist authorized the excavation of the site.

Michael Benoist, Roberts's editor at *National Geographic Adventure,* saw the need for scientific verification and contacted the National Geographic Society department in Washington, D.C., involved in the Genographic Project.[7] This project was billed as an unprecedented effort by the society and IBM to collect one hundred thousand DNA samples from around the globe. The samples would "map humanity's genetic journey through the ages."[8] Family Tree DNA, a Houston laboratory, sold the cheek-swab kits and conducted the tests for the public component of the project. These tests supposedly determined ancestral origins.

Benoist was given Family Tree's name and passed it on to Roberts, who contacted Bennett Greenspan, the CEO and president of the company. Greenspan agreed to the unusual request of comparing hairs from Waldo Ruess's hairbrush to the suspected bones of his brother. Waldo's four children consented to the DNA test and sent the brush to Family Tree, which specializes in genealogical searches, not forensic archeology. Founded in 1999 by Greenspan, the company claimed it was the world leader in genetic genealogy. Greenspan was described on the company's website as an entrepreneur and a lifelong genealogy enthusiast who had turned his hobby into a full-time vocation.

Family Tree notified Roberts and the magazine in early fall of 2008 that a mitochondrial DNA test, which determines maternal lineage, had shown there was no match between the hair and a molar from the grave site. The hair, perhaps one or two years old, was degraded, Greenspan said. Loose hair is regarded as a poor source of DNA, but hair pulled from the scalp with the root intact is a rich source of cellular material. What Roberts did not mention in his story was that there was a 100 percent match with a Family

Tree laboratory technician, meaning the technician had contaminated the samples with his DNA.[9] "So our confidence was diminished," said Brian Ruess, the spokesperson for the family.[10] However, Family Tree determined that the molar was "probably" of European and not Native American origin.[11] This tilted the evidence toward Ruess, but more proof was needed.

Through a friend in November 2008, Roberts located Dennis Van Gerven, an anthropologist at the University of Colorado at Boulder who had one previous experience with reconstructing skeletal remains using photographic superimposition to identify aged human body parts. Referred to as "an acclaimed skeletal biologist" in a university press release, Van Gerven was known for his collection of Nubian mummies.[12] He was also known as the anthropologist who had worked with a law professor colleague on the Hillmon Case. A shooting had resulted in the death of a man in Lawrence, Kansas, in 1879, but no one knew who was buried in the grave identified as Hillmon's. The body was exhumed in 2006. DNA samples were taken from two distant relatives of the two men thought to be in the grave. There was no match because the DNA had leached from the one bone that was tested. Then Van Gerven went to work. Using Adobe Photoshop, an image enhancement and manipulation program, he superimposed a photograph of the corpse over photos of the two men. There was a match with Hillmon's photo, indicating the bones were his. This technique was not ideal, Van Gerven wrote. He said a genetic match was a more positive means of identification.

Van Gerven had the opportunity two years later to use photographic superimposition in another high-profile case. It would be only the second time he had employed the technique. Before Roberts contacted him, he had no idea who Everett Ruess was. After Roberts's repeated entreaties, Van Gerven agreed to attempt to identify the bones because it seemed like an enjoyable project.

He visited the burial site on the Navajo reservation in late January 2009. What Van Gerven saw was a jumble of partially covered human bones and bits of leather. He quickly determined there would be more work than he had anticipated. Van Gerven carefully collected the bones, including the lower jaw, and returned with them to the University of Colorado. Again using Photoshop, he found a match between a partial facial reconstruction of the bones and two portraits of Everett taken by Dorothea Lange. Van Gerven noted that the technique had limitations. But each view matched, he said, as did everything else: age, approximate height, and the condition of the teeth. Months later, in a draft paper being prepared for a peer-reviewed journal, Van Gerven wrote: "With the conclusion of our morphological analysis it was clear that every aspect of the Comb Ridge skeleton corresponded remarkably to Everett Ruess. It was also clear that the final arbiter in this case would be genetic testing."[13] Brian Ruess said later that he took the facial reconstruction "with a grain of salt because it was result oriented. They were starting with the assumption that it was Everett and trying to make a jawbone fit that image."[14] The editors at *National Geographic Adventure* thought differently. The dubious photographic match convinced them to publish Roberts's story, although they had another feature article in reserve. There was a rush to publish "the most compelling story" for the anniversary issue, not only to satisfy reader interest but also to stem the serious decline of advertising revenue.

The National Academy of Sciences made public its critical report on forensic science that February, and while not referring to the Ruess case, it provided a useful context for judging the science being applied to it. In the report, a committee of the national academy gave DNA science high marks for reliability. The chances of a false positive from DNA analysis were rated as "minuscule." There was less reliability among non-DNA forensic disciplines, such as those depicted in detective novels and the *CSI* television series. The committee added in a press release: "With the exception of nuclear DNA analysis, the report says, no forensic method has been rigorously shown to have the capacity to consistently, and with a high degree of certainty, demonstrate a connection between evidence and a specific individual or source."[15] In other words, Van Gerven's method did not have a high degree of certainty. In a few months, the Ruess case would expose the Achilles' heel of nuclear DNA analysis.

Van Gerven looked for someone to conduct the DNA testing on the Ruess bones and settled on his close friend and University of Colorado colleague Kenneth S. Krauter. Krauter, the director of the DNA Sequencing and Bioinformatics facilities in the Department of Molecular, Cellular, and Developmental Biology, had worked on the Human Genome Project. He was an expert in molecular biology and genetics, not forensic biology, which requires a different type of DNA expertise. Like Van Gerven, Krauter was not familiar with Ruess, thought the project seemed "interesting and fun," and had only one previous experience attempting to identify old bones, those being from Van Gerven's Hillmon project.[16] His lab was equipped to analyze high-quality, not age-decayed, DNA samples. In other words, both scientists would be working without the proper tools and procedures, outside their respective areas of expertise, and with no understanding of the intense public interest in their results. It was a classic setup for a spectacular failure.

Krauter's test results were not going to be ready before the editorial deadline for the April–May anniversary issue of *National Geographic Adventure*. But armed with seeming confirmation of a spectacular revelation and facing the deadline for an important issue and the magazine's declining advertising revenue, the editors decided to go ahead with Roberts's story in February. Assembling all his evidence, Roberts concluded that the mystery "seems at last to have been solved."[17] The magazine arrived on newsstands on April 21.

The story was quite compelling, but there were bothersome inconsistencies and details, irrelevant or forced facts, and blind trust in a seventy-five-year-old oral account of a murder in Roberts's seamless narrative. His argument was too perfect, I thought. It had holes that should have been acknowledged, or the story should have been held until all the questions were resolved.

My reservations began with the scientific evidence on which Roberts and the magazine's editors had based the article. What particularly bothered me was Family Tree's determination that the tooth's DNA indicated European origin. That finding was dubious, depending on partial and very questionable results, and the firm was clearly not qualified to run the tests—witness the contamination of the samples. With only one previous photographic identification, Van Gerven was also unqualified, and he lacked seriousness of purpose. This was a lark for him. The anthropologist had employed a result-oriented process that depended on a computer program designed to manipulate photographic images.

The greatest discrepancy in Roberts's narrative account was that Ruess's two burros had clearly been found in Davis Gulch, not Chinle Wash. There was no way Everett could have acquired two more burros and reequipped himself in that wilderness. Roberts termed the burro issue "troublesome." He solved it by questioning the very existence of the burros in Davis Gulch and whether they had actually belonged to Ruess. This was a huge stretch that failed, at least in my mind, to validate Nez's account or explain why Roberts had written in his 1999 article that the burros had been found in Davis Gulch.[18] Also, the text and photographs indicated that the artifacts discovered with the bones did not match Everett's possessions but rather were those of a Native American.

There were other factual matters and interpretations used to buttress Roberts's case that made me feel uncomfortable, such as why the *NEMO* inscription found in Grand Gulch by the guide Ken Sleight in the 1960s—most probably the work of a wannabe Everett—was suddenly significant.[19] It proved to Roberts that Everett, who had not previously been in the area, had detoured on his trek to Chinle Wash and left his mark. A small desert whirlwind, known as a dust devil, had visited Maldonado and others as they left the burial site, "lingering, appearing to die out, then starting again." Roberts implied that the experience, recounted to him by Maldonado, indicated Everett's spirit was present. The transformation of a natural phenomenon into spiritual proof of corporeal existence felt forced. Then there was the troublesome matter of the Navajo's aversion to handling bloody remains, particularly those of white strangers, and why Nez went to the trouble of hauling the body and the saddle up the ridge for burial. Other serious concerns emerged in the next few months, such as Roberts's and Van Gerven's not acknowledging the existence and then downplaying the applicability of Everett's dental records, which did not match the recovered jaw.*

What Roberts and his team had going for them by that time was a more than solid DNA confirmation by a laboratory at a reputable university that the bones belonged to Ruess. This "irrefutable" evidence pushed the bothersome questions to the background. How could such an incontrovertible DNA result ever be wrong?†

———————— ■ ————————

Word that there was a positive DNA match leaked out a few days after publication. Krauter and *National Geographic Adventure,* backed by two National Geographic Society publicists in Washington, D.C., made the official announcement on April 30. A femur taken from the burial site had been compared to saliva swabs from Ruess's two nephews and two nieces, his closest living relatives. The results were presented as irrefutable. Krauter added, "I believe it would hold up in any court in the country."[20] A National Geographic press release added to the certainty:

———————

*As a former newspaper and magazine journalist, I understood the intense pressure to produce a truly remarkable story on deadline for an anniversary issue, especially for a magazine in financial difficulties. In fairness to Roberts, I have asked myself what I would have done under similar circumstances. I would have immediately sought an independent expert or experts to assess the complex scientific data, as I have done for this book and other writing projects. I also routinely ask those experts who have given me information to comment on the accuracy of the corresponding portion of the draft manuscript, a practice that would not have helped Roberts in this case because his experts were wrong.
†I trusted the accuracy of DNA tests at that time, and I had some impressive company—the committee of the National Academy of Sciences that had just issued its report. I could only conclude that some of the bones belonged to Ruess and some, along with the artifacts, belonged to one or more Native Americans, which would have made the burial site more of a body dump. What I was doing was exactly what Roberts had done, forcing disparate facts to conform.

The test examined the inheritance of some 600,000 markers using gene chips from the Affymetrix Corporation and found that the saliva samples and the DNA extracted from the femur share approximately 25 per cent of those markers by inheritance. Nieces and nephews are expected to hold about one-quarter of their genetic markers in common with an aunt or uncle. The test provides essentially irrefutable evidence of a close blood relationship between the Ruess family DNA and the bone DNA. Subsequent tests comparing the bone DNA with 50 unrelated people confirmed the results, with considerably less than 1 per cent of markers shared in this way.[21]

"This was a textbook case," Krauter said. "We had a large number of markers and, when comparing the bone DNA and the Ruess samples, the mode of inheritance of those markers was exactly what you'd expect for the relationship between an uncle and a niece or nephew."[22] At the end of the press release there was advertising and subscription information for the magazine along with the society's mission statement. Clearly, a recognized and trusted brand was involved in these proceedings.

The article Krauter and Van Gerven drafted that summer for submission to a peer-reviewed journal, which they said would answer any remaining questions, stated that the software they used had been 99.9 percent accurate in prior control studies. (The advantage of DNA testing, the National Academy of Sciences report said, was that the likelihood of a false positive could be quantified. In this case that chance was limited to one-tenth of 1 percent.) Their unequivocal conclusion was: "A genetic comparison demonstrates *beyond a doubt* that the Comb Ridge skeleton is related to the Ruess brothers and sisters at the level of an uncle" (emphasis mine).[23]

The public response to the validation of the discovery was massive. People who had never heard of Ruess were now aware of him. His fans were either delirious with joy or ambivalent. Everett Ruess's greatly increased stature in the seventy-five years since his death can be measured by the gush of news following the DNA announcement. *Solved* was the dominant word applied to the mystery from coast to coast in such media outlets as the Associated Press, National Public Radio, *Salt Lake Tribune, Portland Oregonian, San Francisco Chronicle, San Jose Mercury, Los Angeles Times* (which missed the fact that Ruess was a local boy), *Denver Post, New York Times, Navajo Times,* smaller newspapers, radio and television stations, websites, and blogs (even *Outside* magazine, the competition, noted the announcement in a blog post).[24] Readers' comments accompanied the online articles. A sampling follows:

- Holy cow. I heard about Ruess on my first trip out west, and always wondered how it could even be hoped to find him. Simply amazing.
- There have been a handful of these somewhat misanthropic nature-lovers who preferred the solace and majesty of nature to the constraints and conventions of modern civilization. For a few, it was their demise.
- Cheers to you, Everett. May not all our mysteries be discovered nor solved. Because when I wander in the canyon country, I like to think your spirit whispers out there too, guiding my footsteps and lighting my dreams.
- Everett Ruess was my embodiment of youthful wanderlust in the Southwest years and years before I ever heard of Christopher McCandless.
- I think more than anything I just don't want Everett to be found. I think of him out there wandering still; maybe someday I will run into him.
- Ruess was a brilliant young man with a very large and pure heart and I'm sorry to finally learn that he was killed. I'm not disappointed that the mystery has come to an end, but that someone so remarkable was taken from us much too early.
- It's hard not to harshly judge Aneth Nez for not reporting the murder. Family and friends must have suffered for decades.
- Nez probably didn't report the murder because he thought he would himself fall under suspicion. And for good reason.
- The burro thing bothers me. In fact, it seems critical as everyone involved says Everett would never go someplace like Comb Ridge without them.

——————◼——————

The DNA analysis seemed unassailable, but Van Gerven's photo reconstruction was vulnerable. Paul Leatherbury's archeological credentials were less impressive than those of the two University of Colorado academics. He had graduated with a bachelor's degree in anthropology and archeology and worked nine years as an archeologist for the Park Service in Grand Canyon National Park. In the spring of 2009 he was working as a geographic information systems specialist in the Monticello, Utah, office of the Bureau of Land Management. Through the books of Wallace Stegner, Edward Abbey, and Bud Rusho, he, like others, had developed a consuming interest in Ruess. Scott Thybony, who was working on a book on Ruess and Dan Thrapp, mentioned his reservations about the identification to Leatherbury. Leatherbury was interested in putting together a photo exhibit of Ruess but was diverted by the bones issue.

In late April, Leatherbury found Everett's dental records that Stella and Christopher Ruess had forwarded to the Gallup police in 1935. Waldo had saved them, and they were listed in the online guide to the Ruess Family Papers in the Special Collections section of the University of Utah library as being in box 5, folder 2. They were clearly identified in the guide: "This folder includes Everett's dental records." Dental records can be a key factor in identifying a skeleton. There was no mention of dental records in Roberts's story. He had missed them in his searches in the university's archives.[25]

Leatherbury was the first to examine the dental records after the publication of the 2009 article in *National Geographic Adventure*. Roberts was second. He misread the records when he finally found them in early May. Roberts said there was no overall dental chart to show the extent of the work, but he was mistaken. He sent Van Gerven photocopies of the records. Van Gerven was publicly silent on the matter.

There was no question of the dental records' authenticity, an issue that Roberts would raise later. The work in the records was performed at the College of Dentistry at the University of Southern California in December 1932 and January 1933, a period when Ruess was in Los Angeles. It consisted of two gold inlays on the first and second molars on the right side of the lower jaw and gold foil placed on the first molar. The records' folder contains a chart marked with the Palmer notation method showing the location of the work, two bills for dental services, and a notation of a March 1934 X-ray, which also corresponds to a time when Everett was in Los Angeles.[26] The envelope in which the records were sent to Stella Ruess, with the printed return address of the College of Dentistry on the stationery, was postmarked July 16, 1935, a date corresponding to the time when the family sought the records from USC and then forwarded them to Gallup to determine if a burned body was their son's.

Leatherbury began peppering Van Gerven with questions. What kind of dental work had been performed on the lower right molars of the jaw that he had recovered? What was the extent of wear of the lower teeth? No dental work had been performed, Van Gerven replied, on any of the recovered teeth. At Leatherbury's insistence, he repeated this assertion more than once. The wear on the teeth was consistent with a Navajo diet, Van Gerven said. He thought Everett had regularly eaten Navajo food, but Everett's shopping lists indicated that he had a predominantly Anglo diet. Also, he had been on the reservation for only short periods over three years. The implication that Leatherbury drew from this evidence was that the teeth belonged not to Everett but rather to a Native American, thus contradicting the findings of Roberts, Family Tree, and the Colorado team.

Leatherbury also asked Van Gerven if there were any signs of trauma to the skull. No indications of trauma, Van Gerven said, again more than once. Roberts's article mentioned "a dent in the back of the skull, suggestive of a mortal blow," seemingly validating Nez's story that Utes had beaten Everett to death.

Leatherbury sent the dental records to Brian Ruess on June 4, pointing out the discrepancies between them and the jaw. There was no response. The dental records were of no importance to the University of Colorado team. "We considered the dental records," Van Gerven said, "but found them to be ambiguous and incomplete."[27] He was getting fed up with Leatherbury's persistent questions and dispatched an angry email to "any and all interested parties" on June 14, which read in part:

> Does someone actually think that the DNA evidence is so weak that it requires confirmation from the dental record? Does someone seriously want to announce a rejection of a 600,000 nucleotide match based on two fillings and some dental wear? If so then those people had better be prepared to present some unknown Ruess uncle who also died out there who was physically a twin to Everett. I am not kidding here; that is the alternative. I repeat, that is the only alternative explanation here. I'm done now because this entire issue has become absurd and I am not interested in endlessly, and I mean endlessly, responding to people who don't or won't understand the power of the science that has been brought to bear here. If a mistake was made here it was getting the results out before a [peer-reviewed] publication [published it]. . . . In any case, people will simply have to wait because this kind of endless response is pointless. Please forward this to any and all interested parties now and in the future if you need a response from me.[28]

Roberts thought Leatherbury was going to make a startling public revelation about the dental records at the presentations of his evidence in Moab, Utah, on June 21 and Salt Lake City on June 22. But that was not his plan. Leatherbury was concerned on a personal level about the correct identification of the bones. The DNA evidence was compelling, he said, but it was not foolproof and, besides, was beyond most people's comprehension, including his own. He put together a thorough PDF file on the physical evidence and circulated it to a few select people, including Brian Ruess, who forwarded it in late August to a third DNA lab, the Armed Forces DNA Identification Laboratory in Rockville, Maryland.[29]

Unbeknownst to Leatherbury, the Utah state archeologist Kevin Jones also had issues with the identification of the bones, and he was in a position to raise questions publicly. Jones got his master's and doctor's degrees in anthropology from the University of Utah and had been the state archeologist since 1995.[30] He was a member of all the requisite professional societies and had a list of publications, papers, posters, and lectures on regional subjects, particularly Range Creek in central Utah. Jones had spent time at this site, which was rich in ancient Fremont culture artifacts and bones, with Roberts, who had been researching stories for *National Geographic* magazine and *National Geographic Adventure*.[31] A bearded, burly man, Jones rode a motorcycle to work and played the mandolin in a bluegrass band. He was protective of his archeological turf and felt excluded from the Navajo reservation, a state within four states that encompassed the Navajo Nation and had its own archeologist.

Jones had questions after reading and assessing the *National Geographic Adventure* article. He called Roberts on April 28 and offered to arrange another DNA test. Roberts said he had to consult with "the principals," which Jones took to mean the Ruess family. Roberts never called back. The state archeologist then chose another route. His superiors initially objected but then allowed him to post a mild critique on the state history website on June 17. "Everett Ruess—A Suggestion to Take Another Look" was the first public questioning of Roberts's conclusions.[32] Few read the obscure posting.

Jones thought the bones and two Lange photos did not match, the worn teeth were those of a Navajo, the lower jaw was exceptionally crowded and did not correspond to Everett's, and there were weak points in Aneth Nez's story, such as the two unexplained burros and why a Navajo would handle the bloody remains of a white stranger. To Jones, it seemed there had been a rush to publish the article in the anniversary issue. He did not trust the story and called for a third DNA examination of the bones, this one by an independent lab with experience in assessing older remains.[33]

At this point I played a minor role in what was unfolding. I had arrived in Salt Lake City the Wednesday before a June 22 forum at the university on the discovery of the bones to continue my research in the Ruess archive. I interviewed Jones on Thursday morning and continued calling for folders in the Ruess archive that afternoon until I reached the dental records, which I knew were important. Jones, being the state archeologist, was the proper person to assess them, so I left a telephone message for him on Saturday. His colleague, Derinna Kopp, a physical anthropologist, viewed the records on

Monday morning before that evening's program. Neither Jones or Kopp had been aware of their existence prior to my message.

An analysis of the records and photos of the bones led Jones and Kopp to conclude that they belonged to a Native American.[34] They subsequently checked with the state's forensic dental expert, Dr. Reed L. Holt, for his opinion. Holt saw no sign of fillings in the photographs and concluded that the surfaces of the molars had been worn by stone-ground food, consistent with an exclusively Native American diet. "Based on the dental records and pictures I have been given," Holt wrote, "I would question the positive identification of the skeleton as Everett Ruess."[35] His findings were not made public, but they reinforced his colleagues' conclusions and helped bolster Jones's and Kopp's positions within the state bureaucracy when their assessment was attacked.

The forum at the University of Utah had been arranged by Dr. Richard Ingebretsen, a physician who taught courses in forensic pathology and DNA analysis at the university. He was also the founder and president of Glen Canyon Institute, whose goal was to restore Glen Canyon and the Colorado River to their free-flowing conditions, and the vice chair of the board of the Southern Utah Wilderness Alliance. Wild rivers and wilderness were the utopias of these two groups, and Everett Ruess was their inspiration. During his introduction, Ingebretsen called the discovery and identification of Everett's remains "one of the most incredible events in modern times."[36]

He handed the microphone to Roberts, who functioned as master of ceremonies. Also on the dais were Denny Bellson, Brian Ruess, his sister Michele Ruess, and Bud Rusho. Vaughn Hadenfeldt, a guide and Bluff resident, and Greg Child, who took the photos for the *Adventure* article, were also present. Hadenfeldt and Child had helped Bellson and Roberts at the burial site. Bellson had retained a pro bono lawyer and a literary agent, and Roberts was planning a book. Some of the same participants had given a talk the previous night in Moab, and there would be similar presentations that fall in Escalante and Bluff. But the Salt Lake forum was the largest and most comprehensive discussion. Reed Auditorium in Orson Spencer Hall on the university's campus was filled to capacity with three hundred people intent on learning the fate of Everett Ruess.

There was unanimity among the speakers that the University of Colorado's DNA match was conclusive. Brian Ruess told the hushed audience that the family was convinced the bones were their missing uncle's "beyond a statistical certainty." He added:

The issue is one of closure. This can be dragged on forever. Everyone can challenge every last piece of evidence. Everybody has an alternative theory. There will never be resolution of every single question because there was no one there. We don't have a journal as to where he went, why he went, how he went. What we can be certain of is that our family is convinced that the DNA evidence is credible.

When it came time for questions from the audience, Kevin Jones asked about the dental records. To Roberts, they were the "suspect" dental records. Yes, they were a problem, he said, but do they raise a question mark about the DNA? Not really. What had to be considered, he continued, were the "very questionable" dental records versus the "really, really foolproof DNA." Of the burro problem, Roberts said, "I haven't solved it yet."

∎

Three days after the forum, Jones emailed Michele and Brian Ruess that in his "considered opinion" the bones belonged to a young Indian male. He urged them not to cremate the bones and consign the ashes to the ocean, as was the family custom. Jones offered the family, at no cost, the opportunity to work with the DNA laboratories at the Smithsonian Institution or Baylor University, both of which were experienced in assessing older bones. He said the Colorado lab lacked experience in extracting and analyzing DNA from skeletal remains. Brian Ruess replied that he would consult his siblings. He later declined the offer, but there were indications that the family was already considering a third DNA analysis.

News stories by staff writers for the *Salt Lake Tribune* and the *New York Times* and papers subscribing to the Associated Press appeared in early July with such headlines as "Utah Scientists Question Everett Ruess DNA Findings" *(Tribune)* and "Solution to a Longtime Mystery in Utah Is Questioned" *(Times)*. The day after the *Times* article ran, and with a reference to that story, an item appeared on the *National Geographic Adventure* website under the headline "Everett Ruess Update: Believers and Skeptics." Roberts was quoted: "This mystery has created new mysteries that are even more unsolvable. But what surprises me is the passion and even anger this has stirred up. You can understand the family getting passionate, but even supposed impartial bystanders are getting hot under the collar."[37]

None reacted more angrily than Richard Ingebretsen. He launched a scathing attack on Jones and Kopp, labeling them "incompetents" and "conspiracy theorists" whose questioning of the identification of the bones was "nothing short of idiotic." His criticisms of their work were contained in a letter sent on university stationery to their superiors. The state's historical and archeological abilities, he said, lacked credibility, and he threatened to use his position on the boards of two environmental groups to convince them "to avoid working with your organization."* Jones felt the backing he received from his bosses on this issue was tepid. His job teetered in the balance as the letter made its way to the governor's office and the office of the president of the university.

Feelings had also spiked on the University of Colorado campus in Boulder. In a magazine article, Van Gerven was quoted as comparing Jones's concerns to conspiracy theories "like the JFK killing and Obama birthers."[38] That nettled Jones. What surprised him most, he said later, was the anger directed toward him by critics with a scientific background. "Those were not the types of responses I would have expected. It made me wonder what else was going on."[39]

I had been in contact with Jones and Kopp in Salt Lake City and Krauter and Van Gerven in Boulder. It was my policy not to tell either pair what the other was thinking or doing. The silence through September and early October was deafening, so I emailed the two Colorado scientists in mid-October and asked how they were proceeding on their article. They immediately responded that they agreed with the Ruess family that Jones had raised enough doubts about the physical and DNA evidence to take another look. Their DNA identification had been called into question, they were reassessing their analysis, and there would be an announcement by Brian Ruess the following week. On October 22, Ruess sent the following email to interested parties:

> After further DNA testing, the Ruess family is now convinced that the remains found last year and reported to be those of Everett Ruess are in fact the remains of someone else.

---

*Richard J. Ingebretsen to Michael W. Homer, chair, and Philip F. Notarianni, director, Utah State History, July 2, 2009. What upset Ingebretsen, he said later, was that the state agency had not made an independent laboratory assessment of the bones. "In my mind they are guilty of what Mr. Roberts was guilty of—going public before they were absolutely sure of their findings." Ingebretsen, personal communication, January 20, 2010. Ingebretsen had not bothered to determine where the bones were before writing his letter—and still was not aware six months later that they were in the possession of the Ruess family, to do with as it wished. The family had declined Jones's offer to find an independent laboratory, so Ingebretsen's fulmination was without merit.

Because of concerns as to whether the skeletal remains found on Comb Ridge in May of 2008 were actually those of Everett Ruess, the Ruess family decided to seek independent scientific confirmation of the initial findings. The family contacted the Armed Forces DNA Identification Laboratory (AFDIL) in Rockville, Maryland. AFDIL, which is part of the Office of the Armed Forces Medical Examiner of the Armed Forces Institute of Pathology (AFIP), performed an additional round of DNA extraction and analysis from samples taken from the same skeleton.

The AFDIL's studies determined that [the] remains were not those of Everett Ruess using Y-STR testing and mitochondrial DNA (MtDNA) sequencing. Taken together, the MtDNA and Y-STR evidence establishes the remains are not related to Everett's closest living relatives. Subsequent reanalysis by the original [Colorado] DNA team could not duplicate their original results.

As a result of the AFDIL findings and the reanalysis, the Ruess family has accepted that the skeletal remains are not those of Everett Ruess. The bones and associated artifacts will be returned to the Navajo Nation Archeologist for disposition.

The family wishes to thank all the parties of the original research team for their interest in solving the mystery of Everett's disappearance as well as those who felt it was important to undertake additional study before concluding the identity of the remains found at Comb Ridge.

The Ruess family would also like to extend its gratitude to all those who have drawn inspiration from Everett's life and work. We hope that their enthusiasm will continue whether or not the mystery is solved. Additionally, we offer our empathy to families everywhere who have lost and never found a loved one. They know, as we do, the subtle and continuous presence of a family member who has disappeared.[40]

Rather than calling a full-blown press conference or at least putting out a press release, as had been done to announce the DNA confirmation, *National Geographic Adventure* placed the following on its website: "We are not aware of the details of the new study. But given the strength of the previous evidence, we'd like to know more about the facts and procedures of the new testing before updating our investigation."[41] Internally, features editor Michael Benoist said he knew the magazine had made a grave mistake: "AFDIL was the right lab. I definitely know the landscape better at this point."[42]

At about this time a paperback book published by the National Geographic Society began appearing in bookstores. It celebrated *Adventures*'s tenth anniversary and contained the magazine's "best" articles during that time. Roberts's

2009 article was included. A postscript noted that the Colorado DNA results had confirmed the story's findings.[43] In an introduction, the magazine's editor, John Rasmus, said Roberts had solved the mystery of Everett Ruess's disappearance. Perhaps, Rasmus wrote, further dimensions would be added to this story within the covers of the magazine in future years.[44] But that was not to be.

In early December the National Geographic Society announced that it was ceasing the publication of *Adventure* nine months after its tenth anniversary. There would be no February–March 2010 issue containing a planned story by Roberts explaining what had happened. Declining advertising sales—the page count had gone down 44 percent since the first of the year—were cited as the reason for immediately shutting down the magazine. There had been an interested buyer, but the National Geographic Society was not about to sell the yellow rectangle, which signified excellence, to an outsider.[45] The magazine's readers were greatly disappointed. A media website cited such work as Roberts's story as the reason why the publication had won four National Magazine Awards.

———————■———————

So, in retrospect, what went wrong, according to David Roberts, Dennis Van Gerven, and Kenneth Krauter? Although *National Geographic Adventure* no longer existed in February 2010, its website was still functioning, and Roberts offered his justifications online.[46] He did not evaluate his journalistic effort but focused on Van Gerven's and Krauter's science. In Roberts's view, all were blameless.

Roberts credited Van Gerven with conducting "a thorough forensic analysis" before the publication of the article. He cited no errors or omissions that Van Gerven might have committed nor his lack of experience in this forensic specialty. Roberts wrote, "Van Gerven, who performed the facial reconstruction, was dumfounded by the new results." He quoted Van Gerven as stating: "I will go to my grave believing that we could not exclude [the match] based on the best anatomical evidence. A random skeleton was found that by chance alone matched sex, age, and stature. That in itself is remarkable."[47]

Yes, it was quite remarkable that human bones were found near where Aneth Nez said a murder had been committed. But they were Native American bones, which made one wonder exactly what Nez had witnessed, what he had participated in, and what he had done on his own. There was no way to know the true circumstances the story was designed to fit.[48] What Nez witnessed was altered over seventy-five years in the natural way stories passed down through several retellings are radically transformed. His version of what occurred was consecutively filtered by himself, his daughter, her brother, Roberts, readers of *National Geographic Adventure,* the media, and reading and viewing audiences. To label the story an oral tradition, as Roberts and Maldonado did, gave the one-time crime report a legitimacy it did not deserve. An oral tradition is something that is repeated over and over and becomes embedded within the fabric of a culture. Memory, especially recollections extending back three-quarters of a century, is extremely unreliable. It "is distorted by our beliefs, desires, and interests," in the words of Paul Bloom, a professor of psychology at Yale University. Reviewing a book on the imperfections of perceptions, he added that over a long period of time memory fades and becomes an illusion. "Simply talking about something that happened distorts your memory; you come to remember not the event itself, but the story you told."[49]

Roberts's first mistake was taking Nez's story at face value. The result was that the principal impetus of subsequent actions became proving that the bones belonged to Ruess, not disproving this. Roberts, a commercial DNA laboratory, a university DNA laboratory, an anthropology professor, and a Navajo archeologist determined there was a fit between the bones and Ruess. It took Leatherbury, Jones, and a disinterested military laboratory some two thousand miles distant to establish otherwise.

Vaughn Hadenfeldt, the Bluff, Utah, guide, had worked with Roberts on numerous writing projects and knew Danny Bellson. He was the one who alerted Roberts to Bellson's discovery and said of Nez's story at the Salt Lake forum that Navajo oral traditions were not given enough credence, a point Roberts made in the article. After it was all over, Hadenfeldt said he still believed "the core" of the story. "I think there was a white kid out there, but whether you can connect him to Everett Ruess is a whole other thing. I think Nez had more to do with that killing than he let on."[50]

As for Krauter, Roberts said on the National Geographic website that his mistakes were not due to human errors but rather because he had employed "relatively new technology in an unprecedented way." The Affymetrix software, Roberts said, was "unproven for forensic work." Krauter had not known the software could produce false readings for small samples of DNA.[51]

In separate sets of questions for Van Gerven and Krauter, I asked what went wrong. Van Gerven's answers were short and brusque. "I'll be frank. I have almost forty years in, and as with Ken this was a fun, momentary problem. I didn't then and don't now see this as in any sense important to me or my career." He said that even had the analysis been correct, he wouldn't have included it on his vita, and added an exclamation mark to emphasize that point. Van Gerven was amazed by the public response. "I never in my mind anticipated the number of people for whom the disappearance of one young man seventy years ago could become such a central focus of their lives and interests. I remain astounded."[52]

In contrast to Roberts and Van Gerven, Krauter admitted he made serious mistakes. He placed the matter in a wider context and demonstrated how human errors can lead to scientific failures. Krauter pointed out that Nez's story, the opinion of a Navajo archeologist, the Texas DNA laboratory, Van Gerven, he, and Roberts had contributed to an avalanche of proof that the bones belonged to Ruess. These findings, each with a low probability of error in itself, when combined seemed overwhelming and should have led to a correct conclusion—except that they didn't.[53]

On a technical level, the mistake wasn't only due to the software: it was the totality of problems "associated with the analysis of tiny amounts of human DNA present in environmentally exposed samples." Krauter admitted his lack of expertise in this subspecialty. "It is definitely an advantage to be experienced in the nuances of forensic DNA analysis since there is considerable 'craft' involved in anticipating potential artifacts.[54] This is not my occupation." Krauter practiced a different type of genetic analysis: his laboratory was set up to analyze "relatively high-quality DNA samples."[55]

What he had done, in effect, was use the wrong instrument in a surgical procedure for which he was not trained. He had employed "a cutting-edge, high-resolution genotyping process" when the "tried-and-true 'older' technology" employed by the Armed Forces DNA Identification Laboratory was the appropriate tool for the task. (Krauter found the Armed Forces' DNA laboratory findings "extremely convincing.") On the positive side, Krauter had learned the limitations of the new technology. He added: "Obviously, no one likes to be wrong, especially when there is a light shining in one's face, but we erred. I possibly could have figured out that I had erred had I spent more time and energy trying to tear apart the data more than I did. As I said, this was done as an intellectual exercise and was probably not given the attention that it deserved. That was my real failure in this case."[56]

———————◾———————

The matter of the misidentified bones raises important issues beyond the boundaries of a biography, and I can touch upon them only briefly here. The certainty of DNA identification, as illustrated by this case study, seems shaky. If computer software, human errors, and hubris were to blame here, then what about in other cases? Culpability was spread among many parties in the Ruess matter. There was, Krauter said, an "unanticipated weakness" in the software.[57] Well, the same could be said about a journalist, a magazine, and scientists who wanted to make the bones fit Ruess and did not consider credible evidence that contradicted their findings.

Three different laboratories produced three different results. This basic fact says something about the state of forensic and DNA science. The first two labs were not set up to accurately analyze older DNA samples; the last one was. Special equipment, chemicals, computer programs, lab layouts, training, and procedures are needed to properly test such a sample, and the results must be replicable. But how does an outsider, such as a journalist or a lawyer, know what a particular laboratory is capable of achieving, and how can DNA laboratories be prohibited from taking on work they are not qualified or equipped to handle? Roberts, the magazine editors, and the Ruess family learned about the complexities of DNA analysis the hard way—from personal experience. But they also should have been warned about limits by the experts they approached. The fact that they weren't indicates a certain arrogance or carelessness within the ranks of this particular branch of science.

This case study also has legal implications. DNA evidence is frequently presented in court, but few lawyers, juries, or judges are knowledgeable about its complexities. How many parties to criminal cases or civil actions—such as people seeking to determine paternity—can adequately assess the evidence, let alone afford a second and even a third test?* The last test of the bones was conducted by one of the most credible laboratories in the country. The Armed Forces DNA Identification Laboratory undertook the test at no cost to the Ruess family because of its uniqueness and applicability to determining the identity of skeletons to be found years hence in the deserts of Iraq and Afghanistan. That favor was not about to be extended to everyone.[58]

———
*Shortly after I wrote this sentence, a story appeared in the *New York Times Magazine* about the use of "cheap and accurate" DNA tests to determine children's paternity. There was a growing use of those tests for that purpose, the article stated. Ruth Padawer, "Losing Fatherhood," *New York Times Magazine,* November 22, 2009.

Wilderness Song

I have been one who loved the wilderness;
Swaggered and softly crept between the mountain peaks;
I listened long to the sea's brave music;
I sang my songs above the shriek of desert winds.

On canyon trails when warm night winds were blowing,
Blowing, and sighing gently through the star-tipped pines,
Musing, I walked behind my placid Burro,
While water rushed and broke on pointed rocks below.

I have known a green sea's heaving; I have loved
Red rocks and twisted trees and cloudless turquoise skies,
Slow sunny clouds, and red sand blowing;
I have felt the rain and slept behind the waterfall.

In cool sweet grasses I have lain and heard
The ghostly murmur of regretful winds
In aspen glades where rustling silver leaves
Whisper wild sorrows to the green-gold solitudes.

I have watched the shadowed clouds pile high;
Singing I rode to meet the splendid, shouting storm
And fought its fury till the hidden sun
Foundered in darkness, and the lightning heard my song.

Say that I starved; that I was cold and weary;
That I was burned and blinded by the desert suns,
Thirsty and chilled and sick with strange diseases,
Lonely and wet and cold, but that I kept my dream.

Always I shall be one who loves the wilderness;
Swaggers and softly creeps between the mountain peaks.
I shall listen long to the sea's brave music;
I shall sing my songs above the shriek of desert winds.*

---

*The poem was reprinted countless times after its first publication in the *Los Angeles Daily News* of May 19, 1935. One of its most memorable uses was when Harry Partch set five of its lines to music. At the time Partch was with the Federal Writers Project in Los Angeles and had come across a copy of the poem at the home of Alec W. Anderson in Covina, where Everett and his friends had gathered to listen to classical music. "Fragments of the poem so well expressed, in essence, my own feelings and experiences that I immediately set them to music." Partch to Mr. and Mrs. Ruess, April 16, 1939. Partch would go on to become one of America's most innovative composers.

Father and Son Dialogue

The questions and answers, contained in separate letters, are joined here to form a meaningful dialogue. Everett asked the questions and Christopher provided the answers in 1933.[1]

1. Is life only sensation?

Is Beauty of the senses or of the soul? Life is more than sensation, receiving impressions. Something is done with those impressions. They do something with one another. There is Beauty in the first process and also in the second and in the third. Life is full of beauty to those awake to see or feel or perceive it.

2. Is service the true end of life?

No, but rather happiness THROUGH service. The race, life, is important, more than the individual. Only as we play our part as a part of the whole, aware of interrelatedness, do we really and fully live. You and I are like the right hand or the right eye or the big toe—we are grotesque when living apart. The fool hath said in his heart—I am all that is important.

3. Can a strong mind maintain independence and strength if it is not rooted in material independence?

Yes, as many great souls prove. They were not independent. Dependence and independence are alike harmful to the best life. No dependent or independent man can play a high part in life—but only the interdependent man. Great souls today have issued a Declaration of Human Interdependence.

4. Are not all people dependent upon one another?

Yes, that is their glory. As Paul writes of the parts of the body in one of his epistles. It takes all kinds of stones to build a Gothic cathedral—which shows the glory of the incomplete made into completion. Just as man and woman are dependent on one another, child and parent, etc.

5. Do all things follow the attainment of Truth?

No, not unless you create a new definition of the truth. It takes ALL three "ideas of the reason" to define the whole of culture or to define God. He whose life is exclusively devoted to Truth, or to Goodness, or to Beauty, is a very fractional man, though such exaggeration may be needed to a great degree in the division of spiritual labor. This age is in trouble because it has exaggerated TRUTH, it is lopsided. There is no ultimate conflict when all three are stressed and as Aristotle says we "see life sanely and see it whole."

6. Is bodily love empty or to be forgotten?

No, it is part of life. It is not all of life. I do not see that it should ever be out-grown, but it changes form, it begins animal and always remains healthily animal, but it is refined and sublimated.

7. Can one ask too much of life?

Yes, many do. We should have faith in life in cause and effect, in action and reaction. We owe much more to the past than any one of us can give to the present or to the future. It is not for us to play highway robber and hold up life. The great souls probably never ask such a question. But the greatest givers have got most from life, whether Jesus or Edison.

8. Does life have infinite potentialities?

Yes, so far as we can conceive infinity. Certainly incalculable, immeasurable is the contribution and joy open to you or to me. As Tagore says, Life is immense.[2]

9. Must pain spring from pleasure?

Not always. Not equal pain from equal pleasure. Death springs from or grows out of life, but we cannot say but that one is as good and as beautiful as the other; Whitman says they are equally great. One is not more painful and inglorious than the other—birth and death—but what glory lies between! However, psychologically we seem to know pleasure largely by contrast and contrast seems necessary for our minds to make distinctions. No black, no white. No high, no low.

10. Are pain and pleasure equally desirable and necessary?

They are both good for us if we have the will to extract the sweet from the bitter. No one need seek pain, he will get plenty without searching. He need not seek pleasure, he will get more if he gets it indirectly. He needs rather to go his way regardless of both pain and pleasure. The highway or road will give him some pain but the pleasure will be worth the pain. Pleasure is perhaps the wrong word—joy or ecstasy may be better. Ecstasy is the highest of this family of words. It means such happiness that we literally seem to stand outside of ourselves in exaltation.

11. Is the goal of life, thought, and love untouched by the material?

No, God made the material also. Walt Whitman said, I am the poet of the material also. It is a narrow theology or philosophy of life that despises aught that God has made. All are but arts of the one stupendous whole. The Hebrew said that God saw ALL that he had made, and pronounced it GOOD. However, there is a due proportion, as in making a good cake, or a good meal. I may want some salt or pepper, but not the whole shaker spilled on my food!

12. Is pleasure right for all, but selfish for one?

There is no sin or wrong in pleasure except it be at the cost of another soul or life, to aggrandize ourselves by the degradation of another. Selfishness is not evil, it is good, but it must be the larger and not the narrower selfishness. A man's real self includes his parents, his wife and children, his friends, and neighbors, his countrymen, all his fellowmen. He should be selfish both at the center and at the circumference, selfish for ALL. I doubt that there is a real conflict, but there is a harmony. It is not beautiful for a man to sacrifice himself for his child and thus spoil his child. Parents who do not practice give and take, fairness, in this relation make pigs and tyrants out of their children. These children are not being brought up to face reality, are they?

13. Can one be happy while others are miserable?

Yes, a callous man can have a callous happiness. But a noble man cannot be nobly happy while others are miserable. In that sense a man like Jesus never except for moments of rest and retreat can be happy, for he had compassion upon the multitude. Great lovers have a happiness higher than our ordinary happiness. There is a happiness in identification of oneself with others, in bearing their burdens, even their sins. Great souls are not worried much about happiness. "Wist ye not that I must be about my Father's BUSINESS." Jesus and Socrates and Lincoln were not constantly concerned about their pleasure or their happiness.

14. Can one be fine without great sacrifice?

Not the finest. For such a one has been spared great experience. Such a one has not really lived. He has just played at life. Yet he need not be maimed by sacrifice to know reality. Sacrifice is in quality as well as in quantity. Sacrifice may be so great as to amputate life and may be silly or futile. There is sacrifice and sacrifice. One need not be sadist or masochist, neither are sound persons.

15. Can one make great sacrifices without submerging oneself?

Yes, wives of great men, mothers of great sons, teachers of leaders, have found their lives by losing their lives. He that loseth his life for my sake shall find it, says Jesus. You would now begin to find great things for your opening soul in a good modern version of the Gospels. Get one and read it slowly like any other book, and receptively. A seed fulfills itself by losing itself in the ground. So did the men at Thermopylae.

16. Should one submerge oneself in sacrifice?

That depends. Not for the sake of sacrifice, that would be masochism. He that loseth his life for my sake, said Jesus, shall find it. So says the Great Idea or the Grand Old Cause at any time. A man should follow the gleam. He should be wise, not a fool, but a man must sometimes be a fool for the glory of God. There are no better words in which to express the thought.

17. Does not one serve most by doing what one does best?

Yes, if the world needs that or can use that service. On the other hand, it may be selfish, where it is done to please oneself solely, without regard to the needs of one's time or one's fellows. As to art, beauty, the whole always needs that, but it flourishes best when one is part of a world that has found itself and is going somewhere, when art is the expression of the time.

18. Is it possible to be truly unselfish?

No, because even Jesus fed his ego: a man who dies for a cause does express himself, achieves his goal perhaps. God does not ask unselfishness in an absurd sense. Asceticism and self-mortification, and all that sort of thing, are abnormal attitudes. A man must be first a healthy animal. Then he must be more than an animal too. He must be a human.

19. How is it possible for anyone to give more than he is given?

It is not possible. Edison may have done so, and Jesus, and even Ben Franklin, perhaps any great artist, if you value beauty highly enough. Not many can do this, because for a million years or more humans have worked and suffered and lived and died to give us fire, clothes, the wheel, and myriads of everyday accepted things, to say nothing of more recent gifts.

20. Can one give by receiving?

Sometimes. There is a grace of receiving as well as a grace of giving. To accept some things from some people permits self-expression and joy to them. But we must not deceive ourselves and make parasites of ourselves in this respect. We too should give and serve. The meanest man, says Emerson, is he who receives and gives not. But we do not always give back to the giver; a man sends a boy through college and that boy becomes a man and sends some other boy through college. That is a common way of repayment.

21. Is there any fulfillment that endures as such, besides death?

I doubt if death fulfills. It seems to end but I doubt that it ends much. Not one's influence or the influence of one's work. Perhaps even the echoes of your voice may go on forever. Some instrument might pick them up years or ages hence. Beauty is an ultimate fulfillment, as is goodness, as is truth. These are ends in themselves, and are for the sake of life. Many things are worth while that are not enduring. Eternity is just made of todays. Glorify the hour.

22. Is there anything perpetual besides change?

Yes, the tendency to change, to unroll or evolve, and possibly the direction of change. The fact, if so, that things hold together, make sense, is perpetual. Why should we object to change? Maybe it is the essence of life.

23. Is passage from the sensual to the intellectual to the spiritual a correct progression of growth, and if so, should that growth be hastened?

Why not live in all three at the same time? Why such sharp demarcations? A house has a foundation, a first story, and a second story. Why not all three at the same time? "Nor flesh helps spirit more now than spirit flesh" or the like is a saying of Browning's. The Greeks separated flesh and spirit. We moderns tend not to do so, but to respect all parts of creation, each in its place.

ACKNOWLEDGMENTS

For thirty-five years I have been using the Special Collections archives at the J. Willard Marriott Library at the University of Utah. The material lodged there has helped me to write such books as *A River No More, Sagebrush Country, Fallout, Wallace Stegner and the American West,* and finally the biography of Everett Ruess. I may have been the one researcher who most often commuted to the library from a campsite, either in the mountains near Park City or on the outskirts of downtown Salt Lake City, depending on the season.

The Special Collections space underwent a number of room changes and re-modelings over that period, and I experienced them all. But the unfailing courtesy, friendliness, helpfulness, and knowledge of the staff have been constant. Gregory C. Thompson, the associate director for Special Collections, has helped me on each project and given me insights no one else possessed, including where to get my Volkswagen camper repaired in Salt Lake. He also encouraged me to apply for a J. Willard Marriott Library Fellowship, which helped with research expenses for this book. Elizabeth A. Rogers, the archivist who arranged and is in charge of the Ruess collection, answered queries promptly and nudged me in a few directions I might not have taken on my own. At the end, Kristin M. Giacoletto was a great help with the photographs.

A biography of Everett Ruess was not an easy sell. Editors on the East Coast as far back as 1998 blinked their eyes and asked me, Who was Ruess? When I told them, they closed their eyes and went to sleep, metaphorically speaking. Gibbs Smith of Layton, Utah, was interested, but I thought it best to stick with University of California Press, which has published many of my books in hardcover and paperback editions. Sheila Levine, the associate director and publisher, said yes and put me in touch with Kim Robinson, who had just come on board to acquire titles about California and the West. Sheila has been my guardian angel at the press for a number of years, and I thank her. Kim, who is more responsive than any other book editor I have ever dealt with, was persistent, and rightly so, in pointing out needed editorial changes. This is my third book that Dore Brown has capably shepherded through the intricacies of the production process.

A number of people helped me with specific information: Diane Orr and Tom Carey on who the mysterious Frances was; Dr. Michael Whitt and Dr. Colin Hamblin on Everett's physical condition; Meg Newcomer on bipolar disorder; Jonathan Kirsch on legal matters; Scott Thybony on Ruess and Dan Thrapp; W. L. ("Bud") Rusho on the search for Ruess; and Paul Leatherbury on the dental question. Sue Fearon and Grant Johnson of Escalante Canyon Outfitters got me into Davis Gulch on two separate occasions. My friend Gary Ireland and son, Alex Fradkin, kept me company. The Bancroft Library at the University of California, Berkeley; the Utah State Library in Salt Lake; and the libraries and archives of the various national parks and monuments that Everett visited contained material on Ruess and his time. I should emphasize here that I thought the historical context in which Everett lived was an important element in this book because, as the saying goes, no adolescent is an island unto himself.

I was out of my depth on the science involved in the bones issue, so I used Lori Baker, a physical anthropologist at Baylor University, and Derinna Kopp, a Utah state archeologist, as advisors on DNA matters and Mark Griffin, who teaches bioanthropology at San Francisco State University, as an advisor on Dennis Van Gerven's work. All are specialists in older bones. Portions of the last chapter were read by Kevin Jones, Ken Krauter, Paul Leatherbury, and Mark Dowie, the former publisher of *Mother Jones* and an award-winning magazine journalist who advised me on journalism issues.

Carl Brandt, Dianne Fradkin, Connie and Michael Mery, Doris Ober, and Kim Robinson read the entire manuscript. Carl is my literary agent, Dianne is my wife, the Merys are intelligent friends, Doris is my first professional reader, and Kim is the acquiring editor. The press also had three peer reviewers read draft versions of the manuscript. I can say I have never benefited more from the comments I have received. I am, of course, ultimately responsible for any errors.

NOTES

The vast majority of documents and photographs pertaining to Everett Ruess are in the Everett Ruess Family Papers in the Special Collections division of the J. Willard Marriott Library at the University of Utah. Most of the papers were donated to the library by Everett's brother, Waldo, an inveterate collector of materials pertaining to the family. Thank goodness for people like Waldo. Waldo's daughter Michele donated a portion of the fifty-one linear feet of the collection.

Much of the material about Everett's time came from the Bancroft Library at the University of California, Berkeley; the libraries and archives of the various national parks and monuments Ruess visited; and local public libraries scattered throughout the West. This was the first time I used Google extensively to research a book, always making sure I sought further links to provide confirmation or seek a more primary source of information than was first presented on the computer screen. Google makes me look very knowledgeable. Contained within these notes are the references for quoted material, further explanations of what is stated in the text, and my relevant personal experiences so readers can understand why I was drawn to this story and how, through their experiences, they can relate to Everett.

I. DAVIS GULCH

1. The politically correct term for the Anasazi is now *Ancestral Puebloans*. But *Anasazi* has a certain resonance the neutered phrase lacks; thus I adhere to the old word.

2. Various other landscape features from Antarctica to Alaska and Florida

were named after La Gorce, who was editor of the magazine and president of the society in the early 1950s. The U.S. Board of Geographic Names made the official designations and changed La Gorce to LaGorce per its standard treatment of geographic names.

II. WANDERERS

1. See, for example, Evan Balkan, *Vanished!: Explorers Forever Lost* (Birmingham, Ala.: Menasha Ridge Press, 2008), 51–74; Rob Schultheis, "Beyond the Edge," *Backpacker,* November 1988: 34; and Nicosia, "Another 10 Bizarre Disappearances," Listverse, http://listverse.com/2009/02/23/another-10-bizarre-disappearances/.

2. Sheila Nickerson, *Disappearance: A Map* (New York: Doubleday, 1996), 228.

3. Géza Róheim, *The Eternal Ones of the Dream: A Psychoanalytic Interpretation of Australian Myth and Ritual* (New York: International Universities Press, 1945), 13.

4. Bob Callahan, ed., *A Jaime de Angulo Reader* (Berkeley, Calif.: Turtle Island, 1979), xiii.

5. Mark Twain, *The Adventures of Huckleberry Finn* (New York: Penguin Books, 1986), 307.

6. J. D. Salinger, *The Catcher in the Rye* (New York: Back Bay Books, 2001), 257.

7. Ibid., 246.

III. THE LEGACY

1. Bertha Knight Power, *William Henry Knight: California Pioneer* (reprint of a privately printed book, Whitefish, Mont.: Kessinger Publishing, 1932), 27.

2. Ibid., 64, 71.

3. Ibid., 123, 124.

4. Quoted in ibid., 179.

5. Quoted in Waldo Ruess, letter to James D. Hart, director, Bancroft Library, April 16, 1980.

6. Quoted in Power, *Knight,* 182.

7. Christopher Ruess, "Life History of Christopher Ruess," 15-page typed document on "Old Age Counselling Center" stationery, April 25, 1942.

8. Carey McWilliams, *Southern California: Island on the Land* (Salt Lake City: Peregrine Smith Books, 1973), 128.

9. Ruess, "Life History," 4. In the poem "Christopher, 1878–1954," written by Stella after her husband's death, she said the name meant "bearing Christ."

10. Ruess, "Life History," 5.

11. Ibid.

12. Ibid., 8.

13. Stella Knight, letter to an unnamed uncle, December 1900.

14. Ruess, "Life History," 7. Ruess studied under such giants in their fields as William James and Hugo Münsterberg, psychology; Josiah Royce and George Santayana, philosophy; Charles Townsend Copeland, English; and Nathaniel Shaler, geology.

15. "You have no right to go, unless you are equally willing to be prevented from going." This portion of a sentence was taken from Emerson's essay "The Over-Soul."

16. The Unitarians and the Universalist Church joined in 1961 to form the Unitarian Universalist Association.

17. Commission of Appraisal of the American Unitarian Association, *Unitarians Face a New Age* (Boston: Commission of Appraisal of the American Unitarian Association, 1936), 16.

18. Ibid., 152.

19. Daniel Walker Howe, *The Unitarian Conscience: Harvard Moral Philosophy, 1805–1861* (Cambridge, Mass.: Oxford University Press, 1970), 188, 199.

20. Reyner Banham, *Scenes in America Deserta* (Salt Lake City: Gibbs M. Smith, 1982), 217, 219.

21. Ruess, "Life History," 8–9.

22. Christopher Ruess, letter to William Knight, April 8, 1906.

23. "Secretary's Third Report," Harvard College class of 1900, June 1910.

24. Stella Ruess, "Fifty Golden Aprils with Christopher Ruess," April 2, 1914, in "Everett Ruess: Notes on His Childhood and Early Years from His Mother's Journal," prepared for Irene Allen of Escalante, Utah, January 18, 1942, unpaged.

25. Portions of Stella's journal, including one in which she describes the garden, were furnished by her granddaughter Michele Ruess.

The family's—and Everett's—first home was at 827 Fifty-Seventh Street, now in Emeryville.

26. Stella Ruess, undated, untitled fragment.

IV. GROWING UP

1. Everett's places of residence were: Oakland, California, March 1914 to September 1915; Fresno, California, September 1915 to October 1917; Los Angeles, October 1917 to August 1918; Brookline, Massachusetts, September 1918 to July 1920; Brooklyn, July 1920 to May 1922; Palisades Park, New Jersey, May 1922 to September 1924; Los Angeles (a temporary move by Everett and his mother to care for Stella's ailing father), March 1923 to September 1923; Valparaiso, Indiana, September 1924 to July 1928; Los Angeles, July 1928 to 1934.

2. Although his two brothers had greater incomes most years, Christopher's

parents thought he should provide for them as they had for his university education. In return, before dying his mother deeded the family home to Christopher.

3. Christopher Ruess, "Life History of Christopher Ruess," 15-page typed document on "Old Age Counselling Center" stationery, April 25, 1942, 11.

4. Lewis E. Myers & Company, "The Home Teacher," sales brochure, 1913. This booklet was sold with the desk when Ruess worked for the company. The desk is now a collectors' item.

5. Stella Ruess, "Everett Ruess: Notes on His Childhood and Early Years from His Mother's Journal," prepared for Irene Allen of Escalante, Utah, January 18, 1942, 1.

6. Stella Ruess, typed section of journal (1917–28), 2.

7. Stella Ruess, "Fifty Golden Aprils with Christopher Ruess," April 2, 1921, in "Everett Ruess: Notes on His Childhood and Early Years from His Mother's Journal," unpaged. My family constructed a home on that same hillside, within easy walking distance of the trolley on Bloomfield Avenue. I was raised approximately where the Ruess family ate their picnic, and I frequently took the trolley to the end of the line in West Caldwell to visit a friend.

8. Stella Ruess, typed section of journal, 2.

9. Everett Ruess, "His Journal, Vol. II, Kept by His Mother," April 4, 1923.

10. Stella Ruess, typed section of journal, 3.

11. Everett Ruess, "All Boy, Age 11, Secret Diary," ed. Stella Ruess, 1925.

12. Bertha Knight Power, *William Henry Knight: California Pioneer* (reprint of a privately printed book, Whitefish, Mont.: Kessinger Publishing, 1932), 245.

13. The composite that follows is drawn mainly from the 1925 edited diary, a journal kept by Everett from March 15 to October 2, 1927, and letters to his brother and father from 1925 to 1928. Starting in the Valparaiso years, there was a huge upsurge of written materials produced by Everett that would last through the remainder of his short life. For a biographer, what makes that record particularly trustworthy is that the journal entries and the letters to his mother, father, brother, and friends were not made for public consumption.

14. Everett Ruess, "All Boy," January 15, 1925.

15. Everett Ruess to Christopher Ruess, April 29, 1925.

16. Everett Ruess to Christopher and Waldo Ruess, December 11, 1927.

17. The trip was going to be a humdinger. George P. Putnam, the sponsor, promised a "palatial boat" to Europe, a train across the continent, a steamer to Mombasa, a train to Nairobi, and a safari. There would be a story in *Boys' Life* and a book published by Putnam's firm, G. P. Putnam and Sons.

Interestingly, Putnam later married Amelia Earhart, who disappeared over the Pacific Ocean two years after Everett vanished.

18. Christopher Ruess to W. B. Brown, March 4, 1928.

19. Everett Ruess, "All Boy," April 13, 1925.

20. Ibid., May 3, 1925.

21. Ibid., May 26, 1925.

22. Ibid., June 20, 1925.

23. Stella Ruess, draft of "Youth Is for Adventure" (partial photocopy), undated, a manuscript she wrote after Everett's death and attempted to get published. The page is marked "Acknowledgments 3, XII."

24. In another list Everett said he had merit badges in forestry, bird study, safety first, wood carving, leather work, and art and that he was working on badges in photography, insect life, and botany. His father said that he could have had more merit badges if there had been more examiners in the various subjects.

25. Everett Ruess, "All Boy," July 20, 1925.

26. Everett Ruess, "1927 Valparaiso Journal," 101.

27. Everett Ruess, "All Boy," August 26, 1925.

28. Christopher Ruess to Everett Ruess, September 24, 1927.

29. Everett Ruess, "1927 Valparaiso Journal," 22.

30. Everett Ruess, "All Boy," October 3, 1925.

31. Everett Ruess, "1927 Valparaiso Journal," 121.

32. Ibid., 25–26.

33. Everett Ruess, "All Boy," October 18, 1925.

34. Ibid., October 30, 1925.

35. Everett Ruess, "1927 Valparaiso Journal," 85–86.

36. Everett Ruess, "All Boy," December 31, 1925.

37. Christopher Ruess, "Life History," 11.

38. Everett Ruess to Billy (probably a Valparaiso friend), July 31, 1928.

39. Everett Ruess, paged journal for 1925 in which he added entries for 1928, September 15, 1928, 258.

40. Carey McWilliams, *Southern California: Island on the Land* (Salt Lake City: Peregrine Smith Books, 1973), 198, 200.

41. Ibid., 238, 351.

42. Ibid., 364. I am not alone in my opinion of McWilliams. Kevin Starr, who has made a career out of writing about California, noted that "no one mastered his region more completely than this young journalist, social historian, and literary critic." Kevin Starr, *Material Dreams: Southern California through the 1920s* (New York: Oxford University Press, 1990), 313. McWilliams lived in Los Angeles from 1922 to 1951 and then left California to edit *The Nation* in New York City.

43. Starr, *Material Dreams,* 319.

44. Daniel Hurewitz, *Bohemian Los Angeles and the Making of Modern Politics* (Berkeley: University of California Press, 2007), 78, 393.

45. Waldo Ruess, notes for Stella Ruess's obituary, May 10, 1964 (the day of her death).

46. Everett Ruess to Waldo Ruess, October 16, 1929. The description of the performance comes from Helen Caldwell, *Michio Ito* (Berkeley: University of California Press, 1977), 28, 86, 88–89.

47. The Tabard is a London inn mentioned in the first few lines of Chaucer's *Canterbury Tales*.

48. The Otis Art Institute, where Everett took classes for six months, is now known as the Otis College of Art and Design.

49. Everett Ruess to James (perhaps his Valparaiso friend James Wharton), August 12, 1929.

50. Everett Ruess to Billy (perhaps a Valparaiso friend), July 31, 1928.

51. Everett Ruess, "Trails," March 22, 1929.

V. ON THE ROAD

1. Everett Ruess to his parents, June 28, 1930. I use "his family" when the letters are addressed to his mother, father, and brother. "His parents" refers to letters addressed to his mother and father. When he writes letters to a single family member, that person is designated.

2. Everett Ruess to Stella Ruess, June 30, 1930. As I move into Everett's letters that were reprinted by W. L. Rusho in *Everett Ruess: A Vagabond for Beauty* (Salt Lake City: Peregrine Smith Books, 1983) and the more recent *The Mystery of Everett Ruess* (Layton, Utah: Gibbs Smith, 2010), it is worth noting that Rusho edited some, mostly for repetition. When they were available, which is true in most cases, I have used the original letters contained in the Ruess collection at the University of Utah library. Rusho's books do not include the new letters that came to light when the Ruess collection was opened to the public a few years ago. I leave it to someone else to edit the complete letters of Everett Ruess and those letters from others contained in the collection that give a fuller view of his character and life.

3. Nancy Newhall, ed., *The Daybooks of Edward Weston* (New York: Aperture, 1990), 175, 179.

4. Ibid., 173.

5. Everett Ruess to Christopher Ruess, July 1, 1930.

6. Everett Ruess to Christopher Ruess, July 3, 1930.

7. Everett Ruess to Bill Jacobs, July 7, 1930.

8. Harry was also known by his middle name. Harry Leon Wilson Sr. was well known at the time as a former editor of the humor magazine *Puck* and for his many short stories, plays, and novels, including *Ruggles of Red Gap*. He had also worked for the Bancroft History Company, but after Everett's grandfather had departed.

9. Brother and sister lived and attended schools in various places. Charis said the curriculum at Hollywood High School "seemed like a joke to us after the rigors of private school." Charis Wilson, *Through Another Lens: My Years with Edward Weston* (New York: North Point Press, 1998), 27.

10. Everett Ruess to Stella Ruess, July 4, 1930.

11. Newhall, *Daybooks*, 173.

12. Everett Ruess to Waldo Ruess, July 5, 1930.

13. Everett Ruess to Christopher Ruess, July 11, 1930.

14. Everett Ruess to Waldo Ruess, July 17, 1930.

15. Everett Ruess to Waldo Ruess, July 19, 1930. Marked prominently on the brochure for the present-day Point Lobos State Preserve is the warning: "Dangerous cliff and surf conditions exist throughout Point Lobos—use extreme caution."

16. Everett Ruess to his family, July 24, 1930.

17. Ibid.

18. Christopher Ruess to Everett Ruess, July 30, 1930.

19. Everett Ruess to his family, August 5, 1930.

20. Ibid.

21. The best reference for this policy of "something for everyone" with particular reference to Yosemite is Stanford E. Demars, *The Tourist in Yosemite, 1855 to 1985* (Salt Lake City: University of Utah Press, 1991).

22. Alfred Runte, *Yosemite: The Embattled Wilderness* (Lincoln: University of Nebraska Press, 1990), 152.

23. Superintendent C. G. Thomson, Yosemite National Park, annual report to the director of the National Park Service, 1933. Camping in the valley is now limited to 414 spaces. A contemporary camper wrote in his reminiscences of the park in the 1930s, "I know others disagree, but for me this was the Golden Age of Yosemite." Peñalosa, *Yosemite,* 136.

24. Many of the details of the firefall come from Acting Superintendent E. P. Leavitt, letter to Miss Agnes L. Scott, September 20, 1928.

25. Horace M. Albright and Frank J. Taylor, *Oh, Ranger!* (Stanford, Calif.: Stanford University Press, 1928), 144.

26. I was one of those gawkers when my father and I visited the park in 1949, and I wrote the 1968 story in the *Los Angeles Times* about the end of the firefall.

27. Albright and Taylor, *Oh, Ranger!,* 39.

28. Everett Ruess to his family, August 5, 1930.

29. Ibid.

30. Everett camped nearby, taking advantage of the companionship and free meals he was offered by the employees. Meals, cots, and bedding then cost $2 a day at the series of six High Sierra Camps spread through the backcountry of the national park. Now the same services cost approximately $150 a day and are available only by lottery.

31. Everett Ruess to his family, August 9, 1930.

32. Ibid.

33. Everett Ruess to his family, August 12, 1930.

34. Everett Ruess to his family, August 15, 1930.

35. Everett Ruess to his family, undated.

36. Everett Ruess to his family, August 22, 1930.

37. Ibid.

38. Ibid.

39. The superintendent was C. G. Thomson, known as the Colonel to his staff. Formerly the superintendent of Crater Lake National Park in Oregon, he was known for his administrative abilities and dynamic personality and took over Yosemite in 1929, where he was responsible for much construction.

40. Stella Knight Ruess to J. C. Rowell, February 2, 1931. Bancroft's bookstore collection had been sold to the university, which housed them in the Bancroft Library. "Poems in Trees" was published by Bryant Press.

41. Stella Ruess to Waldo Ruess, October 12, 1935.

42. Christopher Ruess to Mr. Bean, "Suggestions to Ameliorate Evil Effects of the Depression on the Morale of Children and Adults," Los Angeles County Probation Department, March 14, 1933.

43. Christopher Ruess, "Life History of Christopher Ruess," 15-page typed document on "Old Age Counselling Center" stationery, April 25, 1942, 12. In 1932 Christopher edited the proceedings of a conference at the University of Southern California that had advocated the advantages of probation. He also wrote an article in the February 1934 issue of *Los Angeles County Employee* advancing the argument that "supervised freedom" was good economics and provided better community protection than "hard punishment."

44. Waldo Ruess to H. L. Watkins, November 26, 1933.

45. Ibid.

46. Ibid.

47. Everett Ruess, "Desert," September 26, 1930.

48. Not surprisingly, Hollywood High School is now known as the School of the Stars for all of the actors who have attended it, and its symbol is an Arabic sheik resembling Rudolph Valentino. "Sheik pride!" is the school's rallying cry.

VI. LAN RAMEAU

1. Everett Ruess to Waldo Ruess, January 14, 1933.

2. Ibid.

3. Cornel Lengel to Everett Ruess, September 22, 1931.

4. Everett Ruess to Waldo Ruess, January 14, 1931.

5. James N. Gregory, *American Exodus: The Dirt Bowl Migration and Okie Culture in California* (New York: Oxford University Press, 1989), 34. The Haggard family was traveling in a 1925 Chevrolet that pulled a two-wheel trailer. It took them four days to reach Bakersfield, California, where Merle would develop the Bakersfield sound in country music.

6. Susan Croce Kelly, *Route 66: The Highway and Its People* (Norman: University of Oklahoma Press, 1988), 62.

7. *The WPA Guide to California* (repr., New York: Pantheon Books, 1984),

608–10, 618. The book was originally published in 1939 and is an excellent guide to the time. For Arizona, *The WPA Guide to 1930s Arizona* (repr., Tucson: University of Arizona Press, 1989) serves the same purpose. The Arizona guide was originally published in 1940.

8. Arizona State Teachers College is now Northern Arizona University.

9. Lan Rameau [Everett Ruess] to Bill Jacobs, February 13, 1931. The 1925 film was about conquering races in the West and Navajo-white relations in Monument Valley.

10. In 1933 Ruess remained in California, spending most of his time in the Sierra Nevada.

11. Al Wetherill, quoted in Gary Topping, *Glen Canyon and the San Juan Country* (Moscow: Idaho University Press, 1997), 99. I am also uncomfortable in Anasazi ruins. I feel I am both a voyeur and a trespasser but have been drawn to as well as repelled by such places of abandonment.

12. John Wetherill, quoted in Frances Gillmor and Louisa Wade Wetherill, *Traders to the Navajo* (Albuquerque: University of New Mexico Press, 1953), 256.

13. *De Chelly* is derived from the Navajo word *tsegi,* meaning "rock canyon," and is pronounced *d'shay.*

14. Reyner Banham, *Scenes in America Deserta* (Salt Lake City: Gibbs M. Smith, 1982), 143. Most of the promotional activity and moviemaking emanated from Harry Goulding's Monument Valley Trading Post and Lodge, twenty-four miles north of Kayenta. Goulding credited his "good friend John Ford" with popularizing the valley. Ford filmed *Stagecoach,* starring John Wayne, in Monument Valley in 1938.

15. John Wetherill, "Notes on Navajo Proposed Park," 1932, private collection.

16. Hal K. Rothman, "Navajo National Monument: A Place and Its People," Southwest Cultural Resources Center Professional Papers number 40 (Santa Fe, N.M.: National Park Service, 1991), 29. As one way to protect ruins, the act provided for the creation of national monuments by executive order, thus bypassing Congress. Richard Wetherill received the most fame and notoriety of the brothers, but John had a more lasting presence in the region. Richard discovered and excavated the Cliff Palace ruin at Mesa Verde, and along with naming that ruin applied the Navajo word *anasazi* to the ancient peoples who had occupied it. The term was picked up by others and applied to the ancient culture that preceded modern "Native" Americans in this region. Richard also discovered Keet Seel, one of three ruins in Navajo National Monument. He excavated Chaco Canyon, the great Anasazi ruin in New Mexico, where he settled and was murdered by a Navajo in 1910. By *discover,* of course, I mean he was the first white man to record the presence of these ruins in a document that has survived and been given credence. People lacking written languages had been present and seen the ruins before the whites did.

17. John Wetherill, "Supplementary Report for April, Southwestern Monuments," May 1, 1934.

18. Lan Rameau to Waldo Ruess, February 13, 1931.

19. Keith Warren to Stella Ruess, March 11, 1931.

20. Lan Rameau to his parents, undated [February 1931].

21. Ibid.

22. Lan Rameau to Bill Jacobs, March 1, 1931. Everett handwrote a more extensive shopping list with the same items on H. T. Goulding Trading Post stationery. Hand drawn on the back are sketches of Anasazi and Navajo designs and symbols, including the drawing of a skull. At the time Everett was camped at Say-Kiz-Y Pass, near the post.

23. Lan Rameau to his family, March 21, 1931.

24. Lemuel A. Garrison, *The Making of a Ranger* (Salt Lake City: Howe Brothers, 1983), 77. There is a debate over whether a horse or a burro makes a better pack animal. The author of a book favoring horses wrote that burros have "a sardonic sense of humor" and are sneakier than horses. They need to be handled with a firm hand. Joe Back, *Horses, Hitches, and Rocky Trails* (Boulder, Colo.: Johnson Books, 1997), 48, 51.

25. Lan Rameau to his family, March 21, 1931.

26. Ibid.

27. Lan Rameau to his family, April 2, 1931.

28. *Aghaa'lá* means "much wool," possibly because the Navajo used the coarse basalt of the volcanic column to scrape the hides of deer, whose hair would accumulate around the rock.

29. *Tsegi* here is pronounced *tsay-yhi*.

30. "Visit to Betatakin," undated fragment.

31. John Wetherill's Keet Seel Visitor Log, Navajo National Monument, NAVA-600, Hubbell Trading Post Natural Historic Site Museum Storage Facility, Ganado, Arizona.

32. Lan Rameau to Bill Jacobs, April 18, 1931.

33. Evert Rulan to Waldo Ruess, May 2, 1931.

34. Ibid.

35. Ibid.

36. Lan Rameau to Waldo Ruess, April 19, 1931.

37. Evert Rulan to Bill Jacobs, May 2, 1931.

38. Ibid.

39. Evert Rulan to Bill Jacobs, May 10, 1930.

40. Ibid.

41. There are no dates on either missive and no salutation on the letter, but both are clearly from Ruess to Jacobs. Judging from their contents, the note was sent in late March or early April and the letter was written in the summer of 1932—bookends to the breakup of the three boys' friendship in Roosevelt, Arizona, that year.

42. Christopher Ruess to Waldo Ruess, September 17, 1935.

43. W. L. Rusho, ed., *Wilderness Journals of Everett Ruess* (Salt Lake City: Gibbs Smith, 1998), 42, 58; Everett Ruess to Frances Schermerhorn, May 1934. The first two intimacies occurred in 1932, the last in 1934.

44. W. L. Rusho, ed., *Everett Ruess: A Vagabond for Beauty* (Salt Lake City: Peregrine Smith Books, 1983), viii.

45. Mark A. Taylor, *Sandstone Sunsets: In Search of Everett Ruess* (Salt Lake City: Gibbs Smith, 1997), 93; Rusho, *Wilderness Journals*, 15; Gary James Bergera, ed., *On Desert Trails with Everett Ruess* (Salt Lake City: Gibbs Smith, 2000), 115–116.

46. Diane Orr, personal communications, December 23, 2009, and June 17, 2010. I am struck by the similar ambiguity of another desert wanderer, T. E. Lawrence, otherwise known as Lawrence of Arabia. Everett read Lawrence's *The Seven Pillars of Wisdom* and his translation of *The Odyssey*. I see nothing unusual in such an ambiguity in sexual orientation. When I hitchhiked alone through Europe in my early twenties, I was continually accosted by gay Englishmen. These experiences made me wonder who I was. At the end of my journey, in Rome, an Italian woman poet with whom I fell in love gave me a copy of *The Seven Pillars of Wisdom* as a gift. She said I reminded her of the author for a number of reasons, including the fact that Lawrence was my middle name.

47. Evert Rulan to Bill Jacobs, May 10, 1931. Everett recounted the same incident in a letter to his family the same day. Stella deleted the reference to the theft when she edited the letter for possible publication after his disappearance. Rusho did the same in his books.

48. Hampton Sides, *Blood and Thunder* (New York: Doubleday, 2006), 228, 231.

49. Everett Ruess, "Impromptu, no. 1," exercise for a UCLA English class, September 30, 1932.

50. T. H. Watkins, *Righteous Pilgrim: The Life and Times of Harold L. Ickes, 1874–1952* (New York: Henry Holt and Co., 1990), 544–45.

51. Evert Rulan to Billy [Bill Jacobs], May 23, 1931.

52. Ibid.

53. Evert Rulan to his family, May 23, 1931.

54. *WPA Guide to 1930s Arizona*, 407.

55. Evert Rulan to his family, June 8, 1931.

56. Ibid.

57. The school, founded in 1902 by a Cambridge University graduate, was an outdoor, western equivalent of an eastern prep school. Its alumni included two sons of President Theodore Roosevelt.

58. Randolph Jenks with Kathryn Reed Brandt and Paul Randolph Sutton, *Leaving the Golden Age of the 1920s for Adventure in the West: Memoirs of Randolph Jenks* (privately printed, 2003), 31.

59. Evert Rulan to Bill Jacobs, June 8, 1931.

60. Ibid.

61. Ruess used the term *kyak,* while one of his favorite publications, *Boys' Life,* published by the Boy Scouts of America, designates them *kayak boxes.* A book on packing and horses spells it *kyack* and identifies this as an old-fashioned term for panniers. Back, *Horses,* 30.

62. Evert Rulan to Bill Jacobs, June 30, 1931.

63. Like *Pegasus, Pericles* was of Greek origin. The Athenian statesman and orator who bore the name had been so distinguished that his time became synonymous with the golden age of Greece.

64. Evert Rulan to Bill Jacobs, June 30, 1931.

65. I have floated down the Colorado River and through the canyon twice. I can't recall how many times I have visited the south and north rims or hiked into and out of the canyon. On my first visit, in 1949, I rode a horse down the north rim. I dictated the following observation into my tape recorder on my most recent visit: "You are never prepared for it, this incredible multilayered, multicolored surprise. There is no warning. It's too grand, too grandiose, too overwhelming in space and time. And then you try to figure out how to relate to it the rest of the time you are there. I think the only way you can is occupy and concentrate on a small space, as Everett did."

66. Michael F. Anderson, *Polishing the Jewel: An Administrative History of Grand Canyon National Park* (Grand Canyon, Ariz.: Grand Canyon Association, 2000), 25.

67. For an accurate comparison, costs must be adjusted for inflation. Seven dollars in 1931 was the equivalent of one hundred dollars in 2010, about half the current room rate at El Tovar excluding meals.

68. Anderson, *Polishing the Jewel,* 33.

69. Everett Ruess to Pat Jenks, August 6, 1931. As of this date, he becomes inconsistent in his use of names.

70. Evert Rulan to Christopher Ruess, July 16, 1931. He wrote two nearly identical versions of this trip: the first to his father and the second four days later to Bill Jacobs. Nearly identical descriptions sometimes appeared in his letters and journal entries.

71. Evert Rulan to Bill Jacobs, July 20, 1931.

72. Aldo Leopold, *A Sand County Almanac* (repr., New York: Oxford University Press, 1989), 170.

73. Everett Ruess to his family, August 18, 1931. By this time Everett had filled five hundred pages of the journal that was subsequently lost and asked his parents to send him another of the same size.

74. Evert Rulan to his family, August 28, 1931.

75. Evert Rulan to Bill Jacobs, August 27–28, 1931.

76. Donal J. Jolley, September monthly report, October 2, 1931; J. H. Allen, September monthly report, October 6, 1931.

77. Evert Rulan to his family, September 9, 1931.

78. P. I. Adams to S. K. Ruess, September 11, 1931.

79. Evert Rulan to his family, August 28 and September 11, 1931.

80. Evert Rulan to Bill Jacobs, September 30, 1931.

81. Everett Ruess to Waldo Ruess, October 9, 1931.

82. See Scott Thybony, *Hermit Trail Guide* (Grand Canyon, Ariz.: Grand Canyon Association, 2005); and Debra L. Suphen, *Sinews of Dirt and Stone,* Historical Research Study for Grand Canyon National Park (Grand Canyon, Ariz.: National Park Service, 1992), 74, 80. The remnants of the camp were set on fire and provided a spectacular blaze for sightseers from the rim in 1936. The trail is minimally maintained and patrolled by the Park Service. Pieces of the fitted and ridged sandstone trail floor and low walls remain in place.

83. Everett Ruess to Waldo Ruess, October 9, 1931.

84. Ibid.

85. F. D. Southard to Mr. and Mrs. Ruess, March 14, 1938. Seven years later the couple remembered Everett distinctly.

86. Everett Ruess to Stella Ruess, October 23, 1931.

87. Ibid.

88. Lyndon L. Hargrave, "The Influence of Economic Geography upon the Rise and Fall of the Pueblo Culture in Arizona," *Museum Notes* (Museum of Northern Arizona), December 1931: 1. Hargrave was a noted southwestern archeologist of the 1930s.

89. Charlie R. Steen et al., *Archeological Studies at Tonto National Monument, Arizona,* vol. 2, *Southwestern Monuments Association Technical Series,* edited by Louis R. Caywood (Globe, Ariz.: Southwestern Monuments Association, 1962).

90. Nancy C. Dallett, *At the Confluence of Change: A History of Tonto National Monument* (Tucson: Western National Parks Association, 2008), 70.

91. Everett Ruess to Waldo Ruess, November 13, 1931.

92. Ibid.

93. Everett Ruess to Bill Jacobs, November 26, 1931.

94. Everett Ruess to his parents, November 28, 1931.

95. Everett Ruess to Stella Ruess, December 6, 1931.

96. Rusho, *Everett Ruess,* 68.

VII. THE MISFIT

1. Stella Ruess, *Los Angeles in Block Print* (Hollywood: Bryant Press, 1932).

2. Alfred L. Law to Everett Ruess, October 27, 1932.

3. Everett Ruess to his family, March 30, 1932.

4. Everett Ruess to his family, undated.

5. Everett Ruess to his parents, April 20, 1932.

6. Eleanor Reynolds to Stella Ruess, June 10, 1936.

7. Everett Ruess to Waldo Ruess, July 12, 1932.

8. Everett Ruess to Waldo Ruess, May 7, 1932; Everett Ruess to his family, May 25, 1932.

9. The first entry for Everett's 1932 journal is dated May 13. A version edited by Stella Ruess exists in the Ruess archives at the University of Utah. It is not reliable. For instance, she deleted the section dealing with the unpleasantness between the friends. I have used the unedited version in W. L. Rusho, ed., *Wilderness Journals of Everett Ruess* (Salt Lake City: Gibbs Smith, 1998), 18–19. The 1932 and 1933 journals and letters were published as one volume, *Everett Ruess: Combination Edition* (Salt Lake City: Peregrine Smith Books, 2002), with little changed from the original paperback versions.

10. Everett Ruess to Bill Jacobs, undated. The quote is from a poem by Carl Sandburg.

11. Now the dirt-surfaced State Highway 288, designated a scenic roadway, the trail continues north of the rim as State Highways 260 and 377.

12. Rusho, *Wilderness Journals*, 19–20.

13. Ibid., 21.

14. Everett Ruess to Waldo Ruess, July 12, 1932.

15. Rusho, *Wilderness Journals*, 25, 27, 28.

16. Ibid., 32.

17. Ibid., 33.

18. Ibid.

19. Ibid., 32, 33, 35.

20. The ranch is still there, with a sign identifying it on the west side of Highway 377. Two of Claude Despain's ten children live there now, but they had not been born when Everett visited in 1932. Charlotte, then eight years old and now Charlotte Despain Crandall, lived in nearby Heber in 2010. We talked on the phone in April 2010. Although Everett mentioned Charlotte in his journal, she could not recall him seventy-eight years later. She did have vivid memories of Tom Reed, who had visited the ranch frequently. He was something of a rake among his Mormon neighbors, she said.

21. Rusho, *Wilderness Journals*, 36.

22. Ibid., 37.

23. I extracted this history of Zeniff from the files of the Navajo County Historical Society in Holbrook, Arizona, and from Leland J. Hanchett Jr., *The Crooked Trail to Holbrook* (Phoenix: Arrowhead Press, 1993). When I visited Zeniff in March 2010, the only resident I could find was a San Francisco patent attorney who had moved there with three adopted children who had drug problems.

24. Rusho, *Wilderness Journals*, 44.

25. Everett Ruess to his family, June 14, 1932.

26. Rusho, *Wilderness Journals*, 47.

27. Ibid., 48.

28. Everett Ruess to Bozo [Bill Jacobs], June 20, 1932.

29. Rusho, *Wilderness Journals,* 49–50.

30. Ibid., 51.

31. Ibid., 53–55.

32. Ibid., 56.

33. Everett Ruess to his parents, April 19, 1934.

34. The Hubbell family operated the Ganado trading post from 1878 to 1965. Ganado was the center of the family's mercantile interests, which included twenty-three similar establishments at one time. The National Park Service purchased the trading post in 1967, and it is now a National Historic Site.

35. Martha Blue, *Indian Trader: The Life and Times of J. L. Hubbell* (Walnut, Calif.: Kiva Publishing, 2000), 271.

36. Rusho, *Wilderness Journals,* 57.

37. Since Everett's supposed Navajo diet was a factor in the misidentification of his bones in 2010, here is the exact quote: "The Navajo diet of squawbread, mutton, and coffee does not appeal to me." Everett Ruess to his family, July 9, 1932. He had earlier sworn off beans, which made him sick.

38. Rusho, *Wilderness Journals,* 58–59.

39. At the time, Gillmor was a graduate student living with the Wetherills at their Kayenta trading post and working with Louisa on Gillmor's master's thesis, which would become their book *Traders to the Navajos* (Albuquerque: University of New Mexico Press, 1953). Gillmor would go on to teach at the universities of New Mexico and Arizona and write other books on the Southwest and on Mexico.

40. Rusho, *Wilderness Journals,* 61. The damaged stone walls of the Dunaway house are still visible across the street from the Garcia Trading Post, which is now a Holiday Inn. A Best Western motel in Kayenta bears the name of the Wetherill Trading Post.

41. Christopher Ruess to Everett Ruess, July 5, 1932.

42. There are levels of disclosure in the correspondence. Everett was most open with his feelings for a while with his friend Bill Jacobs, secondly and most consistently with Waldo, and lastly—with more carefully worded versions—with his parents. When Everett and his brother wrote to each other it was with the understanding that the correspondence was personal and not to be shared with their parents, unless otherwise specified.

43. Everett Ruess to Waldo Ruess, July 12, 1932. There is a variation of this part of the letter in Everett's journal entry for the same day: *God, how the wild calls to me. There can be no other life for me but that of the lone wilderness wanderer. I think I will extend my leave another year. I'd get a couple of good horses and a good saddle. The wild has an irresistible fascination for me. After all, the lone trail is the best.* Rusho, *Wilderness Journals,* 62.

44. Francis Mark Mondimore, *Bipolar Disorder: A Guide for Patients and Families* (Baltimore: Johns Hopkins University Press, 2006), 246. *Completed* is the adjective used by the American Psychiatric Association to distinguish actual deaths from unsuccessful attempts. With effective treatments, the rate for the general population has dropped to 15 percent, but suicide rates for teenagers have tripled in the past half-century, during which time suicide was the third leading cause of teen death. Depression led to most of these suicides. Kay Redfield Jamison, *Night Falls Fast: Understanding Suicide* (New York: Vintage, 1999), 21–22.

45. Emil Kraepelin, *Manic-Depressive Insanity and Paranoia* (Edinburgh, Scotland: E. S. Livingstone, 1921; repr., Memphis, Tenn.: General Books, 2010), 5. Originally published in German in 1896, this classic work has appeared in a number of editions.

46. Kay Redfield Jamison, *An Unquiet Mind* (New York: Alfred A. Knopf, 1995), 6.

47. Mondimore, *Bipolar Disorder,* 12.

48. Jamison, *Touched with Fire: Manic-Depressive Illness and the Artistic Temperament* (New York: Free Press, 1994), 46, 62.

49. Quoted in Mondimore, *Bipolar Disorder,* 25.

50. Kraepelin, *Manic-Depressive Insanity,* 79.

51. In addition to the above citations, I read other books and articles on the subject. Another first-person account, Susanne Antonetta's *A Mind Apart: Travels in a Neurodiverse World* (New York: Jeremy P. Tarcher, 2005), was particularly helpful.

52. Rusho, *Wilderness Journals,* 63.

53. Ibid., 67–68.

54. Ibid., 68. Everett translated *naneskadi* as meaning "squaw bread" in Navajo. It is also known as fry bread, a traditional Indian dish.

55. Ibid., 69, 71. The problem arose from his monotonous diet over the three previous weeks, which lacked such micronutrients as iron, vitamin A, and iodine. Lack of iron causes fatigue, lack of vitamin A causes eyesight problems, and lack of iodine would have heightened Ruess's bipolar moods. Dr. Colin Hamblin, personal communication, March 30, 2011.

56. Ibid., 72. Everett thought the fall led to Jonathan's death, but there are other possibilities. He noted that the horse had been behaving strangely over the previous few days. Larkspur and locoweed are poisonous to livestock, and perhaps Jonathan ingested some.

57. I am familiar with Canyon de Chelly, having lived there with the guide Chauncey Neboyia and his family for one week in the early 1970s. Like Everett, I heard the call of crows flying across the canyon, during my 2010 tour with a guide of Canyon del Muerto. The dirt road we took passed the site of Old Yellow Mustache's camp. I walked a short distance up Twin Trail, which leads to the Navajo community of Del Muerto, on the rim. The ruins where Everett left the saddle and blankets were visible on the north side of the trail. Park regulations prohibited my

searching them. I was assured by a knowledgeable guide that the items were no longer in their hiding place.

58. Everett Ruess to Stella Ruess, July 28, 1932.

59. Rusho, *Wilderness Journals,* 75.

60. Ibid., 77.

61. Ibid., 79.

62. Ibid., 80.

63. Ibid., 81–82.

64. Ibid., 82–83.

65. "Wanted by the NPS," National Park Service news release, March 31, 1931.

66. Richard West Sellars, "A Very Large Array: Early Federal Historic Preservation—The Antiquities Act, Mesa Verde, and the National Park Act," *Natural Resources Journal,* Spring 2007: 299. Sellars was a historian with the National Park Service in Santa Fe.

67. Everett Ruess to his family, August 3, 1932.

68. Fritz Loeffler to Stella Ruess, June 29, 1936.

69. Everett Ruess to Christopher Ruess, August 18, 1932.

70. Ibid.

71. Ibid.

72. Everett Ruess to his family, August 25, 1932.

73. Ibid.

74. Everett Ruess to Christopher Ruess, August 30, 1932.

75. Everett Ruess to Fritz Loeffler, March 23, 1933. Everett said the snake was a rare species, found only in the canyon. He killed a total of eight rattlesnakes that year. In March 1933, Loeffler was running a patent office in New York City.

76. Everett Ruess to Waldo Ruess, November 2, 1932.

77. Grace Meinen to Stella Ruess, January 8, 1936. Everett dedicated two poems to Meinen. He wrote to Mrs. Meinen, as he referred to her, twice from the Sierra Nevada the next year.

VIII. THE BOHEMIAN

1. Everett Ruess to Eleanor and Ben Reynolds, December 1932.

2. Everett Ruess to Fritz Loeffler, March 23, 1933.

3. W. L. Rusho, ed., *Wilderness Journals of Everett Ruess* (Salt Lake City: Gibbs Smith, 1998), 97, 99; Everett Ruess to his family, June 5, 1933.

4. Everett Ruess to his family, June 16, 1933.

5. Everett Ruess to Lawrence Janssens, June 1933.

6. Everett Ruess to his family, July 5, 1933. The two sentences are at the end of a three-page letter and bear no relationship to what precedes them. They are obviously a reply to a query from his family about whether he was having a nervous breakdown.

7. Richard J. Orsi, Alfred Runte, and Marlene Smith-Baranzini, *Yosemite and*

Sequoia: A Century of California National Parks (Berkeley: University of California Press; San Francisco: California Historical Society, 1993), 26.

8. The material in this paragraph and the next comes from the superintendent's reports to the director of the National Park Service for June, July, August, and September 1933—the period when Everett was in the park—and for the entire year of 1933.

9. Lemuel A. Garrison, *The Making of a Ranger* (Salt Lake City: Howe Brothers, 1983), 85.

10. Ibid.

11. Ibid., 74.

12. Rusho, *Wilderness Journals*, 101.

13. Ibid., 102.

14. I presume he read it in translation, but one never knows with Everett.

15. Rusho, *Wilderness Journals*, 105.

16. Garrison, *Ranger*, 72.

17. Horace M. Albright and Frank J. Taylor, *Oh, Ranger!* (Stanford, Calif.: Stanford University Press, 1928), 78.

18. Superintendent John R. White, monthly report to the NPS director, September 7, 1933.

19. Garrison, *Ranger*, 56, 57. The current policy at Sequoia and Kings Canyon National Parks is to remove nonnative trout from certain lakes to give the mountain yellow-legged frog a chance to survive. As I was working on this book, state and federal environmental impact statements were being prepared to make a final decision on how to deal with the trout population. The plan was to create "clusters of fishless habitat" so the native species could recover. Such habitat brought to mind the "barren waters" of long ago.

20. I duplicated that hike in the summer of 2010. The lakes were no longer being stocked. Only native fish were present, and they were too wily to bite, a ranger told me. As a result, I saw no fishing activity.

21. Everett Ruess to his family, June 16, 1933.

22. Rusho, *Wilderness Journals*, 125.

23. Melvin H. Johnson to Stella and Christopher Ruess, March 21, 1939.

24. A remarkable portrait of a June day in the life of Beetle Rock is contained in Sally Carrigher, *One Day on Beetle Rock* (Berkeley, Calif.: Heyday Books, 2002).

25. Everett Ruess to Melvin H. Johnson, July 5, 1933. Pershing Square was a small park in the center of downtown Los Angeles.

26. Ibid.

27. Rusho, *Wilderness Journals*, 131.

28. Everett Ruess to Stella Ruess, July 30, 1933.

29. Rusho, *Wilderness Journals*, 143. I have no idea what the reference was. I searched the summit logs preserved at the Bancroft Library at UC Berkeley, but the one for that date is missing.

30. Rusho, *Wilderness Journals,* 143.

31. Ibid., 154. On an extended, lone backpacking trip in the Uintah Mountains of Utah, I heard the background murmur of a cocktail party and wrote about the experience in *Sagebrush Country.* Like Everett, I had been alone for many days and had a restricted diet.

32. Rusho, *Wilderness Journals,* 154; Everett Ruess to his family, August [illegible], 1933.

33. Rusho, *Wilderness Journals,* 158, 159.

34. Everett Ruess to Waldo Ruess, August 11, 1933.

35. Rusho, *Wilderness Journals,* 161, 162, 170.

36. Ibid., 171, 173.

37. Rusho, *Wilderness Journals,* 179. The lake was named for a poem that appeared in a 1923 issue of the *Sierra Club Bulletin,* which located the lake in a land "of treacherous beauty and awe."

38. Everett Ruess to his parents, September 6, 1933.

39. Rusho, *Wilderness Journals,* 200.

40. The information in this paragraph was compiled from the park superintendent's reports to the director of the Park Service for the summer and early fall months of 1933 and from the superintendent's annual report for the year.

41. Everett Ruess to his parents, October 2, 1933.

42. Wes Visel to Mr. and Mrs. Ruess, August 23, 1936. Everett later sent Visel a block print of a Carmel scene.

43. Kevin Starr, *The Dream Endures: California Enters the 1940s* (New York: Oxford University Press, 1997), 121.

44. Linda Gordon, *Dorothea Lange: A Life beyond Limits* (New York: W. W. Norton, 2009), 68.

45. Everett Ruess to his family, October 24, 1933.

46. Everett Ruess to his parents, October 24, 1933. He wrote two letters that day; see previous note. Besides a mezzanine art gallery and bookshelves on the ground floor, there was a lecture hall in Elder's store, which was a cultural center on the city's premier shopping street. The Depression did not have much effect on Paul Elder & Company, whose stores occupied a number of different locations over its seventy-year lifetime in San Francisco, Santa Barbara, and New York.

47. Another member of Group f/64 was Sonya Noskowiak, Weston's former lover whom Everett had met in 1930 at the Weston home.

48. Everett Ruess to his family, October 29, 1933.

49. Everett Ruess to his family, October 31, 1933.

50. The annual children's parade turned into a massive gay street party that ended in 1976 with a small riot, at which time the action moved to Castro Street, where it came to an end in 2006 with a shooting.

51. Everett Ruess to his parents, November 2, 1933.

52. Dean Luckhart, "Emerson Knight: Landscape Architect 1882–1960," *Landscape Architecture* 2 (January 2, 1962), unpaged.

53. Everett Ruess to Stella Ruess, November 5, 1933.

54. Everett Ruess to his family, November 12, 1933.

55. Everett Ruess to Christopher Ruess, December 13, 1933.

56. The book was *Breakdown: The Collapse of Traditional Civilization* by Robert Briffault (1932). It received a lot of attention on publication. The author, a British surgeon, historian, and novelist, was quoted in *Time* magazine as stating: "Yes, I think Americans are hopelessly stupefied by the humbug, hypocrisy, ballyhoo, and make-believe maintained by their leaders and their institutions—the church, the State, and the schools." *Time,* People section, July 18, 1932.

57. Everett Ruess to Christopher Ruess, December 13, 1933.

58. Everett Ruess to Waldo Ruess, December 13, 1933. In one of the many changes Stella made in Everett's letters when they came into her possession after he disappeared, the reference to intimacy with a girl was deleted. Of course, she may have recognized that the "girl" was married to a friend of the family and thought the reference inappropriate.

59. I had doubts about Frances being Everett's girlfriend. The filmmaker Diane Orr led me to Frances Schermerhorn. Orr had forgotten her last name but said she had a son named Charles, whom Orr had talked with in the 1990s. A Charles Schermerhorn and his son, who has the same first name, are mentioned in Everett's letters to his parents. I asked Orr if that was Frances's last name, and she said it was. The Schermerhorns' son had said his mother's diary documented the times she spent with Everett, all of them in unromantic circumstances. Their mutual interest was music. Diane Orr, personal communication, June 17 and July 29, 2010. I didn't feel that I had solidly documented who Frances was. I tried various searches with no luck and then enlisted the help of Tom Carey, a librarian in the History Center at the San Francisco Public Library. He found the 1930 census information on the Schermerhorns at www.ancestry.com, a subscription site. Mystery solved.

60. Everett Ruess to Frances Schermerhorn, December 14, undated, and December 19, 1933.

61. Everett Ruess to Waldo Ruess, December 22, 1933.

62. Everett Ruess to Frances Schermerhorn, May 5, 1934. Everett's letter probably came into the possession of the Ruesses when they sent a plea to friends who had been in contact with him for his correspondence.

63. Everett Ruess to Emerson Knight, December 29, 1933.

64. Everett Ruess to Christopher Ruess, January 2, 1934.

IX. VANISHED

1. Everett Ruess to Christopher Ruess, January 2 and 7, 1934.

2. Just as his family picnicked within one block of the house where I was raised

in Montclair on their 1922 outing in New Jersey, Everett passed within one block of where I now live in Point Reyes Station on his way to Tomales. His evocative block print of a fisherman's shack and rowboat on Tomales Bay, near my home, now hangs in my office.

3. Everett Ruess to his family, February 9 and 12, 1934.

4. Everett Ruess to his family, February 18, 1934. Rockport, twenty-five miles north of Fort Bragg, has had a rocky history since its founding in 1877. The economic fortunes of the company logging town, its associated mills, and its rock-bound harbor have caused it to go from boom town to ghost town. When Everett visited it, the settlement was just beginning to slip into oblivion. There was a brief revival in the 1940s. When I visited Rockport in 1966, it was a ghost town again.

5. Ibid.

6. Everett Ruess to his parents, February 26, 1934.

7. Everett Ruess to his family, March 2, 1934. There is no record of a photo of the Tomales rancher in the Dorothea Lange Collection at the Oakland Museum of California.

8. Ibid.

9. Everett Ruess to Waldo Ruess, "Monday Night" [1934].

10. In 1945 Christopher Ruess described Anderson as the librarian of the music library at Cornell University and the organist at the Presbyterian Church in Covina for twenty years.

11. Everett Ruess to Waldo Ruess, "Monday Night" [1934].

12. Ibid.

13. Waldo Ruess to his parents, April 17, 1934.

14. Everett Ruess to Bill Jacobs, May 5, 1934.

15. Everett Ruess to Edward Gardiner, May 5, 1934.

16. Everett Ruess to Frances Schermerhorn, May [1934]; Everett Ruess to his parents, May [1934]. The letters are nearly identical.

17. Everett Ruess to Carl Skinner, June 1934.

18. Everett Ruess to Bill Jacobs, June 17, 1934.

19. Everett Ruess to Stella Ruess, May 5, 1934.

20. Everett Ruess to Bill Jacobs, June 17, 1934.

21. Everett Ruess to his parents, June 30, 1934.

22. Everett Ruess to Bill Jacobs, June 29, 1934.

23. Ibid.

24. Everett Ruess to his parents, June 30, 1934.

25. Roger W. Toll to Horace M. Albright, April 28, 1931. Toll was in charge of assessing potential national parks. After Albright resigned in August 1933, the impetus for creating the park lessened in Washington, D.C., although the expedition's fieldwork continued until 1938. By that time it was clear the Navajo wanted no such park.

26. "The Rainbow Bridge–Monument Valley Expedition," *Science,* Aug. 11, 1933.

27. A new car could be purchased for as little as $500 then.

28. Lyndon L. Hargrave, "A Recently Discovered Basket Maker Burial Cave in the Tsegi," *Museum Notes* (Museum of Northern Arizona), October 1934: 13.

29. Vernon DeMars, "A Life in Architecture," Regional Oral History Office, University of California, Berkeley, 1992, 70.

30. Everett Ruess to his parents, July 22, 1934.

31. H. Claiborne Lockett and Lyndon L. Hargrave, "Woodchuck Cave, a Basketmaker II Site in Tsegi Canyon, Arizona," Bulletin 26, Museum of Northern Arizona, 1953. Lockett was the senior author, as he had done most of the work in the field and at the museum when he returned to write the report. Woodchuck Cave was rated the expedition's most important archeological excavation in 1934.

32. Ibid.

33. H. Claiborne Lockett to C. G. Ruess, February 13, 1939.

34. Ibid.

35. Everett Ruess to Waldo Ruess, August 19, 1934.

36. Everett Ruess to his parents, August 25, 1934.

37. Everett Ruess to his parents, September 10, 1934.

38. Everett Ruess to Stella Ruess, September 1934. I was in Mishongnovi in the early 1970s to attend a meeting on mining coal on Black Mesa and returned in 2010 to view the plaza where the dance was held. The plaza was an immaculate space amidst the general disarray of the village. When the Antelope clan kiva was rebuilt in the 1980s, the flooring was discovered to have come from the original mission church. A three-mile race up a canyon and a trail to the mesa precedes the dance. The day of my second visit, the women's society had spread cornmeal at the top of the trail in preparation for its dance.

39. Ibid.

40. Ibid.

41. Everett Ruess to Stella Ruess, September 27, 1934.

42. Everett Ruess to Ned Frisius, September 27, 1934.

43. Everett Ruess to Stella Ruess, October 15, 1934.

44. Everett Ruess to his parents, November 4, 1934.

45. Everett Ruess to Waldo Ruess, November 3, 1934.

46. Maurice Cope to Stella Ruess, February 25, 1935.

47. It was called Smoky Mountain because cattlemen had noticed smoke from burning coal rising from cracks in the ground, hinting at the vast coal reserves in the region that would attract a utility company in the early 1970s. The Southern California Edison Company wanted to build a coal-burning power plant on the nearby Kaiparowits Plateau. Economics and environmental concerns doomed the project.

48. Everett Ruess to Waldo Ruess, November (?), 1934. The letter, written on the Escalante Rim and mailed a few days later in Escalante, has a question mark for the exact date.

49. Lenora Hall LeFevre, *Boulder County and Its People* (Springdale, Utah: Art City Publishing Co., 1973), 261.

50. Everett Ruess to Waldo Ruess, November (?), 1934.

51. Neil Liston, outtake from Diane Orr's documentary *Lost Forever* (Beecher Films, 2000). The Special Collections at the University of Utah house nearly thirty hours of *Lost Forever* outtakes, which are the best record of the last two weeks of Everett's life, the search for him, and various scenarios of his disappearance. Neither the outtakes nor the documentary come to any definite conclusion. In the late 1990s Orr and her crew interviewed virtually everyone who was alive and had some relationship to the story. The collection has no catalogue; thus there is no way to refer precisely to a particular outtake. In some outtakes the person being interviewed is identified by name or can be identified by other means, but in others the interviewee can't be identified.

52. Unless otherwise noted, the description of Escalante comes principally from Lowry Nelson, *The Mormon Village: A Pattern and Technique of Land Settlement* (Salt Lake City: University of Utah Press, 1952); and Nethella Griffin Woolsey, *The Escalante Story* (Springdale, Utah: Art City Publishing Co., 1964).

53. Norm Christiansen, *Lost Forever*.

54. Edward A. Geary, *The Proper Edge of the Sky: The High Plateau Country of Utah* (Salt Lake City: University of Utah Press, 1992), 150.

55. Everett Ruess to Waldo Ruess, November (?), 1934.

56. Everett Ruess to his parents, November 11, 1934. This was the last letter he wrote.

57. Ibid.

58. Ibid.

59. Unknown, *Lost Forever* outtakes.

60. Christiansen, *Lost Forever* outtakes.

61. Everett Ruess to his parents, November 11, 1934.

62. "History Project Participants Talk about Lives," interview with Melvin Alvey, *Deseret News,* April 20, 2006. Available at www.deseretnews.com/article/635201010/History-project-participants-talk-about-lives.html, accessed February 10, 2011. Alvey tells the same story in his *Lost Forever* outtake.

63. Everett Ruess to Waldo Ruess, November (?), 1934.

64. The sheepherders were identified as Jack Woolsey and Adlin Lay in Nethella Griffin Woolsey's 1964 book and Clayton Porter and Addlin Lay in Rusho's 1983 book.

X. THE SEARCH

1. Both criteria are embedded in the federal Wilderness Act of 1964.

2. C. Gregory Crampton, "Historical Sites in Glen Canyon: Mouth of Hansen Creek to Mouth of San Juan River," Anthropological Papers, number 61,

Glen Canyon Series number 17 (University of Utah, December 1962), 6–19. In his report on historical sites in Glen Canyon, Crampton noted: "The region is scarcely known to tourists and vacationers. One who appreciated the canyon wilderness of the Escalante was the youthful and sensitive Everett Ruess, who disappeared from his solitary camp in Davis Gulch (or canyon), a lower tributary of the Escalante, in November 1934. The mystery of his disappearance has not been solved." In a similar 1964 report, Crampton, who wrote a number of publications about this region, noted that Ruess's "two burros were located in Davis Gulch" in 1934. Crampton, "Historical Sites in Cataract and Narrow Canyons, and in Glen Canyon to California Bar," Anthropological Papers, number 72, Glen Canyon Series number 24 (University of Utah, August 1964), 66.

3. This is a rare letter that has survived from Stella to Everett. Whether that was because she didn't write often, he didn't save her letters, or she destroyed them as she did her husband's journals, I don't know.

4. Mail sent to Ruby's Inn—adjacent to Bryce Canyon National Park—Everett's designated address for this period, was forwarded to the Marble Canyon post office, which returned it to the sender after a certain length of time. The address on Stella's letter, "Escalante Rim," more closely matched the Escalante post office; thus it was sent there.

5. The outfit or gear would have consisted of a pack saddle and a riding saddle, saddle blankets or pads, halters and halter ropes, lash ropes and lash cinches, kyaks, duffel bags, and canvas to cover the kyaks.

6. Gail Bailey, outtake from Diane Orr's documentary *Lost Forever* (Beecher Films, 2000). There are newspaper accounts of what Bailey found and the condition of the burros, but this outtake is the only extant firsthand account. Although old and ailing at the time of the interview, Bailey had a command of events that was more acute than the questions of his interviewers.

7. *Salt Lake Tribune,* June 8, 1935.

8. The accounts of the first searches are confusing and have minor differences. I have woven together the stories that appeared in the *Salt Lake Tribune* and the *Deseret News* with W. L. Rusho's 1982 interviews with the searchers and Diane Orr's outtakes. Rusho commented on a draft of this section.

9. The searcher's inscription, *Walter Allen, March 6, 1935,* is visible to this day; *NEMO 1934* disappeared some time ago.

10. *Salt Lake Tribune,* March 10, 1935.

11. Everett Ruess to Stella Ruess, September 27, 1934.

12. Robert H. Lister to J. D. Jennings, July 28, 1957.

13. Florence C. Lister to Diane Orr, undated. The one typewritten page is headed *Lister addendum.* Orr, a Salt Lake filmmaker, gave me a copy. The goods could have been taken from Davis Gulch or someplace else and dumped in Cottonwood Gulch. Who smashed them, and for what purpose? They seem very likely to

have belonged to Everett, especially considering Stella's almost certain confirmation that some belonged to him.

Florence and Robert Lister were noted archeologists who specialized in the Indian cultures of the Southwest. The archeological crew consisted of Robert Lister and two Escalante wranglers and helpers, Alvey and Lloyd Gates. They most probably found the gear in the southerly or left fork of the canyon on July 24, 1957. They spent the night, investigated the right fork the next day, and then left for Davis Gulch, where they spent the next two days. Florence said the crew saw the *NEMO* inscription in Davis Gulch. To add to the confusion over names, they referred to Bement Arch as Nemo Arch in their July 28, 1957, report to J. D. Jennings. Alvey was curious and briefly returned on his own with a friend to Cottonwood Gulch the next spring. He wrote Christopher in summer 1958: "I believe, Mr. Ruess, that it would be wise if it could be arranged, to give the Cottonwood area another careful search. I'm sure that it lies outside the region where most of the other searches for Everett were made." No one was interested in making such an effort twenty-four years after Everett disappeared. The rising water level of Lake Powell has since covered the site. Alvey was a science and mathematics teacher at Escalante High School and maintained a small museum of local artifacts. After his death, the museum was burglarized and burned in 1995. I do not know whether it contained any artifacts from Cottonwood Gulch.

14. Jesse D. Jennings to Robert H. Lister, October 24, 1957.

15. Waldo Ruess to Sheriff George Middleton, March 5, 1960.

16. Neal Johnson to Christopher Ruess, March 14, 1935.

17. Christopher Ruess to Waldo Ruess, September 22, 1935.

18. Donal J. Jolley, "Report on Search for Everett Ruess Who Is Supposedly Lost near the Colorado River," Enclosure 619 330, Department of the Interior, April 24, 1935.

19. Randall Henderson to Waldo Ruess, September 12, 1953; Henderson, *On Desert Trails: Today and Yesterday* (Los Angeles: Westernlore Press, 1961), 135–137. One of the Escalante men was Edson Alvey. In a series of letters in 1963, after he had sold *Desert Magazine,* Henderson held to the rustler theory but could cite no new facts.

20. Edward A. Geary, *The Proper Edge of the Sky: The High Plateau Country of Utah* (Salt Lake City: University of Utah Press, 1992), 172.

21. Waldo Ruess to Norman Christiansen, May 15, 1985. Waldo related the same story, with minor variations about the visit, in a letter to "Stan," whom I presume was Stan Jones, on June 10, 1980. Jones wrote guidebooks about the Lake Powell area. Ruess repeated the story about the two rustlers a third time in a July 21, 1963, letter to the mystery writer Erle Stanley Gardner, adding that he had been told one man "went insane" ten years later but the residents of Escalante felt there was not enough evidence to link the putative rustlers to the murder or "warrant talking out about the matter." Waldo was attempting to interest Gardner in

looking into his brother's death. Gardner's secretary replied that the writer said he had read about Everett's disappearance "and has always wanted to look into this. When he gets time, he hopes to read more about it." Thelma S. Lyon to Waldo Ruess, November 19, 1963.

22. Compare Everett's signature with what some members of the civic clubs' search party carved on the canyon wall of Fiftymile Creek: "E Rues [sic] Hunters, June 6, 1935. FB, RS, HC, AT, HS, LCC." When I used Google to search for *Nemo* in January 2010, I got 21.9 million results. It is a name for bands, towns, landscape features, movies, arcade games, businesses, observatories, various ocean-related devices, and so forth. A book for river runners states that *NEMO* stands for "Nature Enhances My Oblivion." W. H. Church, *River Runner Reverie* (Salt Lake City: Universal Youth Club, 1972).

23. About the author of the *Odyssey,* Lawrence wrote in his translator's note: "Few men can be sailors, soldiers, and naturalists. Yet this Homer was neither land-lubber nor stay-at-home nor ninny. He wrote for audiences to whom adventures were daily life and the sea their universal neighbor." Perhaps Everett would have written in the same manner. T. E. Shaw [T. E. Lawrence], translator, *The Odyssey of Homer* (New York: Oxford University Press, 1932).

24. Walter James Miller and Frederick Paul Walter, translators and annotators, in Jules Verne, *Twenty Thousand Leagues under the Sea* (Annapolis, Md.: Naval Institute Press, 1993), 67.

25. Verne, *Twenty Thousand Leagues,* 388.

26. Christopher Ruess to Ray C. Carr, June 5, 1935.

27. My account of the trip is drawn from three sources. "June Trip to Utah Etc., C & S, 1935," handwritten diary in a UCLA blue book used for examinations. "Log of the Pilgrimage in Search of Everett Made by Stella and Christopher June 21 to July 3, 1935, Arizona—Utah—Nevada—California," undated. Within this text is the note "(Revisions of Stella's notes by typist Christopher throughout)." Unfortunately, the detailed log ends midway through June 26. A less detailed account was handwritten by Stella sometime after 1940 and ends on the return trip through Nevada.

28. The dates Richardson gave in the February 21, 1934, letter for Everett's appearance at the trading post were unclear. Stella did not give much credence to Richardson's account.

29. Nequatewa wrote *Truth of a Hopi* (Flagstaff, Ariz.: Northland Press, 1967). His biography, by Alfred S. Whiting, is *Born a Chief* (Tucson: University of Arizona Press, 1993).

30. In appreciation for what they had done, the Ruesses sent the Allens a copy of the *Harvard Classics* for their young son and daughter and copies of Stella's *Los Angeles in Block Print* for the sixteen Escalante searchers.

31. Christopher Ruess to Mr. and Mrs. John Wetherill, July 6, 1935.

32. Christopher Ruess to Ray C. Carr, October 25, 1935.

33. Kelsey Presley to Stella Ruess, August 1, 1935.

34. Christopher Ruess, diary entry, August 11, 1935.

35. Quoted in Gary James Bergera, ed., *On Desert Tails with Everett Ruess* (Salt Lake City: Gibbs Smith, 2000), 74, 93.

36. Christopher Ruess to John U. Terrell, August 29, 1935.

37. "Another Search Looms in Utah for Local Artist," *Los Angeles Times,* October 20, 1935.

38. Christopher Ruess to Paul Poponoe, December 13, 1935.

39. Governor Henry H. Blood to Mr. and Mrs. Christopher Ruess, May 7, 1935; Ray E. Carr to Christopher Ruess, January 20, 1936.

40. Waldo Ruess to his parents, April 12, 1935.

41. Waldo Ruess to his parents, July 26, 1935.

42. Christopher Ruess to Waldo Ruess, September 17, 1935.

43. Christopher Ruess, diary entry, November 13, 1935, sent to Waldo Ruess.

44. Stella Ruess to Lillian Anderson, December 13, 1935.

45. Waldo Ruess to his parents, November 28, 1935.

XI. HEALING

1. Maynard Dixon to Stella Ruess, March 6, 1935.

2. Edward Weston to Stella and Christopher Ruess, January 22, 1938.

3. Hala Jean Hammond to Stella and Christopher Ruess, December 24, 1937.

4. Lawrence Janssens to Stella and Christopher Ruess, August 1, 1935.

5. Alan Booth to Stella and Christopher Ruess, December 25, 1937.

6. Harry F. Nurnburger to Stella and Christopher Ruess, January 4, 1937.

7. Eleanor Reynolds to Stella Ruess, June 10, 1934.

8. Fritz E. Loeffler to Stella and Christopher Ruess, June 29, 1936.

9. J. Sedgley Jory to Stella and Christopher Ruess, December 17, 1937.

10. Lon Garrison to Stella and Christopher Ruess, August 21, 1936.

11. Bill Atwood to Mrs. and Mrs. Ruess, August 21, 1936.

12. Emerson Knight to Stella Ruess, April 7, 1935.

13. Harriet G. (illegible) to Stella Ruess, December 14, 1935.

14. Anna Gast to Stella Ruess, April 30, 1935.

15. Ida H. Hodgin to Stella and Christopher Ruess, February 6, 1936.

16. Maybelle G. Phelps to Stella Ruess, March 30, 1935.

17. Sara Pence to Stella Ruess, June 1, 1935.

18. "The Duchess" to Stella and Christopher Ruess, June 25, 1935.

19. May Peery Heeb to Stella Ruess, May 7, 1935.

20. Christopher Ruess to John U. Terrell, May 27, 1938.

21. Mary A. Blair to Stella and Christopher Ruess, June 16, 1952.

22. Burton Bowen to Christopher Ruess, April 1, 1942. *Evert Rulan* was one of Everett Ruess's aliases, a fact that had been published by the date this particu-

lar piece of information was given to the family. Bowen added a second *t* to the first name.

23. Caradonna Bittel to Stella and Christopher Ruess, March 30, 1944.

24. A report of an Everett sighting near Monterrey, Mexico, had been published in *Desert Magazine* in December 1939.

25. Caradonna Bittel to Stella Ruess, January 29, 1960; Caradonna Bittel to Stella Ruess, [early 1961].

26. Frederick L. Allen to Christopher G. Ruess, November 17, 1936. The principals were the Park Service ranger Maurice Cope, H. Jennings Allen of Escalante, John Wetherill of Kayenta, and John U. Terrell at the *Salt Lake Tribune*.

27. Frederick L. Allen to Fred C. Hathaway, December 24, 1936. Both were officers of the life insurance company. I don't know if the prizes were awarded after the 1938–39 school year.

28. Hamlin Garland to Stella and Christopher Ruess, March 21, 1937. Garland, a prolific author who had won the 1922 Pulitzer Prize for biography, was interested in psychic phenomena at this time. Two years later he urged the Ruesses to consult with Arthur Ford of the Institute of Psychic Science, on whose board Garland served: "It might be that at some of his circles you would beg a reliable message." Hamlin Garland to Mr. and Mrs. Ruess, December 23, 1939.

29. Christopher Ruess to Frank Silvey, February 2, 1938.

30. Marie M. Ogden to Stella and Christopher Ruess, July 3, 1938.

31. John P. O'Grady, *Pilgrims to the Wild: Everett Ruess, Henry David Thoreau, John Muir, Clarence King, Mary Austin* (Salt Lake City: University of Utah Press, 1993), 16, 17.

32. Quoted in Gary James Bergera, ed., *On Desert Trails with Everett Ruess* (Salt Lake City: Gibbs Smith, 2000), xi, xiii.

33. Randall Henderson to Hugh Lacy, May 15, 1939.

34. Hugh Lacy, "What Became of Everett Ruess?" *Desert Magazine,* December 1939: 37.

35. Randall Henderson to Christopher Ruess, August 22, 1939.

36. *On Desert Trails with Everett Ruess,* with introduction by Hugh Lacy and foreword by Randall Henderson (El Centro, Calif.: Desert Magazine Press, 1940; reprint, Palm Desert, Calif.: Desert Magazine Press, 1950). See also Gary James Bergera, ed., *On Desert Trails with Everett Ruess,* commemorative edition (Salt Lake City: Gibbs Smith, 2000). The book was praised by the author Edward Howard Griggs, who compared it to works by Henry David Thoreau and John Muir. It was the inspiration for a radio play by the Los Angeles City College station, which was repeated because of listener demand.

37. Frank Hilliard to Stella and Christopher Ruess, June 25, 1943.

38. Nelson Trusler Johnson to Stella Ruess, December 28, 1940. Johnson was a longtime State Department expert on China. Chungking was heavily bombed by the Japanese in 1939 and 1941. Waldo's "only claim to fame" was a photograph

of the bombing that ran in *Life's Picture History of World War II*. Waldo Ruess to "the President, Bancroft Library," April 13, 1987.

39. Evelyn Gentry Caldwell to Stella Ruess, June 26, 1944. Caldwell authored a National Institute of Health study on the pathology of homosexual and heterosexual males, finding little difference between the two, and was active in gay rights causes in Los Angeles. She received many professional honors.

40. Wallace Stegner, *Mormon Country* (New York: Duell, Sloan and Pearce, 1942), 330.

41. Ibid., 321–22.

42. Stegner regretted not extending Abbey's writing fellowship at Stanford, as Abbey had requested, to cover his writing of this book. Philip L. Fradkin, *Wallace Stegner and the American West* (New York: Alfred A. Knopf, 2008), 130.

43. Edward Abbey, *Desert Solitaire: A Season in the Wilderness* (New York: Simon and Schuster, 1990), 242. When Abbey wrote about Ruess he was going "by memory and hearsay only," which was why there are some minor errors in this book. He thought Everett deserved a book-length biography.

44. Edward Abbey, *Confessions of a Barbarian: Selections from the Journals of Edward Abbey, 1951–1989* (Boston: Little, Brown and Company, 1994), 185.

45. Ed Abbey to Waldo Ruess, July 12, 1970.

46. N. Scott Momaday, "Everett Ruess: The Dark Trail Into Myth," *American West*, April 1987: 66–70. Stegner was an early editor-in-chief and backer of this magazine.

47. The following account comes mainly from Stella's untitled diary of the trip, which I found in the University of Utah archives. It is a masterpiece of descriptive writing that she unfortunately could never shape into a coherent magazine account. Aleson's submission to the *Deseret News* adds a few details.

48. My guess is that this is the same place where I spent a night fifty-seven years later and saw the name *Dunn* carved in the sandstone.

49. The story had two headlines, having run in two editions of the Sunday newspaper. "Canyons Veiling Ruess Mystery" and "Utah Canyons Veil Fate of L.A. Poet," *Los Angeles Times*, June 15, 1952.

50. Christopher Ruess had inherited his mother's house upon her death. He sold it in 1942 to help purchase 531 N. Ardmore. Waldo loaned his parents $1,200 for that purpose. Other than what they owed their son, the Ruesses had no debts at the time.

51. Christopher Ruess to the Social Security Administration, October 5, 1952.

52. The Associated Press, *Los Angeles Times*, *Time* magazine, and other U.S. publications ran stories on this Cold War episode. "Hooligan," *Time*, May 13, 1946, and "Reds Release Angeleno Clerk in U.S. Embassy," *Los Angeles Times*, July 18, 1946, were part of the extensive coverage that must have been embarrassing to his parents.

53. Ken Sleight, interview by Ken Verdoia, undated. This interview was for a documentary about Glen Canyon for KUED, the PBS station in Salt Lake City.

54. Ken Sleight to Waldo Ruess, March 15, 1964.

55. Ken Sleight, personal communications (email and telephone conversation), June 5, 2009.

56. Ken Sleight to Waldo Ruess, September 4, 1964.

57. Ken Sleight, personal communication, June 5, 2009. Paint was not Everett's style.

58. The plaque was later stolen, but one attached to an inaccessible place in Davis Gulch is still there.

59. E. R. Fryer, general superintendent of the Navajo reservation, to Christopher Ruess, January 30, 1942. Fryer and Waldo Ruess knew each other as civilians on the same LST in a convoy headed toward Africa during World War II but didn't make the Everett connection at that time.

60. Gladwell Richardson, *Navajo Trader* (Tucson: University of Arizona Press, 1986), 165–68.

61. Gladwell Richardson to "Mr. V. Summers," January 30, 1947. Calling Vi Summers an interested party is a bit of a stretch. Burton Bowen had put her address as the San Francisco mail drop in an ad he ran in *Adventure* magazine seeking information on Ruess. Richardson wrote a long letter in response explaining his interest in the case. Randall Henderson of *Desert Magazine* advised Richardson to drop his involvement with Bowen unless Bowen had "authentic evidence," since the family had been deluged by many "crackpot letters" and had given up hope that Everett was alive. Randall Henderson to Gladwell Richardson, February 17, 1947.

62. Harry Aleson to Stella and Christopher Ruess, November 27, 1950. As of this date, Aleson had been in Davis Gulch seven times and flown over it twice. He wrote the Ruesses: "Outside of your own family, I believe that I have given more thought to Everett's disappearance than any other man. I know that in your hearts you have 'set Everett free.' But to me, the mystery of it will not be quieted" (ibid). He reported in a letter to Stella just after Christopher's death that there was nothing new to add about Everett's disappearance. Aleson to Stella Ruess, December 22, 1954.

63. Harry Aleson to Stella Ruess, December 10, 1956, and December 17, 1956.

64. Stanley A. Jones to Waldo Ruess, September 15, 1975.

65. Norm Tessman to Waldo Ruess, July 9, 1985; Norm Tessman to Waldo Ruess, January 22, 1986.

66. Allen J. Malmquist to Waldo Ruess, April 15, 1988. This incident is recounted in Scott Thybony, *Burntwater* (Tucson: University of Arizona Press, 1997), 58.

67. The documentaries are *Lost Forever* by Diane Orr and *Vanished!* by Dyanna Taylor. The play was performed in Salt Lake City. The mystery novel is *To Die in Kanab*. The song is "Everett Ruess" by Dave Alvin, from his album *Ashgrove*. *Seitaad ruessi* is the name of the plant-eating dinosaur discovered in southeastern Utah. Google listed nearly 200,000 results for the name *Everett Ruess* in 2010.

Everett and the places he inhabited appear on blogs, websites, YouTube, and Facebook. This is not a complete compilation, just an indication of the many formats in which references to Ruess appear.

68. Wallace Stegner, *Mormon Country* (New York: Duell, Sloan and Pearce, 1942), 330.

XII. RESURRECTION

1. Several people who had a working relationship with Roberts mentioned this tendency to me. Among them was Kevin Jones, the Utah state archaeologist, who thought the Cambridge, Mass., writer had exaggerated certain aspects of a story on Range Creek, a complex of archaeological sites in central Utah. Scott Thybony, a Flagstaff writer, accompanied Roberts into Davis Gulch where Roberts thought he had found a *NEMO* inscription. Thybony was skeptical about the bones story. He thought Roberts's credibility had been hurt in the region because of "the Comb Ridge burial fiasco." Kevin Jones, personal communication, October 29, 2009; Scott Thybony, personal communications, November 8, 2009, and February 25, 2011.

2. David Roberts, "What Happened to Everett Ruess?" *National Geographic Adventure,* April–May 1999: 174.

3. W. L. Rusho, ed., *The Mystery of Everett Ruess* (Layton, Utah: Gibbs Smith, 2010), 252. This book is a new, retitled edition of Rusho's *Everett Ruess: A Vagabond for Beauty* (Salt Lake City: Peregrine Smith Books, 1983) with a brief afterword covering the bones issue. Bud Rusho, whom I have known since the late 1970s, died in March 2011. We had talked and exchanged emails about the bones issue. He did not think Roberts was a careful writer.

4. John Rasmus, "Return to Comb Ridge," *National Geographic Adventure,* April–May 2009: 13.

5. David Roberts interview, *Utah Now,* KUED-TV, Salt Lake City, May 8, 2009.

6. Bellson's story appears in David Roberts, "Finding Everett Ruess," *National Geographic Adventure,* April–May 2009: 74–102. Bellson related it at the June 22, 2009, forum "The Finding of Everett Ruess: A 75-Year-Old Mystery Solved," sponsored by the Glen Canyon Institute at the University of Utah in Salt Lake City. Roberts retold it numerous times in personal appearances and media interviews.

7. Michael Benoist, personal communications, November 6 and 9, 2009.

8. "The Genographic Project: About Genographic: Field Research," National Geographic, accessed February 16, 2011, https://genographic.nationalgeographic .com/genographic/about.html.

9. Benoist, personal communication, November 6, 2009.

10. "The Finding of Everett Ruess: A 75-Year-Old Mystery Solved," transcript of Glen Canyon Institute Forum, Salt Lake City, June 22, 2009. I attended the

forum, took written notes, later recorded the audio portion of the streaming video on the Internet, and made a transcript from that tape recording.

11. Kenneth S. Krauter at the University of Colorado at Boulder, who was next in line to attempt a DNA identification of the bones, received the results of the Family Tree tests. He said Family Tree termed *probable* the bones' being of Caucasian origin, but "these sorts of conclusions are pretty soft in my opinion." Kenneth S. Krauter, personal communication, February 3, 2010.

12. "Professor of Year Van Gerven to Address Legislators March 15," University of Colorado News Center, March 9, 1998.

13. Dennis Van Gerven and Kenneth Krauter, "The Case for Everett Ruess: A Vagabond for Beauty," undated, 12. The authors sent me their draft manuscript in mid-August 2009.

14. Brian Ruess quote is from "The Finding of Everett Ruess," June 22, 2009. Statements about *National Geographic Adventure* are from Benoist, personal communication, November 6, 2009.

15. Executive Summary, "Strengthening Forensic Science in the United States: A Path Forward," National Academy of Sciences, http://nap.edu/openbook.php ?record_id=12589, S-3, S-5, S-7; "'Badly Fragmented' Forensic Science System Needs Overhaul: Evidence to Support Reliability of Many Techniques Is Lacking," February 18, 2009, 1, 2, available online at http://www8.nationalacademies .org/onpinews/newsitem.aspx?RECORDID=12589, accessed February 16, 2010. Nuclear DNA, the most common form of DNA used in forensic analysis, is derived from the nuclei of complex organisms, such as humans.

16. Kenneth S. Krauter, personal communication, February 3, 2010.

17. Roberts, "Finding Everett Ruess," 102.

18. Roberts interview, May 8, 2009; Roberts, "Finding Everett Ruess," 81; Roberts, "What Happened to Everett Ruess?," 143.

19. When I asked Sleight about the discrepancies in Roberts's article, he said, "Lots just doesn't fit." Ken Sleight, personal communication, June 5, 2009. The electronic reconstruction of the Grand Gulch *NEMO* shown by Roberts on a screen in Salt Lake City in June 2009 did not match the letters Sleight had seen. The letters are invisible to the naked eye and needed to be enhanced for the presentation. Roberts gave the writer Scott Thybony precise directions to the site, but Thybony could find nothing. "If he's pinning his 'Everett made it to Comb Ridge' theory on that, he's skating on thin ice—or at least thin scratchings." Thybony, personal communication, June 16, 2010.

20. "Mysterious Disappearance of Explorer Everett Ruess Solved after 75 Years," University of Colorado at Boulder News Center, April 30, 2009.

21. "After 75 Years, National Geographic Adventure Solves Mystery of Lost Explorer," *National Geographic Adventure* news release, April 30, 2009.

22. Ibid.

23. Van Gerven and Krauter, "The Case for Everett Ruess," 20.

24. My source for these news accounts and electronic messages was a Google Alert for *Everett Ruess*. No doubt I missed many other print stories and electronic communications.

25. I assume these searches went back as far as 1999 but cannot say with any certainty because Roberts said he would not answer any questions, as he was writing a book on the subject. David Roberts, personal communication, January 5, 2010.

26. Leatherbury contacted the College of Dentistry and was told that records were destroyed after ten years, so there was no way to view the X-ray.

27. Dennis Van Gerven, personal communication, February 9, 2010.

28. Dennis Van Gerven to David Roberts, June 14, 2009. Because of the request at the end, this email has circulated widely throughout the Internet and appears on several websites.

29. Paul Leatherbury, "Everett Ruess: Dental Record Inconsistencies," PDF file, August 8, 2009. I came across this document by accident. The report was briefly posted online, and then Leatherbury asked that it be deleted. It is rich in primary sources, documentation, and photographs, many of them found in the Ruess archive at the University of Utah and available to any serious researcher.

30. State archeologist is one of six positions in the Antiquities Section of the Utah Division of State History, usually not the most powerful of state agencies. But because ancient ruins and artifacts are a very visible part of the Utah landscape, the job has more importance than its place on the ladder of power might indicate.

31. Kevin Jones, personal communication, October 29, 2009.

32. Kevin Jones and Derinna Kopp, "Everett Ruess—A Suggestion to Take Another Look," Utah State History, accessed February 16, 2011, http://history .utah.gov/archaeology/ruess.html.

33. Jones and Kopp, "Everett Ruess"; Kevin Jones, personal communication, June 19, 2009.

34. Derinna Kopp and Kevin Jones, "Everett Ruess Dental Records," Utah Antiquities Section, June 25, 2009.

35. Dr. Reed L. Holt to Derinna Kopp, July 9, 2009.

36. "The Finding of Everett Ruess," June 22, 2009. See note 10.

37. Alyson Sheppard, "Everett Ruess Update: Believers and Skeptics," *National Geographic Adventure* blog, July 6, 2009, accessed February 16, 2001, http:// ngadventure.typepad.com/blog/2009/07/everett-ruess-update-believers-and -skeptics.html.

38. Amy Maestas, "Enigma Unraveled: Discovering Everett Ruess's Body Turns a Romantic Tale into Suspicion and Superstition," *InsideOutside* magazine, September 2009.

39. Kevin Jones, personal communication, October 29, 2009.

40. Brian Ruess for the Ruess family and Paul Stone for AFDIL, "Ruess Family Accepts Comb Ridge Remains Are Not Those of Everett Ruess," October 22, 2009.

41. "New Everett Ruess DNA Test Raises Questions," *National Geographic Adventure* blog, October 29, 2009, accessed February 16, 2011, http://ngadventure .typepad.com/blog/2009/10/questions-abound-after-new-everett-ruess-dna-test -results.html. There were other media reactions to the third DNA test; see, for example: "CU-Boulder Prof Acknowledges DNA Mistake in Case of Poet Everett Ruess," *Boulder Daily Camera,* October 21, 2009; "New Test Results Deepen Mystery Surrounding Explorer Everett Ruess," University of Colorado News Center, October 21, 2009; "Utah Bones Aren't Those of Wandering Poet Everett Ruess," *Denver Post,* October 22, 2009. The media took less interest in this story than in the original DNA confirmation, so the impression that Everett's bones had been found lingered for some time, especially on the Internet.

42. Benoist, personal communication, November 6, 2009.

43. The book had gone to press before those results were overturned.

44. John Rasmus, ed., *The New Age of Adventure: Ten Years of Great Writing* (Washington, D.C.: National Geographic Society, 2009), 8.

45. "National Geographic Adventure Magazine Folds," *New York Times,* December 4, 2009.

46. David Roberts, "Everett Ruess Update: How the DNA Test Went Wrong," *National Geographic Adventure* blog, February 2, 2010, accessed February 16, 2011, http://ngadventure.typepad.com/blog/2010/02/everett-ruess-how-the-dna-test -went-wrong.html. I checked the website for comments for a number of days. The first and only comment during that week was made by W. L. Rusho, who said he had had a number of doubts when he first read Roberts's story. (Actually, he and I had compared doubts.) The University of Colorado DNA results had deceived him (as they did me), and it was not until the Utah state archeologist Kevin Jones questioned the DNA and the forensic evidence that he swung back to his original doubts.

I have no idea what explanations Roberts will offer in his book, due to be published in July 2011.

47. Roberts, "Everett Ruess Update."

48. For example, violence was endemic in the Comb Ridge area in the late nineteenth and early twentieth centuries. Trouble between the Navajo, Piute, and Ute and non-Mormon and Mormon whites climaxed in the Posey War of 1923. A posse of whites killed two Piute, who were buried on or near Comb Ridge. Gary Topping, *Glen Canyon and the San Juan Country* (Moscow: Idaho University Press, 1997), 37–38.

49. Paul Bloom, "What We Miss," *New York Times Book Review,* June 6, 2010. The two cognitive scientists who wrote the book Bloom reviewed, *The Invisible Gorilla,* devoted thirty-six of its pages to what they called "the illusion of memory." "What we retrieve often is filled in based on gist, inference, and other influences; it is more like an improvised riff on a familiar melody than a digital recording of an original performance," the authors wrote. "We mistakenly believe

that our memories are accurate and precise, and we cannot readily separate those aspects of our memory that accurately reflect what happened from those that were introduced later." In all, there were six illusions stemming from one of psychology's most important experiments, conducted at Harvard University by the authors. The results circulated widely after being published in 1999. The experiment involved a video of two teams, one in white shirts and the other in black shirts, passing a basketball back and forth to each other. Harvard students were told to watch the video and count the number of passes. Midway through the video a woman wearing a gorilla suit walks to the middle of the screen, faces the audience, thumps her chest, and disappears. When asked if they noticed anything unusual, half the subjects said no. This experiment has been repeated many times in different forms and places and with different conditions and audiences, yielding the same result. In the book the authors show how the experiment applies to a large number of seeming events that were really illusions. Christopher Chabris and Daniel Simons, *The Invisible Gorilla: And Other Ways Our Intuitions Deceive Us* (New York: Crown, 2010), 62, 63, 7, 39.

50. Vaughn Hadenfeldt, personal communication, April 26, 2010.

51. Roberts, "Everett Ruess Update."

52. Dennis Van Gerven, personal communication, February 9, 2010.

53. Kenneth Krauter, personal communication, March 27, 2010.

54. *Artifacts* in this case means inaccurate results because of the degraded DNA.

55. Kenneth Krauter, personal communication, March 27, 2010.

56. Kenneth Krauter, personal communication, February 3, 2010.

57. "CU-Boulder Prof," *Boulder Daily Camera.*

58. I sought information beyond the press release from the military lab, but none was forthcoming. A spokesperson, Paul R. Stone, said the lab was working on its own publication and "would not be able to market it if we already provided the same information to you." Stone, personal communication, November 6, 2009. One year later no publication had been produced, because the technician who had worked on the bones project had left the agency. Stone, personal communication, November 30, 2010. No peer-reviewed article in a technical journal, an authentication revered by scientists, exists as of this writing for other experts to judge.

APPENDIX B: FATHER AND SON DIALOGUE

1. Everett Ruess to Christopher Ruess, December 4, 1933; Christopher Ruess to Everett Ruess, December 10, 1933.

2. Rabindranath Tagore of India was the first Asian to win the Nobel Prize in Literature.

SELECTED BIBLIOGRAPHY

This bibliography is more an extended recommended reading list on the subject of Everett Ruess and his time than a listing of all possible works I have consulted or that bear on the subject. I have limited the list to those works that should be available in major libraries, well-stocked bookstores, or online stores selling new or used hardcover and paperback books.

Abbey, Edward. *Desert Solitaire: A Season in the Wilderness*. New York: Simon and Schuster, 1990.

Aitchison, Stewart. *A Guide to Southern Utah's Hole-in-the-Rock Trail*. Salt Lake City: University of Utah Press, 2005.

Albright, Horace M., and Frank J. Taylor. *Oh, Ranger!* Stanford, Calif.: Stanford University Press, 1928.

Anderson, Michael F. *Polishing the Jewel: An Administrative History of Grand Canyon National Park*. Grand Canyon, Ariz.: Grand Canyon Association, 2000.

Antonetta, Susanne. *A Mind Apart: Travels in a Neurodiverse World*. New York: Jeremy P. Tarcher, 2005.

Back, Joe. *Horses, Hitches, and Rocky Trails*. Boulder, Colo.: Johnson Books, 1997.

Banham, Reyner. *Scenes in America Deserta*. Salt Lake City: Gibbs M. Smith, 1982.

Bergera, Gary James, ed. *On Desert Trails with Everett Ruess,* commemorative edition. Salt Lake City: Gibbs Smith, 2000.

Bloom, Paul. "What We Miss." *New York Times Book Review,* June 6, 2010.

Blue, Martha. *Indian Trader: The Life and Times of J. L. Hubbell*. Walnut, Calif.: Kiva Publishing, 2000.

Carrigher, Sally. *One Day on Beetle Rock*. Berkeley, Calif.: Heyday Books, 2002.

Chabris, Christopher, and Daniel Simons. *The Invisible Gorilla: And Other Ways Our Intuitions Deceive Us*. New York: Crown, 2010.

Commission of Appraisal of the American Unitarian Association. *Unitarians Face a New Age*. Boston: Commission of Appraisal of the American Unitarian Association, 1936.

Costello, Peter. *Jules Verne*. New York: Charles Scribner's Sons, 1978.

Crampton, C. Gregory. "Historical Sites in Glen Canyon: Mouth of Hansen Creek to Mouth of San Juan River." Anthropological Papers, number 61, Glen Canyon Series number 17. University of Utah, December 1962.

————. "Historical Sites in Cataract and Narrow Canyons, and in Glen Canyon to California Bar." Anthropological Papers, number 72, Glen Canyon Series number 24. University of Utah, August 1964.

Dallett, Nancy C. *At the Confluence of Change: A History of Tonto National Monument*. Tucson: Western National Parks Association, 2008.

Demars, Stanford E. *The Tourist in Yosemite, 1855 to 1985*. Salt Lake City: University of Utah Press, 1991.

Garrison, Lemuel A. *The Making of a Ranger*. Salt Lake City: Howe Brothers, 1983.

Geary, Edward A. *The Proper Edge of the Sky: The High Plateau Country of Utah*. Salt Lake City: University of Utah Press, 1992.

Gillmor, Frances, and Louisa Wade Wetherill. *Traders to the Navajo*. Albuquerque: University of New Mexico Press, 1953.

Gordon, Linda. *Dorothea Lange: A Life beyond Limits*. New York: W. W. Norton, 2009.

Grant, Campbell. *Canyon de Chelly: Its People and Rock Art*. Tucson: University of Arizona Press, 1978.

Gregory, James N. *American Exodus: The Dirt Bowl Migration and Okie Culture in California*. New York: Oxford University Press, 1989.

Hagerty, Donald J. *Desert Dreams: The Art and Life of Maynard Dixon*. Salt Lake City: Gibbs Smith, 1993.

Hanchett, Leland J., Jr. *The Crooked Trail to Holbrook*. Phoenix: Arrowhead Press, 1993.

Hargrave, Lyndon L. "The Influence of Economic Geography upon the Rise and Fall of the Pueblo Culture in Arizona." *Museum Notes* (Museum of Northern Arizona), December 1931.

————. "A Recently Discovered Basket Maker Burial Cave in the Tsegi." *Museum Notes* (Museum of Northern Arizona), October 1934.

Henderson, Randall. *On Desert Trails: Today and Yesterday*. Los Angeles: Westernlore Press, 1961.

Howe, Daniel Walker. *The Unitarian Conscience: Harvard Moral Philosophy, 1805–1861*. Cambridge, Mass.: Oxford University Press, 1970.

Hurewitz, Daniel. *Bohemian Los Angeles and the Making of Modern Politics.* Berkeley: University of California Press, 2007.

Jamison, Kay Redfield. *Touched with Fire: Manic-Depressive Illness and the Artistic Temperament.* New York: Free Press, 1994.

———. *An Unquiet Mind.* New York: Alfred A. Knopf, 1995.

———. *Night Falls Fast: Understanding Suicide.* New York: Vintage, 1999.

———. *Nothing Was the Same.* New York: Alfred A. Knopf, 2009.

Kelly, Susan Croce. *Route 66: The Highway and Its People.* Norman: University of Oklahoma Press, 1988.

Knipmeyer, James H. *Butch Cassidy Was Here: Historic Inscriptions of the Colorado Plateau.* Salt Lake City: University of Utah Press, 2002.

Kraepelin, Emil. *Manic-Depressive Insanity and Paranoia.* Edinburgh, Scotland: E. S. Livingstone, 1921; reprint, Memphis, Tenn.: General Books, 2010.

Krakauer, Jon. *Into the Wild.* New York: Anchor Books, 1997.

Leader, Leonard. *Los Angeles and the Great Depression.* New York: Garland Publishing, 1991.

LeFevre, Lenora Hall. *Boulder County and Its People.* Springdale, Utah: Art City Publishing Co., 1973.

Lockett, H. Claiborne, and Lyndon L. Hargrave. "Woodchuck Cave, a Basketmaker II Site in Tsegi Canyon, Arizona." Bulletin 26, Museum of Northern Arizona, 1953.

Luckhart, Dean. "Emerson Knight: Landscape Architect 1882–1960." *Landscape Architecture* 2, January 2, 1962.

McWilliams, Carey. *Southern California: Island on the Land.* Salt Lake City: Peregrine Smith Books, 1973.

Momaday, N. Scott. "Everett Ruess: The Dark Trail into Myth." *American West,* April 1987.

Mondimore, Francis Mark. *Bipolar Disorder: A Guide for Patients and Families.* Baltimore: Johns Hopkins University Press, 2006.

Nelson, Lowry. *The Mormon Village: A Pattern and Technique of Land Settlement.* Salt Lake City: University of Utah Press, 1952.

Newhall, Nancy, ed. *The Daybooks of Edward Weston.* New York: Aperture, 1990.

Nickerson, Sheila. *Disappearance: A Map.* New York: Doubleday, 1996.

O'Grady, John P. *Pilgrims to the Wild: Everett Ruess, Henry David Thoreau, John Muir, Clarence King, Mary Austin.* Salt Lake City: University of Utah Press, 1993.

Orsi, Richard J., Alfred Runte, and Marlene Smith-Baranzini. *Yosemite and Sequoia: A Century of California National Parks.* Berkeley: University of California Press; San Francisco: California Historical Society, 1993.

Peñalosa, Fernando. *Yosemite in the 1930s: A Remembrance.* Rancho Palos Verdes, Calif.: Quaking Aspen Books, 2002.

Power, Bertha Knight. *William Henry Knight: California Pioneer.* Reprint of a privately printed book, Whitefish, Mont.: Kessinger Publishing, 1932.

Rasmus, John, ed. *The New Age of Adventure: Ten Years of Great Writing.* Washington, D.C.: National Geographic Society, 2009.

Richardson, Gladwell. *Navajo Trader.* Tucson: University of Arizona Press, 1986.

Roberts, David. "What Happened to Everett Ruess." *National Geographic Adventure,* April–May 1999.

———. "The Mystery of Everett Ruess: Solved," *National Geographic Adventure,* April–May 2009.

———. "Everett Ruess: How the DNA Test Went Wrong." *National Geographic Adventure* website, accessed February 2, 2011. http://ngadventure.typepad.com/blog/2010/02/everett-ruess-how-the-dna-test-went-wrong.html.

Rothman, Hal K. "Navajo National Monument: A Place and Its People." Southwest Cultural Resources Center Professional Papers number 40. Santa Fe, N.M.: National Park Service, 1991.

Runte, Alfred. *Yosemite: The Embattled Wilderness.* Lincoln: University of Nebraska Press, 1990.

Rusho, W. L., ed. *Everett Ruess: A Vagabond for Beauty.* Salt Lake City: Peregrine Smith Books, 1983.

———, ed. *Wilderness Journals of Everett Ruess.* Salt Lake City: Gibbs Smith, 1998.

———, ed. *Everett Ruess: Combination Edition.* Salt Lake City: Peregrine Smith Books, 2002.

———, ed. *The Mystery of Everett Ruess.* Layton, Utah: Gibbs Smith, 2010.

Salinger, J. D. *The Catcher in the Rye.* New York: Back Bay Books, 2001.

Scoyen, Eivind T., and Frank J. Taylor. *The Rainbow Canyons.* Stanford, Calif.: Stanford University Press, 1931.

Sellars, Richard West. "A Very Large Array: Early Federal Historic Preservation—The Antiquities Act, Mesa Verde, and the National Park Act." *Natural Resources Journal,* Spring 2007.

Shaw, T. E. [T. E. Lawrence], trans. *The Odyssey of Homer.* New York: Oxford University Press, 1932.

Sides, Hampton. *Blood and Thunder.* New York: Doubleday, 2006.

Smith, Duane A. *Mesa Verde National Park.* Boulder: University Press of Colorado, 2002.

Solnit, Rebecca. *A Field Guide to Getting Lost.* New York: Viking, 2005.

Starr, Kevin. *Material Dreams: Southern California through the 1920s.* New York: Oxford University Press, 1990.

———. *The Dream Endures: California Enters the 1940s.* New York: Oxford University Press, 1997.

Steen, Charlie R., Lloyd M. Pierson, Vorsila L. Bohrer, and Kate Peck Kent. *Archeological Studies at Tonto National Monument, Arizona.* Vol. 2, *Southwestern*

Monuments Association Technical Series. Edited by Louis R. Caywood. Globe, Ariz.: Southwestern Monuments Association, 1962.

Stegner, Wallace. *Mormon Country.* New York: Duell, Sloan and Pearce, 1942.

Suphen, Debra L. *Sinews of Dirt and Stone.* Historical Research Study for Grand Canyon National Park. Grand Canyon, Ariz.: National Park Service, 1992.

Taylor, Mark A. *Sandstone Sunsets: In Search of Everett Ruess.* Salt Lake City: Gibbs Smith, 1997.

Thybony, Scott. *Hermit Trail Guide.* Grand Canyon, Ariz.: Grand Canyon Association, 2005.

Topping, Gary. *Glen Canyon and the San Juan Country.* Moscow: Idaho University Press, 1997.

Van Dyke, John C. *The Desert.* Salt Lake City: Gibbs M. Smith, 1987.

Verne, Jules. *Twenty Thousand Leagues under the Sea.* Translated and annotated by Walter James Miller and Frederick Paul Walter. Annapolis, Md.: Naval Institute Press, 1993.

Watkins, T. H. *Righteous Pilgrim: The Life and Times of Harold L. Ickes, 1874–1952.* New York: Henry Holt and Co., 1990.

Wilson, Herbert Earl. *The Lore and the Lure of the Yosemite: The Indians, Their Customs, Legends and Beliefs, and the Story of Yosemite.* San Francisco: Sunset Press, 1923.

Woolsey, Nethella Griffin. *The Escalante Story.* Springdale, Utah: Art City Publishing Co., 1964.

The WPA Guide to California. Reprint, New York: Pantheon Books, 1984.

The WPA Guide to 1930s Arizona. Reprint, Tucson: University of Arizona Press, 1989.

INDEX

Note: The initials CR, ER, SR, and WR refer to Christopher Ruess, Everett Ruess, Stella Ruess, and Waldo Ruess.

Abbey, Edward, 179, 184, 187, 247n42,43
accident theories, 152, 155, 173; drowning, 155, 182, 184; fall, 136, 161, 163; quicksand, 151, 157
Adams, Ansel, 117, 119–20
Adams, Virginia, 119n
adolescence, 6, 9–10, 77, 144; bipolar disorder and, 94, 95, 234n44
Adventure magazine, 248n61
The Adventures of Tom Sawyer (Twain), 26
aesthetic ideals. *See* beauty
AFDIL (Armed Forced DNA Identification Laboratory), 198, 202–3, 206, 207, 251–52n41, 253n58
Affymetrix DNA analysis software, 195, 205, 206, 207
Agathla Peak, 60, *fig. 15*
Alameda County, Ruess family in, 18–19, 20, 221nn1,25
Alameda Unitarian Church, 18
Albright, Horace, 42, 72, 110, 132–33, 239n25

Aleson, Harry, 180–82, 184, 185–87, 247n47, 248n62
"All Boy" (ER), 23
Allen, H. Jennings, 150–51, 155, 163, 181
Allen, Mildred, 149, 150, 162, 181, 182
Allen, Walter, 4, 151, 242n9
Alta Peak, 112
Alvey, Edson B., 152, 153, 242–43n13, 243n19
Alvey, Melvin, 144–45, 156n
Alvin, Dave, 248n67
The American (James), 45
American Indian, 32, 170
American Spectator, 19n
American West, 247n46
Anasazi, 54, 219n1; in Canyon de Chelly, 66–67; use of term, 227n16
Anasazi sites and artifacts, 54, 143, 227n11, 227n16; Canyon de Chelly and Canyon del Muerto, 66–67, 98; collecting and governing law, 54, 55–57, 61, 101, 227n16; Cottonwood Gulch, 153; Davis Gulch, 2, 4–5, 157, 181–82; ER's collections, 58, 61,

inscriptions: ER's NEMO inscriptions, 2–3, 5, 151, 157–60, 181, 182, 242n9, 242–43n13; Grand Gulch NEMO inscription, 184, 193, 250n19; by searchers, 3–4, 151, 181, 242n9, 244n22; tourist inscriptions at Mesa Verde, 100

Institute of Psychic Science, 246n28

Into the Wild (film), 9

Into the Wild (Krakauer), 9, 187

The Invisible Gorilla (Chabris and Simons), 252–53n49

Irving, Washington, 93

Italian Navy seaplane incident, Roosevelt Lake, 79

Ito, Michio, 31–32

Jacobs, Bill, 65, 74, 81, 102, 128; ER's advice to, 61; ER's burro shoe gift, 81, 231n96; ER's correspondence with, 59n, 61–62, 63–65, 67, 74, 130, 228n41, 233n42; nature of ER's relationship with, 63–65; and 1932 trip, 83, 84–85, 86, 87, 89

James, Henry, 45

James, William, 221n14

Jamison, Kay Redfield, 94–95n, 96

Janice Meredith (film), 25

Janssens, Lawrence, 170

Jeffers, Robinson, 36, 122

Jenks, Randolph "Pat," 69–70, 184

Jennings, Jesse D., 153, 242–43n13

Jesus Christ, in CR and ER's father-son dialogue, 212, 213, 214

jimson weed, 4

John Muir Trail, 45–46, 108, 114

Johnson, Alice Kinlicheenie, 92

Johnson, Hiram, 18

Johnson, Melvin, 111–12

Johnson, Neal, 154–55, 162, 165, 172

Johnson, Nelson Trusler, 177, 246–47n38

Johnson, Sam, 92

"John Van Dyke and Everett Ruess: A Comparison with the Spirit of Place Tradition" (Perkins), 53–54n

Jolley, Donal, Jr., 74n, 91n

Jolley, Donal, Sr., 74, 155, 162

"Jonathan" *aka* "Bay" (horse), 89, 90, 98, 234n56

Jones, Kevin, 199–200, 201–2, 249n1, 252n46

Jones, Stan, 186, 243–44n21

Jurgen: A Comedy of Justice (Cabell), 122

Kaibab Plateau, 73, 74

Kaibab squirrel, 73

Kaiparowits Plateau, 146, 240n44

Kayenta, 54, 57; ER in, 57, 60, 129–31, 132, 136; ER's parents' visit, 161; Wetherill trading post, 54, 56, 233n39

Keet Seel ruin, 60, 61, 227n16

Keit, Katherine. *See* Ruess, Katherine Keit

Kent, Rockwell, 122

Khan Alam Khan (Khan Ali), 126, 127–28

Kings Canyon National Park, 114, 236n19

Kinlicheenie, Friday, 91, 92

Knight, Alfred, 12

Knight, Bertha, 12, 13

Knight, Daisy, 19

Knight, Ella Waters (grandmother), 12

Knight, Emerson (uncle), 12, 121–22, 125, 171

Knight, Stella. *See* Ruess, Stella Knight

Knight, William H. (grandfather), 11–13, 19n, 22

Kolb, Emery, 186

Kopp, Derinna, 199–200, 201–2

Kraepelin, Emil (quoted), 96

Krakauer, Jon, 9, 187

Krauter, Kenneth S., 192, 194, 195, 202, 249–50n11; "The Case for Everett Ruess: A Vagabond for Beauty," 191–92, 195, 250n13; DNA analysis of Comb Ridge bones, 192, 194–96, 198, 201–2, 205, 206; on faulty DNA analysis, 206; reanalysis, 203

kyaks, 70, 87, 230n61

Lacy, Hugh, 176, 180

Lacy, Mike, 190

La Farge, Oliver, 137

La Gorce, John Oliver, 5, 219–20n2

LaGorce Arch, 2, 5, 157, 181, 184

Lake of the Fallen Moon, 114, 237n37

Lake Powell, 2–3, 147, 242–43n13; 1957 archaeological survey, 152–53, 242–43n13

Lake Tahoe, 12

Lake Tenaya, 44, 45

Lange, Dorothea, 116–17, 118–19, 151–52n, 169; and ER, 104, 118, 119, 120, 122, 124,

series and, 165; Stegner and, 177–79. *See also* "Finding Everett Ruess"; *On Desert Trails with Everett Ruess*; Roberts, David

READING: as a boy, 22, 26; on 1930 trip, 44, 45; on 1931 trip, 62; on 1932 trip, 83, 85, 86, 87, 89, 90–91, 92, 93, 97, 99; on 1933–1934 trip, 110, 111, 112, 113, 114, 117, 121, 122; on 1934 trip, 132. *See also specific authors and titles*

TRAVELS (1930), 34–46; Carmel and Big Sur, 36–40; money, 38; San Luis Obispo and Morro Bay, 34–35; Yosemite, 40–46

TRAVELS (1931), 49–81; Apache Trail and Tonto Basin, 77, 78–81; attitudes about going home, 75, 81; burros, 58, 59–60, 63, 65–66, 67–68, 69–71, 72, 73, 77, 81; camping, 53; Canyon de Chelly, 63, 68; Curly the puppy, 62, 63, 69, 72, 75; equipment and practical skills, 58–59, 60, 61, 63; Grand Canyon, 68, 70–73, 75–77, 170; health, 69–70; Hopi mesas and encounter with Jenks, 68–70; Kaibab Plateau and Zion, 27n, 73–75, 155, *fig. 10*; Kayenta and Navajo National Monument, 57, 60–61; mental state, 57, 61–62, 81; money, 59, 66, 68, 74, 75, 76, 77, 80; name changes, 50, 57, 62–63, 75; photographs, *figs. 9, 10*; plans for, 50, 51–52

TRAVELS (1932), 82–104; attitudes about going home, 102; burros, 83, 86, 87; Canyon de Chelly and Canyon del Muerto, 96–98; Carmel, 104; Curly's leaving, 85; Grand Canyon, 103–4; health, 90, 92, 97, 98, 99, 102; items left behind, 98, 234–35n57; mental state, 84–85, 87, 90, 93, 97–98, 99, 102–3; Mogollon Rim, Zeniff, and Holbrook, 86–89; Mojave Desert, 104; money, equipment, and supplies, 83, 84, 86, 88, 89, 99–100; Navajo country, 90–93, 96–100; pack horses, 85, 86, 89, 90, 98, 99, 234n56; Roosevelt Lake and Tonto Basin, 83–86; Shiprock, Ute country, and Mesa Verde, 99–103; travel journals, 101–2, 232n9

TRAVELS (1933–1934), 105–28; burros, 106, 109, 116; equipment and supplies, 112; health, 106, 113, 114, 115–16, 121, 122; High Sierra and John Muir Trails, 114–15; men-

tal state, 106, 113, 114, 124–25; Northern California coast, 126–27, 238–39n2; parents' visit to San Francisco, 122–24; return to Los Angeles, 128; San Francisco Bay Area, 116–20, 121–26, 127–28; Sequoia National Park, 106, 109–10; Yosemite, 115–16

TRAVELS (1934), 129–45; beginning of, 129; burros, 129, 130, 131, 134, 137–38, 150–51, 155; equipment, supplies, and preparedness, 129, 130, 138, 139, 144–45, 150, 242n5; ER's assessment of, 143; ER's plans for, 105, 122, 139; Escalante to Soda Gulch, 140–45; Flagstaff, Grand Canyon, and Bryce country, 138–40, 161; food and cooking, 144; health and injuries, 138; Hopi mesas and Gallup, 136–37, 161; Kayenta, Chinle, and Canyon de Chelly, 129–31, 136; mental state, 130, 132, 143, 145, 158; missing travel journal, 152, 189; money, 138, 143; Monument Valley and Navajo Mountain, 130–32; parents' retracing of, 160–63; Rainbow Bridge–Monument Valley Expedition, 132–36. *See also* Ruess, Everett: DISAPPEARANCE

WRITINGS AND OBSERVATIONS: about art and being an artist, 32, 38, 62, 76, 77, 97, 105, 122, 138; as a boy, 23, 24, 25–28, 29, 32, 170, 222n13; book proposed after his disappearance, 167, 168, 174–75; death and disappearance hints in, 180; handwriting analysis, 173; Momaday on, 180; on beauty, 17, 97, 130; on death, 93, 123; on friends and relationships, 64, 74, 87, 89, 93, 102–3, 119; on his college experience, 105; on his ideals and aims, 124; on his mental state, 85, 93, 97–98; on his plans and aspirations, 62, 75, 124; on Los Angeles Young Communist demonstration, 128–29; on nature and closeness to God, 24; on pain, 61–62; on solitude and isolation, 74, 86, 87, 90, 93, 97–98, 102–3, 233n43; on the value and grip of life, 114, 130, 132; on towns and cities, 44, 45, 86, 89, 102, 119, 127, 145; on Wagner's *Tristan und Isolde,* 122; on wandering, 93, 100, 233n43; poetry, 24, 32, 33, 38n, 47–48, 104, 105, 118, 209–10; "Program of the 1931 Artists' and Adventurers' Expedition," 51–52; prose

Text:	11.25/13.5 Adobe Garamond
Display:	Adobe Garamond
Compositor:	BookMatters, Berkeley
Indexer:	Thérèse Shere
Cartographer:	Bill Nelson
Printer and binder:	Thomson-Shore, Inc.